Alabama &
Mississippi
Gardener's Guide

Alabama & Mississippi

Gardener's Guide

Felder Rushing & Jennifer Greer

COOL SPRINGS PRESS
Growing Successful Gardeners™
BRENTWOOD, TENNESSEE

Published by Cool Springs Press, P.O. Box 2828, Brentwood, Tennessee 37024

Rushing, Felder, 1952-
    Alabama & Mississippi gardener's guide / Felder Rushing & Jennifer Greer.
       p. cm.
    Includes bibliographical references (p.).
    1. Gardening--Alabama. 2. Gardening--Mississippi.
    I. Title: Alabama and Mississippi gardener's guide. II. Greer, Jennifer. III. Title.
  SB453.2.A2R87 2005
  635.9'09761--dc22
                        2004022210

First printing 2005
Printed in the United States of America
10 9 8 7 6 5 4 3

Managing Editor: Jenny Andrews
Horticulture Editor: Troy Marden
Copyeditor: Sara J. Henry
Cover Design: Sheri Ferguson, Ferguson Designs
Production Artist: S.E. Anderson

On the cover: *Camellia* 'Pink Perfection'

Cool Springs Press books may be purchased in bulk for educational, business, fundraising, or sales promotional use. For information, please email **cgames@coolspringspress.com**.

Visit the Cool Springs Press website at **www.coolspringspress.com**.

Dedication and Acknowledgments

I dedicate my portion of this book to the generations of gardeners before me who blazed a rambling path through unknown territory, making this journey less of a struggle to learn what is new, and more of an insightful stroll down an ever-widening road of gardening knowledge in the "sister states."

I thank my co-author for bringing fresh insight into gardening in our neck of the woods, the university horticulturists who elevated our understanding of natural processes and how they can be tamed, and especially the "garden variety" gardeners who brought us back down to earth with practical, out-of-school experiences that sometime say to just leave things well enough alone.

I would also like to celebrate our hard-working editor, Jenny Andrews, for her super patience and humor, and to acknowledge her horticultural and gardening insights; believe me, it is refreshing to have someone looking over my shoulder who is also a dirt-under-her-fingernails gardener!

—Felder Rushing

To Alabama gardeners—past, present, and future—all friends in the garden of life.

I would like to acknowledge Charlotte Hagood, Jan Midgley, Alabama Master Gardeners, the Birmingham Botanical Gardens, the *Birmingham News*, *Southern Living* and the Alabama Cooperative Extension System.

—Jennifer Greer

Photography Credits

Thomas Eltzroth: 18, 20, 26, 30, 31, 33, 34, 36, 37, 38, 41, 43, 44, 48, 50, 54, 56, 58, 59, 61, 62, 63, 64, 65, 66, 68, 70, 74, 75, 77, 78, 79, 80, 81, 83, 84, 85, 86, 87, 89, 90, 91, 93, 94, 96, 97B, 102, 103, 112, 114, 115, 116, 118, 120, 124, 125, 133, 134, 137, 138, 139, 141, 142A, 143A, 144B, 145A, 146, 150, 152, 154, 158, 159, 160, 163, 166, 171, 172, 173, 174, 177, 181, 184, 186, 188, 189, 191, 196, 197, 198, 199, 207, 209, 210, 212, 224, 228, 232, 234, 242, 248, 255

Jerry Pavia: 13, 14, 16, 21, 25, 27, 29, 32, 35, 39, 42, 45, 51, 55, 88, 98, 100, 101, 104, 105, 117, 119, 121, 126, 128, 129, 130, 135, 143B, 148, 149, 156, 157, 165, 175, 178, 179, 180, 182, 183, 185, 190, 193, 200, 203, 208, 214, 216, 218, 222, 225, 229, 230, 233, 237, 239A

Liz Ball: 47, 53, 57, 69, 72, 76, 82, 92, 106, 108, 110, 123, 127, 132, 151, 164, 167, 176, 187, 194, 195, 201, 205, 206, 213, 217, 219, 220, 240A, 241B

Felder Rushing: 10, 12, 17, 19, 24, 28, 40, 46, 52, 71, 95, 99, 107, 131, 145B, 147, 153, 155, 169, 215, 235, 238, 239B, 243AB, 247B, 250B, 254A

William Adams: 67, 97A, 113, 192, 240B, 245, 246, 247A

André Viette: 49, 109, 111, 122, 204, 226, 227

Pamela Harper: 73, 162, 211, 221, 231

Neil Soderstrom: 142B, 144A, 249, 251, 250A, 252, 254B

Michael Dirr: 168, 202

Charles Mann: 15, 140

Ralph Snodsmith: 170, 223

Cathy Wilkinson Barash: 161

Lorenzo Gunn: 223

Dency Kane: 60

Gerard Krewer: 236

Greg Spiechert: 241A

Mark Turner: 136

Table of Contents

Featured Plants
for Alabama & Mississippi

Annuals
Black-Eyed Susan, 26
Calliopsis, 27
Cleome, 28
Coleus, 29
Cosmos, 30
Foxglove, 31
Geranium, 32
Globe Amaranth, 33
Impatiens, 34
Lantana, 35
Larkspur, 36
Marigold, 37
Melampodium, 38
Pansy, 39
Petunia, 40
Poppy, 41
Scarlet Sage, 42
Snapdragon, 43
Wax Begonia, 44
Zinnia, 45

Bulbs
Blazing Star, 50
Caladium, 51
Crinum, 52
Crocus, 53
Daffodil, 54
Elephant's Ear, 55
Gladiolus, 56
Grape Hyacinth, 57
Lily, 58
Lycoris, 59
Painted Arum, 60
Rain Lily, 61
Summer Snowflake, 62
Tulip, 63

Groundcovers
Ajuga, 66
Asiatic Jasmine, 67
Creeping Juniper, 68
Creeping Lily Turf, 69
English Ivy, 70
Japanese Pachysandra, 71
Mondo Grass, 72
Southern Shield Fern, 73
Vinca, 74
Wintercreeper, 75

Herbs
Basil, 78
Bay, 79
Chives, 80
Cilantro, 81
Dill, 82
Lavender, 83
Lemon Balm, 84
Mint, 85
Oregano, 86
Parsley, 87
Pepper, 88
Rosemary, 89
Sage, 90
Thyme, 91

Ornamental Grasses
Blue Lyme Grass, 95
Broomsedge, 95
Feather Grass, 95
Feather Reed Grass, 95
Fountain Grass, 96
Japanese Blood Grass, 96
Maiden Grass, 96
Pampas Grass, 96
Purple Muhly Grass, 97
River Oats, 97
Striped Cane, 97
Variegated Ribbon Grass, 97

Perennials
Artemisia, 102
Aster, 103
Balloon Flower, 104
Bluestar, 105
Cardinal Flower, 106
Cast-iron Plant, 107
Chrysanthemum, 108
Columbine, 109
Coreopsis, 110
Daylily, 111
Dianthus, 112
Ginger Lily, 113
Goldenrod, 114
Hibiscus, 115
Holly Fern, 116
Hosta, 117
Iris, 118
Japanese Painted Fern, 119
Lamb's Ears, 120
Lenten Rose, 121
Monarda, 122
Narrowleaf Sunflower, 123
Obedient Plant, 124
Oxeye Daisy, 125
Peony, 126
Purple Coneflower, 127
Rose Verbena, 128
Ruellia, 129
Salvia, 130
Sedum, 131
Soapwort, 132
Spiderwort, 133
Stokes' Aster, 134
Summer Phlox, 135
Wild Blue Phlox, 136
Yarrow, 137

Welcome to Gardening *in*
Alabama & Mississippi

Gardening in the "sister states" is exciting! This is true in spite of a few obstacles, such as pockets of difficult soils and daunting weather that gives meteorologists fits and drives gardeners to gamble. In fact, we have hundreds of fantastic plants that love it here, and can reward our efforts many times over. From our rocky higher elevations and canyons, to our rich river bottoms, from prairie outcrops to the Piney Woods and sandy Gulf Coast, we have diversity in our landscape and in what we can grow. Just a few advantages we enjoy include:

- A relatively mild climate that enables us to have flowers twelve months out of the year
- High annual rainfall (and access to inexpensive water during dry summers)
- Decent soils which are fairly easy to work with or improve
- A wide range of plant choices, from temperate to subtropical
- A strong horticultural, landscaping, and gardening tradition
- Excellent botanical gardens and educational resources
- Outstanding commercial nurseries and retail garden centers
- Great gardeners

For sure, our climate is not perfect. In late winter, we experience wildly fluctuating temperatures that confuse plants eager to start growing, followed by a short "English" spring and a long, humid summer, then the hurricane season in August and September. But these challenges are what keep our gardens—and our gardeners—so alive.

Designing a Garden

There are many ways to design and install a garden, depending on your personality, objective, and budget. If you are gardening for the fun of it, want to really get to know plants, and express your own creativity, then do it yourself, learning as you go. But if you need a major landscaping overhaul and would rather have the work done by professionals, you may want to enter into a creative collaboration with a garden designer or landscape architect. Either way, visit different gardens to see a variety of styles before deciding which will best suit your house, property, and personality. Also consider how you will view and how you will use your garden space. Below are a few styles from which to choose:

- Formal gardens, which are more expensive to create and maintain, might include manicured turf, specimen evergreens, classic shrubs (such as camellia, boxwood, and azalea), roses, ivy, a perennial border, and areas for annual bedding plants.
- Low-maintenance suburban gardens have spreading lawns and a foundation planting of shrubs that can be pruned regularly but simply.
- Informal gardens, which follow patterns in nature, are less expensive to create and maintain. They might have less turf and more groundcovers, along with ferns, ornamental grasses, naturalized bulbs, wildflowers, and native shrubs and trees.
- Cottage gardens have practically no lawn but lots of free-flowing beds of small trees, flowering shrubs, heirloom roses, vines, bulbs, herbs, perennials, and reseeding annuals. They are highly personal and can be fairly easy to maintain, depending on the plants chosen.

Armand Clematis

Making a Plant List

Sometimes the sheer number of plant choices can overwhelm a new gardener. If that happens, take it step by step. Start by siting larger, "backbone" types of plants, such as trees and shrubs. Use a variety of evergreen and deciduous plants so the landscape is not boring and there is something interesting to see all year. Choose a few select locations to plant colorful annuals so you get a feeling of "instant gratification" while you figure out the rest of the garden. Then expand on your knowledge every season by adding more annuals, perennials, grasses, groundcovers, and other plants. If you find that you have an affinity for a particular type of plant, learn more about it and include it throughout your garden. This will help give your garden a cohesive look and feel.

Today, gardening clubs or societies often organize around groups of plants (for example, the Daffodil Society or the Daylily Society). Gardeners in these groups share information about the plants, including named selections, that work well in your area. Botanical gardens and arboreta often have contact information for plant groups, and most plant societies have websites. Master Gardeners—an outreach program of the horticulture programs at such universities as Auburn and Mississippi State—are a lively group of local gardeners who are trained and eager to help you with free advice and consultations. For more information on Master Gardeners in your area, contact your county Agricultural Extension Service office.

Matching the Plants with the Site

Now, you are ready for what might be the most important part of the whole process: choosing the right plant or plants for the right site. Obviously, it's not critical if you misplace a few inexpensive annuals, but you certainly don't want to plant a tree in the wrong place and watch it suffer or die. When you are attracted to a particular plant, see if it matches the growing conditions of the site you have in mind (sunny or shady, wet or dry soil, northern or southern exposure, and so on.). Also, look to see if there is a particular species, hybrid, or named selection of the plant that performs better in your area or has some other outstanding feature (disease resistance, fall color, bigger blooms). Check your soil to see if it is heavy clay, loose sand, or just-right loam, and amend it as needed; the amount of soil moisture and drainage capability are also important. Observe light and shade patterns throughout the day (morning sun is less intense, afternoon sun can be too hot for some plants).

Admittedly, at times we all lose our heads over a great-looking but borderline-hardy plant, and bring it home without knowing where we will put it. Or we may be lucky enough to be given such a plant. This can often make choosing a good spot difficult. Before committing it to the ground, do a little research to see how you may be able to adjust your garden (such as extra soil preparation) to fit its needs. Many gardens have locations that will allow you to grow a more finicky plant with a minimum amount of extra effort.

Hardy, Semi-Hardy, and Tropical Plants

Most of the plants in this book are winter hardy throughout both states, with a few exceptions for the northern or higher elevation counties, and a few plants that really don't like the all-year mild climate along the Gulf Coast. Special notes on these are in their individual descriptions, plus a few hints on how to get them to grow out of their normal ranges. In each plant profile, we refer to regions of the state that generally correspond to Hardiness Zones created by the United States Department of Agriculture (USDA); see the Plant Hardiness Map on page 23. Those regions are North (Zone 7a), Central (Zone 7b), and Gulf Coast (Zones 8 and 9).

While zone information is helpful, it refers only to winter hardiness, or minimum temperatures. Our hot, humid summers, as well as our mid-spring frosts, are often equally trying for plants. And many plants can thrive in areas outside their zones, often because any given landscape is full of "microclimates" with slight variations in temperature. Some plants are just more widely adaptable than plant tags might indicate. Once you have mastered the safe bets for your garden, you may want to look around for a good

Black-Eyed Susan and Coral Honeysuckle

microclimate in which to grow borderline plants you are attracted to: An overhanging tree can be an "umbrella" to protect plants from light, late frosts; a concrete driveway will collect heat during the day and radiate it at night to give an extra degree of frost protection to adjacent plants; a low spot in the yard can be a colder "frost pocket."

When to Plant: Fall and Spring

In general, most trees, shrubs, and hardy perennial plants should be planted in the fall so they can take advantage of winter and early spring rains before new growth begins. They can also be planted in the spring and summer, but will require more watering the first year. Just because tomatoes and marigolds appear at the garden centers on March 1 doesn't mean it's time to plant them. Good Friday, the traditional spring planting date for Southerners, often comes too early and the soil is still too cool for good root growth. Summer annuals, tropicals, and semi-hardy plants should be planted in the spring after threat of a freeze or frost has passed. Along the Gulf Coast this date usually falls around April 1; in Central areas, around April 15; in the northern and higher elevation counties, around April 30.

A Climbing Rose in a Southern Garden

Experienced gardeners often plant a few things ahead of time, using protective coverings as insurance against sudden temperature drops. But when planting a large number of bedding plants, it is best to wait—after all, we have a very long growing season, and there is plenty of time to get it all in the ground.

The Good Earth

The best plants can languish in poor soil. Perhaps the best single piece of advice one gardener can give another is to treat the soil as a living, generous thing, not as a prop for plants. But not all soils are created equal. While most are adequate for supporting plant roots, some are better or worse than others for holding moisture, air, and nutrients—all essential for strong root growth. To find out about your soil, dig a hole 6 inches deep and observe the color and texture of the soil. There are three basic soil types:

- Sandy soils tend to be well drained, but need watering often and are low in nutrients.
- Clay soils tend to be richer in nutrients, but are poorly drained.
- Loamy soils are ideal, rich, and well drained.

Next, call your county agent and find out about getting a soil test for a small fee. This will tell you your soil's pH (the relative acidity or alkalinity, which affects how roots grow and the amount of nutrients that may be available), and how to change it if needed. It also helps pinpoint nutrient deficiencies in need of correction. If you have questions, your county agent or a Master Gardener will be able to help interpret the results.

Hawthorn

Building Good Soil

When building a new house, instruct the builder to set aside the topsoil so you can use it in your garden. If you live in a new suburb, however, your topsoil may have already been scraped away during construction. Or, it may have been lost to erosion from pioneer farming practices and made its way to the Gulf of Mexico. You can buy topsoil in bags at a garden shop or by the truckload from a soil products supplier (a by-product of our sprawling development). Soil from a previously wooded site is richer and has fewer weeds than soil from an agricultural area, but comparison-shopping is difficult. Find a company with a good reputation for quality soil.

To improve your soil, start by aerating it. Just loosening the existing soil provides great benefits to plant growth, health, and drought tolerance. Think about this when digging holes for planting. Also, remember to core aerate the soil under lawns regularly. And be sure you have plenty of paths in your garden, so you do not walk on—and compact—soil where you are trying to grow things. Improve poor or poorly drained soils at planting time. Instead of digging out and discarding poor soil, simply add amendments to it, like adding crackers to a bowl of soup. An all-purpose, "good soil" recipe is $2/3$ topsoil and $1/3$ organic matter (cheap potting soil, finely-ground bark chips, compost, leaf mould, composted manure). Some gardeners add sand to clay soils, but organic matter alone is often just fine.

Regularly feed your soil and it will in turn feed your plants. In the fall, spread a 2- to 4-inch blanket of organic mulch (shredded leaves, pine bark, pine straw, grass clippings) on flower beds and around shrubs, which will slowly decompose, enriching the soil with nutrients. In the spring and at planting time for annuals, add a layer of compost on top of your soil then scratch it in with a rake.

Easy Guide to Composting

Everybody, even Mother Nature with her rotting leaves and logs, has his or her own recipe for compost. There tend to be two basic kinds: fast and complicated, or slow and easy. For slow composting, simply find a convenient place to start a leaf pile, and add what you have as you can, and take away what you need when you want it. Pile on leaves, grass clippings, vegetable scraps, coffee grounds, eggshells, used potting soil from old plants, and plant trimmings, and they will start to decompose. Once you get it started, add new materials to one side, and dig finished compost from the other.

For fast compost, make a compost bin at least 3 or 4 feet high and wide out of wood or wooden pallets, or a silo out of hardware cloth or chicken wire held up by very sturdy metal or wooden posts. Pile everything into it, including some sort of nitrogen (cottonseed meal, fish emulsion, coffee grounds, grass clippings) keep it moist, and aerate or mix it up every few weeks. It can be completely finished in just three or four months. Most gardeners who compost this way keep two or three bins going, at different stages of decomposition. Also check with your town officials to see if there is a community compost program from which you can get free or very inexpensive compost already made.

Tips for Wise Watering

Plants need water to grow, but too much causes roots to remain shallow or to even rot. As a general rule, do not over-water. Most established woody garden plants (trees, shrubs, vines) and quite a few perennials and annuals need little or no extra water—they have been growing in small towns and country gardens for decades on just rainfall. But to get the most out of plants, especially tropicals and annuals, be prepared to give them a slow soaking every week or two; remember, for good root growth, infrequent deep watering is better than frequent shallow watering. Newly planted plants need regular watering to get them started, then you can water less frequently unless there are drought conditions.

Consider using soaker hoses or drip irrigation (available at garden centers), which uses thin tubes to deliver water right to the base of plants instead of showering them—which is wasteful and can create ideal conditions for leaf diseases. Note: If you have a sprinkler instead of a drip watering system, water in the morning (not at night) so the foliage can dry during the day.

Fertilizers: Less Is More

Growing ornamental plants isn't like farming, which requires regular feeding to replace nutrients that are harvested or washed away in winter rains. Still most garden plants need an extra touch of "plant food"—fertilizers—in addition to what is available in your native soil. Fertilizers include the most important "big three" nutrients: nitrogen (N) for green growth, phosphorus (P) for flowers and fruit, and potassium or potash (K) for strong roots, stems, winterizing, and general health.

Fertilizers are labeled with a set of three numbers that represent these three ingredients. Choose one with all three

Ornamental Grasses and Purple Coneflower

numbers the same or nearly the same, or slightly higher nitrogen for green plants (lawns, ferns, herbs, leafy shrubs), or slightly higher phosphorus for flowering and fruiting plants (roses, azaleas, daylilies, peppers). There are specialty fertilizers for most groups of plants that, though expensive, are usually very good. Use them at less than the recommended strength for acceptable plant growth. Slow-release fertilizers are just that—they feed plants over many weeks or months, which is much better than commercial or garden-grade fertilizers that start out strong and quickly wash away. If you feed your soil regularly with compost, your plants will be healthier and need less fertilizer.

Mulch Twice a Year

A layer of organic mulch such as pine straw, pine bark, or chipped leaves on top of the soil over plant roots will keep the soil shaded in the hot summer, protect it from dramatic temperature swings in the winter, help prevent weed seeds from sprouting, and slowly decompose to "feed" the soil. A good rule of thumb for determining how much mulch to use (no matter what type) is to spread a layer just thick enough to completely cover the ground, then add that much more to allow for settling and natural composting. Mulch at planting time, and again in the spring or fall, depending on when you plant. Keep mulch away from the base or crown of plants, especially those that need excellent drainage, because it could cause them to rot. Mulch can attract snails and slugs, but the benefits far outweigh the potential problems.

Pampas Grass

Pruning Is Good Grooming

Pruning is good grooming for woody plants, just like haircuts are for people. Basically, there are three things you need to remember about pruning: why, when, and how.

Southern Magnolia

- **Why:** Prune to remove dead wood, to improve flowering and fruiting, to rejuvenate an overgrown plant, or to maintain a desired size or form.
- **When:** Fast-growing plants, such as forsythia, nandina, and roses, should be pruned every year; slower-growing plants may need pruning only every two or three years. Prune spring-flowering shrubs (azaleas, spirea, nandina, hollies) after they finish blooming in the late spring or very early summer. Prune summer-flowering shrubs (roses, althea, hydrangea, crape myrtle, chaste tree) in late winter or early spring before the new season's growth begins.
- **How:** Cut out dead wood and overly long limbs from inside the plant. Thin other branches that are touching and overlapping. Cut back no more than a third of the plant at a time, maintaining the plant's natural growth habit. Remember, pruning is local in effect and new growth will occur below the cut. Do not top trees or shear shrubs (unless it is being used in a formal garden and is a plant that responds well to shearing, such as boxwood), which results in a "witch's broom" look. To produce compact, heavy growth in a crape myrtle, for example, prune it back to 1 foot off the ground. To produce a taller crape myrtle, cut out only small branches. Prune hedges, such as boxwood, so the base of the plant is wider than the top, aiming for a slightly A shape, rather than a V shape. On trees, be careful to prune just to the outside of the growth collar (the slight bulge where the stem meets the trunk or limb) so the wound can heal properly.

The Basics of Propagation

Fifty years ago, every gardener knew how to start plants from seed, divide a clump of a perennial, or root a shrub cutting. These simple skills can save you a lot of money, help you obtain the best selections,

A Southern Landscape with Live Oaks and Summer Annuals

increase your collection of plants, and help you enjoy growing plants perfectly adapted to your climate. Growing annuals from seed is usually simple and straightforward. Keys to success include using fresh seed, planting at the proper depth, and keeping the soil evenly moist and humid until germination occurs. Though many perennials are as easy to get started from seed as annuals, they may take up to a year to flower.

Many plants that grow from clumps of stems coming from beneath the ground can be divided into smaller plants, each with its own roots and stems, to increase your supply of plants. Herbaceous perennials such as daylily, iris, phlox, sedum, yarrow, and oxeye daisy are often divided. The rule of thumb for when to divide is simple: Divide spring bloomers in the fall and winter, and divide summer or fall bloomers in the winter or spring. Get a good amount of roots with each division and discard any pieces with few leaves and roots, since they probably won't thrive.

Woody plants such as hydrangea, spirea, and chaste tree will often send up new shoots from the base of the mother plant. Divisions can be taken from woody shrubs in winter, before new growth begins. Dig around the new shoot carefully, to make sure it has enough roots to make it on its own. Then cut the new plant free with clippers or a knife and replant.

Plants that branch out from a single stem cannot be divided, but many will root from stem cuttings. This is a good technique to use when you want to propagate many plants or want to overwinter a prized basil or tender perennial for use the following year. Some plants, including English ivy, hydrangea, coleus, wax begonia, and geranium, will root in a glass of water. Others work best when inserted in a moist medium such as a mixture of sharp sand, perlite, and peat moss, or even stuck in decent garden soil. Although cuttings of many annuals and herbaceous perennials can be taken whenever the plants are in active growth, timing is more critical with woody shrubs. The best rule of thumb for shrubs and vines is to root evergreens (hollies, ivy, azaleas) in the summer and deciduous plants (roses, crape myrtle, forsythia) in the fall or winter.

Layering is an easy way to root parts of a plant while still attached. It works well for several plants, including vines, creeping juniper, rosemary, and roses. Bend a young branch so that part of it is in the ground, with the tip sticking out (some gardeners remove a small area of bark from the underside of the branch at the midpoint, and dust the cut with rooting hormone). Pile soil over the buried part of the stem and place a brick or stone on top to weigh it down. When it has formed a mass of roots (which usually takes two or three months), sever the branch and replant it.

Environmentally Friendly Pest Control

Every gardener handles pest control differently. The trend is to avoid the routine use of chemicals, for several reasons—including personal safety, economics, and protection of the environment. Hand picking or thumping, mashing, spraying with water, or pruning can get rid of many of the worst offenders.

Spraying with soapy water (especially with special "insecticidal" soaps) and other natural materials (including light horticultural oils) often works as well as chemicals. Choosing and planting pest-resistant species and varieties is a huge step forward, as is simply getting rid of difficult, pest-prone plants. For more information on pest control, see pages 249 through 252.

Gardening is a chance to get closer to nature, not do battle with it. Choosing good plants, siting them in their preferred growing conditions, and doing a thorough job of soil preparation will help your garden be as easy to care for as it is beautiful and productive. The rest of this book is dedicated to just a few of the very best plants for "sister states" gardeners.

Sedum, Black-Eyed Susan, and Miscanthus

How to Use the *Alabama & Mississippi Gardener's Guide*

Each entry in this guide provides you with information about a plant's particular characteristics, habits, and its basic requirements for active growth, as well as our personal experience and knowledge of the plant. We include the information you need to help you realize each plant's potential. Only when a plant performs at its best can one appreciate it fully. You will find such pertinent information as mature height and spread, bloom period and colors, sun and soil preferences, water requirements, fertilizing needs, pruning and care, and pest information.

Sun Preferences

Symbols represent the range of sunlight suitable for each plant. Full sun means eight hours or more, including midday. Part sun means six to eight hours, not midday. Part shade means three or four hours, preferably morning. Shade means less than two hours of sun. Some plants can be grown in more than one range of sun, so you will sometimes see more than one sun symbol.

Full Sun **Part Sun** **Part Shade** **Shade**

Additional Benefits

Many plants offer benefits that further enhance their value. The following symbols indicate some of the more important additional benefits:

 Attracts Butterflies

 Attracts Hummingbirds

 Produces Edible Fruit

 Has Fragrance

 Produces Food for Birds and Wildlife

 Drought Resistant

 Suitable for Cut Flowers or Arrangements

 Long Bloom Period

 Native Plant

 Supports Bees

 Provides Shelter for Birds

 Good Fall Color

Companion Planting and Design

For most of the entries, we provide landscape design ideas, as well as suggestions for companion plants to help you create pleasing and successful combinations—and inspire original compositions of your own. This is where we find much enjoyment from gardening.

Personal Favorites

These sections describe those specific cultivars or varieties that we have found particularly noteworthy, or we recommend other good species to try. Give them a try . . . or perhaps you'll find your own personal favorite.

USDA Cold Hardiness Zones

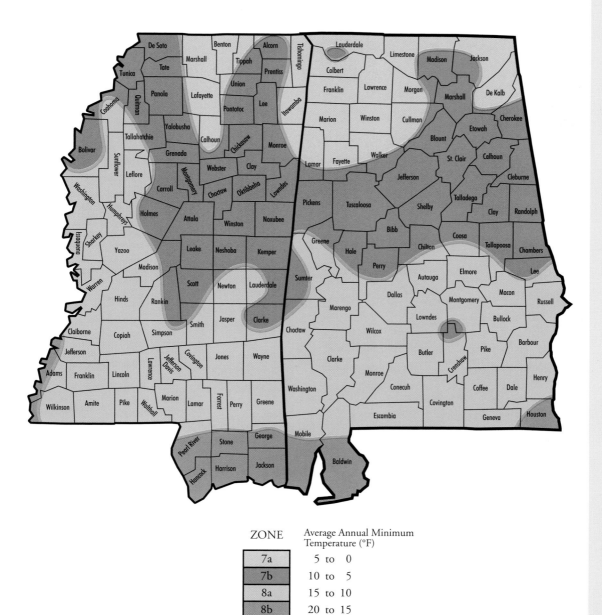

ZONE	Average Annual Minimum Temperature (°F)
7a	5 to 0
7b	10 to 5
8a	15 to 10
8b	20 to 15

Hardiness Zones

Cold-hardiness zone designations were developed by the United States Department of Agriculture (USDA) to indicate the minimum average temperature for an area. A zone assigned to an individual plant indicates the lowest temperature at which the plant can be expected to survive over the winter.

Annuals *for Alabama & Mississippi*

There's no such thing as an instant garden—except with annuals, which give immediate "flower power." Annuals are plants that complete their life cycle within a growing season. These tough plants produce flowers or beautiful foliage from seed over either the summer or winter, before dying from winter freeze or summer heat. Because we have "English winters and Texas summers," our crazy weather sometimes makes it tough on perennials, but annuals can take it. Generally inexpensive and easy to grow, annuals bring seasonal color, fragrance, and texture to the garden. They can be used in many different ways:

- As colorful fillers in perennial or shrub borders
- As mass plantings in beds for impact
- As splashes of color in container gardens
- As attractive foliage plants in shade gardens
- As flowers for cutting to enjoy in arrangements
- As irresistible attractants, bringing butterflies, hummingbirds, and children to the garden

Annual Success

In this chapter, annuals fall into two main categories: bedding plants, such as pansies, petunias, and marigolds, which usually last one season; and old-fashioned reseeding annuals, such as black-eyed Susan, cosmos, and cleome, whose offspring show up every year in the most surprising places. In addition, several plants here are sometimes mistakenly called "biennial" because they live over the winter—including foxglove, larkspur, and poppy. They must be planted in the fall for a spring show. Some plants can be perennial in other parts of the country but usually can't take our fickle winter weather or hot, humid summer nights and are grown as annuals here in the Deep South.

For success with annuals, keep these tried-and-true tips in mind:

- Choose the right annual for the right spot—think "sun" or "shade" when buying plants.
- Buy named selections you know perform well in your area. Botanical garden display beds, university trial gardens, and better garden shops offer clues to choosing these.
- Prepare planting bed soils very well, as annuals have a lot of work to do in a short time. Annuals do best in loamy, well-drained soil with at least one-third organic material.

Cosmos, Angelonia, Zinnia, and Petunia

Coleus 'Rusty'

- Add a slow-acting or controlled-release fertilizer to the soil at planting time, and water growing plants occasionally with water-soluble fertilizers. Never overfeed!

- Dig a hole as deep as the rootball and at least twice as wide.

- Plant annuals properly, being especially careful to tease loose a few roots at planting time (instead of allowing them to stay in a ball) to encourage wide-ranging deep roots.

- Set the plant with the top of the rootball at the same level it was growing in the pot.

- Gently firm the soil around the base of the plant, then water thoroughly to remove air pockets and let the plant settle.

- Cover the soil surface after planting with a layer of pine straw, leaves, or bark mulch to keep roots cool and moist in the summer, and warm and weed-free in winter.

- Water deeply, but only as needed. Too much water is often worse than none at all!

- Pinch or cut off faded flowers (called "deadheading") to encourage bushier growth and more flowers.

One last thing: Because they are usually so easy to grow, annuals are great for children and beginning gardeners. Who among us doesn't remember planting zinnias as a child during summer vacation? Okay, maybe not everyone. But there is a bumper sticker that says: "It's never too late to have a happy childhood." That can be translated to mean it's never too late to plant zinnias!

There are too many great annuals to mention even just our favorites here—they could fill their own book! But on the following pages are a few that sooner or later every good gardener grows. Give them a try, then add others that catch your fancy, and see for yourself how annuals can bring gusto and pizzazz to your garden, no matter how large or small.

Black-Eyed Susan
Rudbeckia hirta

This most beautiful roadside wildflower and its improved varieties have finally become choice spring and early summer annuals (sometimes short-lived perennials) for naturalistic and cut-flower gardens. The plants reseed prolifically over the summer, sprouting in the fall and growing over the winter to bloom the following spring, branching into two or three dozen long, sturdy stems topped with daisy-like flowers. The orange-yellow blooms spread out from a characteristic brown "nose" and can be 2 to 5 inches wide, single or sometimes double. Some varieties are splashed with accents of gold, orange, or red. They provide dependable color in the dry or well-drained garden and long-lasting cut flowers with little or no fuss and bother.

Other Common Name
Gloriosa Daisy

Bloom Period and Seasonal Color
Yellow blooms with black centers in summer

Mature Height × Spread
2 to 3 feet × 2 feet

When, Where, and How to Plant
Sow seeds directly where the plants are to grow, in late summer or early fall (up to two months before the first frost) for blooms late the following spring. Keep the soil moist for a week or two, until seedlings emerge, and thin seedlings to a foot or more apart. Set out young transplants in the spring when the soil warms up. This native wildflower tolerates drought and poor soil, but does best in a rich, well-drained soil. Mulch to control weeds.

Growing Tips
Black-eyed Susan is drought tolerant, but benefits from watering during extended dry spells. Like other wildflowers, it does not need fertilizing unless the soil is nutrient deficient.

Care
Deadhead black-eyed Susan to prolong blooming, but let a few flowers go to seed and scatter the seeds at the base of the plant, to provide volunteer seedlings for next year. Other than a few caterpillars that do minor damage to plants, few pests bother black-eyed Susans—even deer avoid browsing them if at all possible. Powdery mildew may discolor some foliage during wet seasons, but is not generally enough of a problem to warrant spraying.

Companion Planting and Design
In addition to its natural companions of coreopsis and Queen Anne's lace, this simple yellow daisy with the chocolate-brown central cone electrifies a bed full of blue larkspur, magenta phlox, orange daylilies, and red poppies. Easy to grow, they are ideal for meadow or cutting gardens, or for creating dazzling borders in summer and fall. Plants reseed and are good for naturalizing sunny areas, wildflower meadows, and sunny walkways.

Personal Favorites
The award-winning 'Indian Summer' has large flowers with classic dark centers; 'Irish Eyes' has a light green cone that fades to brown when seeds mature. 'Goldilocks' is a low-growing variety. The stunning 'Gloriosa' has large flowers up to 7 inches across with more colors than the species.

When, Where, and How to Plant

All coreopsis are native to prairies and open places, and require sunshine and well-drained soils to survive. Sow calliopsis seed onto open ground, tamping the seed in direct contact with the soil (if seeds are caught up in mulch, they won't sprout). The best success is with seeds sown in the late summer or very early fall, because to flower their best, the small "rosette" plants need to be exposed to winter freezes, which they tolerate with great ease. For uniform stands of plants, keep the seeded areas moist until seedlings sprout, then water a little more deeply two or three times to get plants established; these tough roadside beauties can take it from there. Where possible, tuck them between perennials where mulch is not too thick.

Growing Tips

Calliopsis is very drought tolerant and needs little or no water or fertilizer once established. Tall plants may "flop" during prolonged rainy spells, but if you plant them between or behind other flowers, their flower stems will grow upward toward the light. The very prolific reseeder will "come back" for many years with little help from the gardener; by pulling dead plants up and tapping them around the garden, you will sow seeds in enough places to provide plenty of seedlings by winter.

Care

Deadhead calliopsis to keep new flower stems forming, but always leave a few faded flowers so they can form their little seeds. Save a few seed to sow in the fall. Calliopsis has no real pests.

Companion Planting and Design

Use calliopsis in almost any naturalistic design—mixed borders, wildflower meadows, woodland edges, perennial plantings, even large containers where a filler plant is needed. It is a great companion to dense or spiky plants such as daylily, phlox, blazing star, salvia, sunflowers, or coneflowers.

Personal Favorites

There are a few hard-to-find varieties of this type of coreopsis, including solid burgundy varieties such as 'Mahogany Midget', but the simple, easy-to-grow "plain" one is by far the most satisfying.

Coreopsis, Mississippi's official state wildflower, is usually considered a short-lived perennial—and many species are. But the most prolific species of all is a tall, airy, many-branched annual that readily fills in between other flowers in the late spring and summer, sometimes later, before reseeding everywhere. Its "Indian blanket" flowers, which don't have the prominent central "cone" of black-eyed Susan, have yellow, orange, and burgundy rays, usually with contrasting bands. Its leaves are small and narrow and seem to disappear under clouds of inch-wide flowers. There are other, hard-to-find annual species, but this native plant is one of the most choice filler flowers for the spring and summer flower border or wildflower meadow.

Other Common Name
Plains Coreopsis

Bloom Period and Seasonal Color
Spring and summer flowers of yellow or burgundy

Mature Height × Spread
2 to 4 feet × 2 to 3 feet

Cleome
Cleome hassleriana

Cleome sprouts in early spring when the soil warms, and by mid-June the spectacular, 3- to 5-foot-tall plants sport exotic bottlebrushes in cotton-candy colors. Cleome's large, airy sprays of orchid-like flowers come in white, rose, dusty pink, or lavender. The protruding stamens look like spider legs or cat whiskers, hence the other common names. The leaves are sticky in two ways—they have short spines, and exude a sticky sap that some gardeners find objectionable. The plant looks delicate, but is very durable with a tough, tropical constitution, well suited to our hottest summers. Cut flowers will wilt at first, but perk up quickly in water. It reseeds prolifically (almost too well) to ensure its presence in the flower garden year after year.

Other Common Names
Spider Flower, Cat Whiskers

Bloom Period and Seasonal Color
Pink, white, lavender blooms, from summer to frost

Mature Height × Spread
3 to 5 feet × 2 to 3 feet

When, Where, and How to Plant
Sow cleome seeds when the soil has warmed in late spring, after the threat of frost has passed. Plant cleome in full sun to partial shade in loose, well-drained soil. Cleome is available as transplants in the spring, and seedlings can be moved when they are very small, but it is best grown from seed sown directly in the garden where plants are to flower. This encourages deep root growth, which helps plants resist drought. Keep seeded areas moist until seedlings emerge, usually in ten to fifteen days. After that, water less often, but deeply (to encourage deep roots), until the young plants are well established. Thin to $1^1/2$ to 2 feet apart after the seedlings have at least four leaves.

Growing Tips
Plants respond to deep watering during periods of drought, but generally prefer warm, dry conditions. Cleome needs little fertilizer to flower well over a long period.

Care
When blooming starts to taper off, cut back old flower stems to the main plant to encourage new growth and a fresh flush of blooms. Cleome reseeds, but often comes back as mixed colors. Because they did not evolve in our seasons, the seeds germinate during a long, warm fall or earlier in the spring than is always safe. Usually seedlings withstand cool nights, but sometimes they may die during a prolonged cold spell. There are few, if any, pests to worry about.

Companion Planting and Design
Because of its size, plant cleome at the back of a border, or highlighted against a wall, fence, or tall shrubs. Its airy effect makes it ideal as "filler" with other annuals or low-growing, drought-tolerant perennials such as daylily or iris.

Personal Favorites
Try the Queen series, which grows about 4 feet tall, and includes violet and rose. 'Helen Campbell' is white. 'Sparkler Blush' is a dwarf pink version.

Coleus
Solenostemon hybrids

When, Where, and How to Plant

Set out these very frost-sensitive plants in mid-spring after the soil has thoroughly warmed and all danger of frost has passed. Common coleus can be grown quickly and easily from seed, but new varieties are available only from stem cuttings taken any time the plant is actively growing. Coleus grows in average soil, but it likes rich, moist soil. Set plants at least a foot apart, keeping in mind the size of the plants and the importance of good air circulation, which helps prevent foliage and stem diseases. Coleus grows best in highly amended soils rich in organic material. Mix a controlled-release, all-purpose fertilizer with the soil.

Growing Tips

Coleus likes a steady dose of moisture. Water plants deeply as needed, especially at the first signs of wilting (they quickly regain their composure). Water container plantings more frequently, especially those in full sun. Coleus needs light doses of fertilizer to replace fertilizer that is washed out after repeated waterings. Mulches help keep soils cool and moist.

Care

When possible, pinch off the long spikes of rather insignificant pale blue flowers to preserve the plant's vigor and encourage more colorful leaves. Shear back plants that get out of hand—they sprout back quickly. Root the pieces you cut off to share with other gardeners. Whiteflies and mealy bugs can sometimes be annoying, but rarely require spraying.

Companion Planting and Design

Taller selections are stunning massed in beds; the dwarf forms (6 inches tall) make colorful borders and potted plants. Coleus grows well with shade-loving trailing or creeping groundcovers such as ajuga, moneywort, liriope; tropicals such as asparagus fern; and annuals such as impatiens.

Personal Favorites

There are simply too many good coleus available, most very good plants, to single out any, though the sun-loving 'Plum Parfait' and 'Burgundy Sun' garner lots of attentions at malls and fast-food restaurants when grown in full sun.

Coleus was discovered in the Old World tropics and became a classic Victorian bedding plant. This formerly shade-loving "queen of grandmother's garden" has made an incredible comeback in popularity, largely due to hundreds of dazzling new heat- and sun-tolerant varieties. Its large leaves and spikes of flowers lend a tropical air to any garden. The frilly, toothed, or wrinkled foliage is often splashed and streaked with combinations of green, gold, bronze, cream, copper, cranberry, pink, and purple. For more subdued tastes, there are solid colors of velvety red, rose, bronze, or yellow green. Flowers are good for butterflies, but tend to grow at the expense of foliage, which is the main attraction.

Other Common Name
Painted Leaves

Bloom Period and Seasonal Color
Yellow, green, bronze, mauve, purple foliage from late spring until frost

Mature Height × Spread
6 inches to 4 feet × 1 to 3 feet

Cosmos
Cosmos species

A native of Mexico, cosmos is a cheerful warm-weather annual, popular in children's gardens, cutting gardens, and naturalistic plantings, that takes the heat and humidity of our summers in stride despite its delicate appearance. From late April to midsummer, common cosmos (C. bipinnatus) has large, single or double flowers of pink, white, rose, or crimson that float daisy-like on long stems above a dense mass of feathered, finely divided foliage. Yellow cosmos (C. sulphureus) can grow up to 7 feet tall but usually stays between 2 and 3 feet, with larger, more marigold-like leaves, and deep orange or yellow flowers from summer to fall. They all reseed themselves to the point of nearly being a nuisance.

Bloom Period and Seasonal Color
Pink, white, purple, orange, yellow blooms from summer to frost

Mature Height × Spread
2 to 7 feet × 1 to 3 feet

When, Where, and How to Plant
Sow seeds when the soil has warmed in late spring after the threat of frost has passed. Cosmos grows best in dry, infertile, even sandy soil with excellent drainage; in rich or moist soil, you get abundant leaves, but fewer flowers. Small seedlings can be transplanted, and small plants are generally available in garden shops in late spring. However, it is almost embarrassingly easy to grow from seed sown directly onto bare soil, usually blooming within a few weeks. Keep seeded areas evenly moist until seedlings emerge, then thin to 9 to 12 inches apart.

Growing Tips
Cosmos is drought tolerant, and will quickly rot if kept wet. It requires little or no fertilizer unless the soil is seriously nutrient deficient. Overfertilizing gives you a lot of stems and leaves with few flowers.

Care
Cosmos benefits from being cut back in midsummer to promote a new flush of blooms. With deadheading, cosmos blooms all summer into fall; however, because cosmos reseeds, leave a few seedheads to scatter and do their job. Plantings can thin out over time if left to their own devices, so you may choose to save some seed to replant each spring for a better show of blooms. Tall selections fall over during storms, so use them at the back of the garden or stake them. Whiteflies may be a temporary nuisance, but no sprays are needed.

Companion Planting and Design
Because of its many flowers often in contrasting colors, cosmos is often mass-planted in naturalistic gardens, or used as a companion to denser-flowering plants such as sunflowers, daylily, or coarse-foliage iris, and as a filler for small shrubs or groundcovers.

Personal Favorites
There are several good new strains of cosmos, including crimson 'Dazzler' and the tall red 'Versailles Red', which is one of the best cut-flower cosmos. 'Bright Lights' and 'Klondike' are semi-dwarf, semi-double flowering forms of *C. sulphureus*.

When, Where, and How to Plant

When possible, set out foxglove transplants in the fall well before the first frost, so they can get a winter chill to flower better the following spring. If not available in the fall, set out plants as soon as you can find them in the late winter or early spring before they start flowering. Sow seed in late summer or early fall so plants can get up and going before winter. Keep evenly moist until seedlings emerge. Foxgloves like the morning sun of beds with an eastern or northern exposure, or partial shade at the edge of trees. Be sure to give them afternoon shade. Plant in a rich, loose, well-drained soil. Space 12 to 15 inches apart. Mulch to keep the root zone cool and moist, and to control weeds. Note: Foxglove is the source of a strong heart medicine and can be dangerous when ingested, so keep children and pets from eating any part of the plant.

Growing Tips

Water foxglove deeply no more than once a week to keep plants from rotting. Fertilize with compost or a slow-acting, controlled-release, all-purpose fertilizer in the late winter, but don't force them into tender growth in the heat of summer. Cut faded flowers to force new side shoots and flowers.

Care

Stake tall flower spikes when needed, or simply cut the leaning ones for flower arrangements (this also induces repeat blooming). Slugs and snails may be troublesome in wet weather.

Companion Planting and Design

Foxgloves are effective at the back of a long border or at the edge of a shady woodland garden. Or, if you have just a little space, plant half a dozen foxgloves in the center of a small, circular bed, surrounded by cool-season annuals and biennials, such as violas and parsley.

Personal Favorites

'Shirley' is a giant, speckle-throated foxglove that grows to 3 to 6 feet; 'Excelsior' is a medium tall foxglove; and 'Foxy' is a still more compact variety. 'Alba' is a striking white and makes a fine cut flower.

Tall, exotic-looking European native foxgloves bring a romantic touch to many a Southern spring garden. Foxgloves, which may be very short-lived perennials in the upper parts of our states (especially in higher elevations), range in color from the typical dull pink-purple of the species to strawberry, apricot, lemon, and cream, often spotted or mottled with a darker shade. Each spike rises from a rosette of oblong leaves that usually remains evergreen through the winter. Even without pinching to encourage more bloom spikes, foxgloves bloom for about six weeks in the garden, attracting hummingbirds and inquisitive bees, and daring to be cut and put into flower arrangements. There are several species in addition to the common foxglove.

Other Common Name
Digitalis

Bloom Period and Seasonal Color
White, pastel yellow, pink, mauve blooms in spring

Mature Height × Spread
2- to 5-feet flower spikes × 1- to 2-foot leaf rosettes

Geranium

Pelargonium × hortorum

The old-fashioned, popular plants we call geraniums are not true geraniums (cranesbill). What we most commonly grow is Pelargonium from South Africa, which loves our heat and humidity. Growing 8 to 15 inches or more tall, these "garden" geraniums have thick, sturdy stems and kidney-shaped, fuzzy leaves that are often variegated or have colorful "zonal" markings, and a strong fragrance when bruised or cut. Half-ball clusters of single or double flowers in red, white, pink, salmon, and rose are held above the leaves on narrow, straight stems. In hot, humid July and August, geraniums start to look scraggly. If you cut them back, however, they often bloom again in the cool of fall.

Other Common Name
Garden Geranium

Bloom Period and Seasonal Color
Red, pink, orange, purple, white, salmon blooms from late winter to frost

Mature Height × Spread
8 to 18 inches × 1 foot

When, Where, and How to Plant
Geraniums, which can tolerate light frosts, flower best in cool weather, so set potted plants out in the late winter or early spring; they can also be set out in the late summer or fall for a long flowering period before hard freezes set in. When planting in the soil, wait until the danger of freezing is past in the spring. Geraniums thrive in well-drained, neutral pH soil; add lime if your soil is too acidic. Set plants 12 to 18 inches apart. These plants like afternoon shade in summer, but tolerate southern and western exposures in spring. If planting in a container, allow the plants to become slightly rootbound, as this facilitates abundant blooms. Geraniums are easily propagated from stem cuttings placed in moist, sterile sand.

Growing Tips
Geraniums are drought tolerant. Water only when the soil is dry; do not over-water. If new growth begins to turn yellow, plants need more frequent watering. High-nitrogen fertilizer promotes foliage growth over blooms, so use a "flower booster" type fertilizer with more phosphorus (indicated by the middle number on the fertilizer label).

Care
Deadhead regularly to preserve the plant's vigor and neatness, and to encourage more flowers. Pinch plants back to promote bushiness. Remove yellow or dead older leaves that invite disease in humid climates. Overwinter potted plants indoors in a sunny window, or simply pull them out of their pots, strip off their leaves, shake off the potting soil, and keep the succulent stems dry until replanting in the spring. Spider mites and whiteflies may be troublesome during hot, dry weather.

Companion Planting and Design
Although they work well as bedding plants, geraniums really shine in planters, pots, and window boxes. They bloom best when slightly potbound and the soil dries out a bit between waterings. Use with cascading ivy or vinca, or with dusty miller and spike dracaena.

Personal Favorites
There are many selections, including the Americana and Designer series.

Globe Amaranth
Gomphrena globosa

When, Where, and How to Plant

Gomphrena, native to hot, dry climates, is tough enough to grow in a parking lot. It needs as much sun as possible, and perfectly well-drained, almost poor soils. Sow seed over freshly dug and raked soil as soon as the weather warms for good in the spring, up until midsummer for a fall crop of flowers. Transplant small garden center plants from spring to midsummer, loosening the potting soil to encourage fast side-root growth and tougher plants. No need to mulch this plant, as it loves hot dirt!

Growing Tips

Globe amaranth is extremely heat and drought tolerant. Water only when very dry or risk root rot, and fertilize very lightly if at all—or expect a lot of foliage growth and few flowers.

Care

Gomphrena benefits from being cut back lightly in midsummer to promote bushiness and a new flush of blooms. With deadheading, it blooms all summer into fall; however, because it reseeds, leave a few seedheads to scatter and do their job. The population can thin out over the years, so you may choose to save some seed to replant each spring for a better show of blooms. Tall selections fall over during storms, so use them at the back of the garden. Whiteflies may be a temporary nuisance, but no sprays are needed.

Companion Planting and Design

Because a gomphrena plant by itself lacks a lot of substance, its stiff, airy stems and loads of tight flowers make it a perfect companion to other summer flowers. Tuck it between daylilies, phlox, asters, shrub roses, or other coarse or spiky plants—use it in the garden just as you would a filler in flower arrangements.

Personal Favorites

Purplish magenta 'Buddy' and white 'Sissy' are small, compact varieties best suited for fronts and edges of borders and containers. 'Lavender Lady' is a tall pink variety, and 'Strawberry Fields' is a true red that no summer garden should be without.

This trio of very old heat and drought-tolerant cottage garden flowers, all native to Africa, seldom appear alone: celosia (prince's feather and cockscomb), Madagascar periwinkle, and gomphrena. The first two are so common in garden centers they don't need recommending—but the latter deserves a special highlight. Globe amaranth, with its clover-like heads of magenta or white, is one of the toughest filler plants of the hot summer garden. The common old varieties have remained popular for many generations, but new red and pink varieties have made their splash with new gardeners as well. They are sturdy, low-maintenance companions for most other flowers, and can be cut and dried into "everlasting" arrangements that retain their color for years.

Other Common Names
Bachelor Buttons, Gomphrena

Bloom Period and Seasonal Color
Red, pink, magenta, or white flowers from spring to frost

Mature Height × Spread
6 to 36 inches × 6 to 18 inches

Impatiens
Impatiens walleriana

Impatiens remains one of the most popular and dependable summer annuals for shade. It likes heat, humidity, and partial shade. Water only when they wilt, and they will bloom happily until frost. Impatiens comes in a variety of lipstick colors, ranging from red to lavender to flamingo pink. Dwarf and double-flowering selections exist as well. Impatiens plants are called touch-me-nots because the seed capsule explodes at the slightest touch. As a result, impatiens may naturalize and reseed for years (though offspring might not be the colors you originally planted). The taller, hybrid New Guinea impatiens (I. hawkeri) is often sold in larger pots, rather than as flats of bedding plants. They have distinct yellow and green foliage, bigger flowers, and the ability to tolerate more sun.

Other Common Names
Busy Lizzie, Touch-Me-Not

Bloom Period and Seasonal Color
Red, white, pink, salmon, lilac blooms from spring to frost

Mature Height × Spread
8 to 24 inches × 12 to 18 inches

When, Where, and How to Plant
Set out transplants in the late spring when all danger of frost is past, in a shaded or morning-sun-only bed. Sow impatiens seed indoors in late winter or early spring, if you have a greenhouse or fluorescent lights indoors. Do not cover seeds with soil—they need light to germinate. Keep evenly moist until seedlings emerge. Take cuttings in the fall before the first freeze (they root readily in water). Fertilize regularly and keep the soil moist. Space 12 to 18 inches apart, depending upon the selection and mature size of the plant. If the soil is poor, add organic material. Mulch to keep the root zone moist and to control weeds.

Growing Tips
Water impatiens deeply as often as they need it, which you can tell from their wilting; however, do not keep them wet or their succulent stems may rot at the soil line. Fertilize impatiens regularly to compensate for what washes out during frequent waterings and to help plants keep producing new foliage and flowers; use the fertilizer at half strength or expect plants to get leggy and brittle in the shade. Mulches help keep soil moist, but will prevent a lot of reseeding.

Care
Pinch plants back to promote bushiness. You can even prune them halfway to the ground to rejuvenate leggy or floppy plants. Whiteflies can be a nuisance in hot weather, and slugs and snails will eat some flowers and foliage.

Companion Planting and Design
Plant impatiens in large masses, or in drifts among ferns, caladiums, hosta, liriope, and other shade-loving plants for a natural look. Use them to fill holes in flower borders, or in mixed plantings in containers. Grow impatiens as a houseplant in winter in a sunny window.

Personal Favorites
The Elfin, Dazzler, Accent, Blitz, Impulse, and Twinkle series are all good bets, but nurserymen are constantly coming out with more great varieties.

Lantana
Lantana camara

When, Where, and How to Plant

Set out transplants in late spring when the weather has warmed and all danger of frost is past, in loose, well-drained soil. Lantana tolerates just about any kind of soil—sand, clay, or loam—as long as the drainage is excellent. Be very sure to loosen roots of new transplants—almost "bare-root" them—or the potting soil will keep roots too wet after watering. Eastern or southern sites with some protection increase lantana's chances of surviving winter. Set plants 3 to 4 feet apart, depending upon the selection. Propagate lantana by cuttings taken in the summer or fall.

Growing Tips

Lantana is extremely heat and drought tolerant. Water only when very dry, or risk root rot; fertilize very lightly if at all, or expect a lot of foliage growth and few flowers.

Care

Prune back periodically to promote bushiness. Where lantana is root hardy, in the fall after a frost has burst the bark of the stems, cut the plants nearly to the ground, cover entirely with leaf mulch, and expect new growth to come up from the crown near the roots very late the next spring after the weather has warmed. In dry weather, lantana attracts spider mites. Spray the undersides of leaves weekly with a strong stream of water, or use an insecticidal soap that won't harm butterflies.

Companion Planting and Design

Lantana, especially low-growing or cascading varieties, makes a terrific container plant, particularly in hot sites. All types blend well with tropical foliage plants such as canna. Interplant summer lantana with winter and spring bulbs, which perform during lantana's "off" season and require little or no water in the summer.

Personal Favorites

Lantana comes in several different selections, including 'Dazzler' and 'Patriot Rainbow'. 'New Gold' is a semi-hardy groundcover, and both 'Miss Huff' and the Son series ('Sampson', 'Sonrise', and 'Sonset', developed by a Mississippi nurseryman) are very winter hardy.

Gardeners from Interstate 20 south assume that lantanas are hardy perennials (they are downright weedy close to the Gulf Coast). However, with some old-fashioned exceptions and a few interesting new varieties, gardeners in the northern third of our states use lantana as dependable heat- and drought-loving summer annuals that bloom from spring to autumn's first frost. Ask local Master Gardeners or garden center managers for ones that may live for several years in your area. Lantana's crinkly, pungent foliage serves as a good backdrop for the masses of rounded heads of flowers that are among the very best butterfly attractions for sunny gardens. Note: The bright blue berries of lantana are very poisonous so keep curious children from eating them!

Other Common Name

Yellow Sage

Bloom Period and Seasonal Color

Pink, yellow, orange, red, and purple blooms from summer to frost

Mature Height × Spread

1 to 4 feet × 3 feet or more

Larkspur

Consolida ambigua

Larkspur is a pastel-blooming cottage garden flower in the same family as larger delphiniums, with airy spires of single or double blossoms densely packed along sturdy stems. The single varieties have what looks like a rabbit head in the center. Larkspur grows over the winter (cold weather does not affect it at all), blooms in the spring and early summer, sets seeds, and dies in the heat by late summer, then reseeds prolifically to start the process over again in the fall. It is a welcome seasonal transition plant that bridges fading winter pansies and early spring iris, into the season of daylilies and warm-season annuals. Larkspur is an excellent cut flower.

Other Common Name
Delphinium

Bloom Period and Seasonal Color
Blue, white, pink blooms in spring and summer

Mature Height × Spread
2 to 5 feet × 1 foot

When, Where, and How to Plant
Sow larkspur seed in the late summer or fall; seed will sprout when the weather has begun to cool. Garden stores sometimes remove flower seeds from their shelves in midsummer; buy enough in the spring to plant in the fall—and make a note to remind yourself to plant them later! Keep the soil evenly moist until germination occurs, in one to two weeks. Plant larkspur in rich, loose, slightly alkaline soil. Thin seedlings 6 inches to a foot apart. Larkspur transplants are available, but it's easier to grow them from seed. Transplants set out in spring have a more difficult time getting established before blooming. Also, larkspur looks best when planted en masse for a burst of color, so starting with transplants is expensive.

Growing Tips
In fall, water young plants regularly until they are well established. In spring, water only as needed every week or two. Fertilize plants lightly with compost or a balanced, slow-release fertilizer. Do not overfertilize or you will get a lot of foliage and few flowers. Mulch beneath leaves to control weeds, but do not cover the crown.

Care
Deadhead to prolong blooms, but allow a few plants to set seed. Harvest when capsules turn brown and sow half of them right away, where you want larkspur next year. The seeds remain dormant throughout the summer, but germinate with the cooler weather in fall. Save some seed as insurance against a hard winter. If fall plants are killed, sow saved seeds in late winter or very early spring. Stake them if necessary. There are no major pests.

Companion Planting and Design
Plant these spiky flowers at the back of the border or at the center of an island bed. Larkspur creates a spring watercolor when planted with oxeye daisies, pink phlox, yellow snapdragons, and 'The Fairy' rose, and is a perfect companion to iris and artemisia.

Personal Favorites
The Giant Imperial series grows 4 feet tall. Good cultivars include 'White King', 'Rose Queen', 'Blue Bell', and 'Blue Spire'.

When, Where, and How to Plant

Plant seeds or set out transplants in late spring after all danger of frost has passed. Sow seeds where plants are to grow. Keep them evenly moist until seedlings emerge. Seeds usually sprout within five to seven days, and should be thinned to allow for best growth. Or start marigold transplants from seed in early spring in a greenhouse or direct light of a south-facing window. Some gardeners stagger plantings so they have a new "crop" of transplants for fall color. Plant marigolds in average, well-drained garden soil. If drainage is a problem, plant them in containers and raised beds. Note: Marigolds have long been touted as pest repellents. This is not true, except for repelling soil nematodes when tilled into infested soil. Sorry!

Growing Tips

Marigolds appreciate a good soaking every week or two depending on the weather. Fertilize French marigolds only lightly at planting, or they produce too much foliage and not many flowers. Other selections, such as African marigolds and the new hybrids called "triploids," need repeat fertilization at midseason.

Care

Deadhead spent blooms to prolong flowering. After three months of bloom, marigolds start to look ragged, and can be cut back to resprout new growth or simply replaced with new plants. Spider mites are a serious problem for which most sprays are not very effective.

Companion Planting and Design

Marigolds are among the most versatile summer flowers. Plant them in rows, masses, drifts, or containers. Small ones make terrific edging, while taller ones (the best for cut flowers) should be toward the back of a bed to hide ugly older foliage.

Personal Favorites

French marigolds (*T. patula*) include 'Janie Flame' and 'Aurora Light Yellow'. American hybrids (*T. erecta*) include the Discovery and Climax series, 'Perfection Gold', 'Inca Gold', and 'Antigua Yellow'. 'Little Hero' is a good, heat-tolerant dwarf. Signet marigolds (*T. tenuifolia*) include 'Starfire' and 'Gem'.

Marigolds are among our favorite summer bedding plants, able to tolerate summer heat because of their Mexican heritage. There are several distinct types, notably the French marigolds and much taller African strains, but most are tidy mounds of highly aromatic green, fernlike foliage covered with single or double floral buttons in yellow, gold, red, and bicolor combinations. They provide almost instant color from transplants, but are also very easy to grow from seed. If kept watered, fertilized, and free of spider mites, marigolds can last in full bloom until Thanksgiving. However, new plants or seeds can be set out in the middle of the summer for a dazzling fall display. Single-flowering varieties are best for butterflies.

Bloom Period and Seasonal Color
Yellow, burnt orange, red blooms from spring to frost

Mature Height × Spread
6 inches to 4 feet × 6 to 18 inches

Melampodium
Melampodium paludosum

Any plant that looks as fresh and green as medallion plant does in August—after nightmarish heat and humidity—deserves to be in every garden. This "top ten" summer annual has small, crisp, sunflower-style leaves on a bushy plant covered in almost solid sheets of dime-size or larger buttery yellow daisies. It thrives in our summer climate to put on a dazzling late-summer show, even in very poor soils. Distant kin of the sunflower, melampodium hails from Latin America. The plant blooms from early summer until frost and happily reseeds—some say too happily, and consider it a weed. But what a weed! Choose your variety carefully, because it will be with you a long time.

Other Common Names
Star Daisy, Medallion Plant

Bloom Period and Seasonal Color
Yellow blooms from summer to frost

Mature Height × Spread
18 to 36 inches × 18 to 24 inches

When, Where, and How to Plant
Though melampodium can grow in "parking lot" conditions, it performs best when set out in average soil that is very well drained, in full sun. For fast effect, set small plants out in late spring after the danger of frost has passed, or start transplants from seed in early spring, if you have a greenhouse or a full sun window indoors. If you have time on your hands, sow seed directly where you want the plants, and keep seeded areas evenly moist until seedlings emerge. Do not over-water new plants or they will rot at the soil line.

Growing Tips
Melampodium thrives in drought, but grows best with occasional deep soakings. Wilted plants quickly regain their composure with water. They have no special fertilizer requirements, except to not be overfertilized or they will get top-heavy and flop over. Melampodium plants reseed prolifically, as long as mulches don't interfere with seed coming in contact with soil.

Care
For the most part, melampodium has few needs. It is "self cleaning"—it does not need deadheading to continue blooming—and holds up well in wind as long as its roots have not been rotted by irrigation. The plants have few pests other than occasional whiteflies, which rarely cause serious problems.

Companion Planting and Design
Depending on the variety, melampodium may be used as edging and borders, or in mass plantings in beds. They work well in hot, dry spots such as around mailboxes or alongside concrete walks or patios where reflected heat withers other flowers, and contrast nicely with the cooling effect of blue salvia.

Personal Favorites
One of the most common varieties is the 3-foot tall 'Medallion' (hence its common name), but it tends to get leggy over the summer. 'Derby' is a popular dwarf that grows 8 to 10 inches tall, 'Million Gold' is a prolific-flowering foot-tall plant, and 'Showstar' is a convenient 2-foot selection.

Pansy
Viola wittrockiana

When, Where, and How to Plant
To establish a good root system before the ground gets too cold, set out transplants in mid- to late fall (when you plant spring blooming bulbs), in pots or garden spots where they will get winter sunshine. They can also be set out in early spring for flowering before hot summer sets in. Established plants withstand temperatures down to 10 to 15 degrees. Sow seeds outdoors in August for the following spring or indoors in late winter for spring transplants. Sow seeds where plants are to grow. Keep them evenly moist until seedlings emerge. Plant in rich, well-drained soil. Set plants 6 to 12 inches apart.

Growing Tips
Water until plants are established in the fall. After that, winter rains usually take care of violas, except for potted plants, which may need more attention than those in the ground. Feed regularly with your preferred fertilizer according to directions, at planting and again in late winter. Mulch lightly to protect roots from extreme temperature swings, and to help reduce weeds.

Care
Pinch back new plants, and old leggy ones, to promote healthy pansies and more flowers. Like all cool-weather annuals, pansies begin to wither and die with the approach of summer. Have summer annuals ready to plant in their place in May. Johnny jump-ups often reseed the following fall except in heavy mulches.

Companion Planting and Design
Pansies provide color for beds, borders, hanging baskets, and pots from October to May. They are perfect for edging paths or interplanting with daffodils to carry on after the bulbs have flowered. Hint: Plant single-color pansies or Johnny jump-ups under daffodils, or the yellow or white daffodils will fade in the color confusion.

Personal Favorites
Large-flowered pansies, such as the Majestic Giant series, are showy, but don't bloom as long as hybrids such as the Crystal Bowl series and many other strains. Try different ones for different uses. Violas are smaller flowered plants similar to pansies and sold alongside them; they often come through cold winters better than some types of pansies, and bloom prolifically.

Pansies, the mainstays of our winter gardens, started out as English cottage garden flowers but have now been bred into an amazing selection of varieties. The close cousin Johnny jump-ups (V. tricolor) is an even older, slightly more heat-tolerant plant with generally small purple and yellow flowers. The hybrid violas are mounding green plants topped with cheerful flowers from late fall until early summer when heat burns them out in the South. The flowers have five lovely petals, some with contrasting "faces" in a huge array of colors and contrasts. Viola foliage stays evergreen throughout the worst winter, and their edible flowers make striking garnishes. Johnny jump-ups reseed very well.

Other Common Names
Johnny Jump-Ups, Viola

Bloom Period and Seasonal Color
White, yellow, blue, purple, mauve, red, bronze blooms in fall, winter, spring

Mature Height × Spread
4 to 8 inches × 6 to 12 inches

Petunia

Petunia hybrids

The sweetly scented, funnel-shaped blossoms are classics in the Southern cottage garden. From spring to fall, and sometimes after light frosts, old-fashioned types of petunias ramble wherever a space develops between shrubs and perennials to tie the garden together with reliable banks of color. In the hottest part of summer, most varieties look stressed, especially in lower elevations or in reflected heat, but they come back to life in cooler weather. Flowers are single or double, edged or veined with a contrasting hue. The grandifloras have the largest flowers, up to 6 inches across, but the smaller multifloras have more numerous blossoms, which almost cover the plant. Old-fashioned petunias can reseed.

Bloom Period and Seasonal Color
White, pink, salmon, rose, yellow, purple, blue, red blooms, spring to fall

Mature Height × Spread
8 to 20 inches × 1 to 3 feet or more

When, Where, and How to Plant
Plant petunias in early to mid-spring, so they can get established during cool spring nights. Sow seeds indoors in late winter for spring transplants, or sow old-fashioned, single, reseeding petunias outdoors in the ground in early spring. When sowing seeds where plants are to grow, be sure to mark the spot, as seedlings are dust-size specks. Keep them evenly moist until seedlings emerge. Plant petunias in average, well-drained soil. Morning sun is best, as petunias benefit from afternoon shade in summer. Set plants 1 foot or more apart to give them room to ramble. Mulch to control weeds and keep roots moist.

Growing Tips
Petunias are somewhat drought tolerant, but they like being watered deeply every week or two, in lieu of rain. Feed petunias lightly with a balanced fertilizer (one with all three numbers on the fertilizer label about the same) in the spring and again in the fall, but don't push them too much in the heat of summer (use fertilizer half strength then). Hybrid petunias are subject to root rot if overwatered in our humid summers; avoid this by not keeping plants wet, and making sure their soil is very well drained.

Care
Pinch tips off long branches to promote thick new growth and more flowering, especially in the summer. Whiteflies and slugs may be troublesome.

Companion Planting and Design
Petunias are "good enough" just on their own, in masses or borders. Their nonstop flowering and cascading—sometimes vine-like—growth make them perfect for containers and hanging baskets. Try them with sun coleus, canna, or spiky perennials such as iris or salvias. Plant where their fragrance can be noticed.

Personal Favorites
There are too many good ones to mention (and more coming every year), but a very popular, new type is 'Purple Wave'—it holds up incredibly well in the heat of summer, spreads aggressively, and smells delightful!

Poppy
Papaver species

When, Where, and How to Plant
Poppy plants transplant very poorly, so are nearly always direct-seeded into well-drained soil in winter sunshine. They will not tolerate hot weather and require cold weather to grow properly, so are best sown in the fall (the same time you sow larkspur or set out foxglove transplants or daffodils and other spring bulbs) for overwintering and flowering the following spring. Plant poppies in rich, loamy soil, but do not mulch or they will not sprout. Hint: Mix tiny poppy seeds with sand to help even out the sowing. Keep soil evenly moist until seedlings emerge, and thin seedlings 8 to 12 inches apart. For a longer bloom, make a second sowing after the first seedlings emerge.

Growing Tips
Water during dry spells, but do not keep wet. Poppies are durable in even fairly poor soils, but respond to light feeding in the late winter, before winter-dormant plants begin their fast spring growth. Like all cool-weather annuals, they begin to wither and die with the approach of summer. They reseed if soil is left free of mulch.

Care
Seeds germinate in cooler weather, so sow them in the fall; save some seeds as insurance against a hard winter. If fall plants are killed, sow saved seeds in late winter or very early spring. There are no major pests, though rabbits might nibble on foliage.

Companion Planting and Design
Use poppies as fillers among irises and bulbs, or as clumps of color between other spring-blooming cottage garden plants such as larkspur, foxgloves, and Shasta daises. The poppies are also popular in rock gardens or in masses in meadows or sunny islands.

Personal Favorites
Besides the common Shirley or Flanders Field poppies (*P. rhoeas*) with short, divided leaves and single or double flowers, and Iceland poppies (*P. nudicaule*) with large flowers (up to 6 inches), there are the opium poppies. The potential for illegal drug use has kept this out of mainstream gardens but does not keep dedicated gardeners from sharing seed, and whose seeds are used in baking.

The poppy is a classic cottage garden flower that fills a beautiful niche in informal gardens. Planted around the same time in the fall as spring bulbs, it blooms in the last cool days of spring, after the spring bulbs and before summer perennials. Nothing compares to a drift of the delicate, silken flowers balancing gracefully atop long stems on 18- to 30-inch plants. The crinkled blossoms, usually appearing conveniently around Memorial Day, can be single or double, sometimes edged with a thin line of a contrasting hue. Unusual round seedpods make interesting additions to dried flower arrangements, and look good by themselves in a vase. Most types usually reseed prolifically to come back every year.

Bloom Period and Seasonal Color
White, pink, peach, red, rose blooms in spring

Mature Height × Spread
18 to 30 inches × 8 to 12 inches

Scarlet Sage
Salvia splendens

Many varieties of strikingly pretty, versatile scarlet sage are available in garden centers every spring and summer. Its dense, sturdy spikes of 2-inch tubular bracts seem to glow above bright, grass-green, heart-shaped foliage on dense, shrubby plants, and draw hummingbirds and butterflies from great distances. The red ones are most commonly sold, but it is also available in deep purple, pink, rose, salmon, lavender, and cream. Sold as a sun-loving annual, this tropical perennial holds its color—both flowers and foliage—much better in light shade in the Deep South. It can reseed in some gardens, but is easy to pull up if it becomes a pest. Texas sage (S. coccinea), perennial along our Gulf Coast but grown elsewhere as a reseeding annual, is more heat-, drought-, and sun-tolerant than scarlet sage.

Other Common Name
Salvia

Bloom Period and Seasonal Color
Red, pink, rose, purple, cream blooms from summer to frost

Mature Height × Spread
1 to 3 feet × 8 to 12 inches

When, Where, and How to Plant
Set out store-bought bedding plants in late spring after the danger of frost is past, and replant in mid-summer (if you can find the plants) for a spectacular fall display. Sow seeds indoors in late winter for spring transplants or sow outdoors in the ground in spring after all threat of frost is past. Plant salvia in rich, well-drained soil, setting plants 8 to 12 inches apart depending on the mature size. To direct seed in the garden, sow seeds where the plants are to grow, according to directions on the package. Keep them evenly moist until seedlings emerge. Again, this salvia seems to hold up better in light shade.

Growing Tips
Water plants as needed, but do not keep them wet or allow them to dry out completely. Feed lightly and regularly to promote healthy new growth, deep green leaves, and continuous flowering.

Care
Pinch back scarlet sage to promote new growth and flowering. At midsummer, shear back plants to rejuvenate them, or simply pull them up and replant with more. Whiteflies are sometimes a serious pest, but water and fertilizer help the plants put on fresh new growth.

Companion Planting and Design
The vivid red is stunning in mass plantings, but all annual salvias make perfect contrasts to petunias, daylilies, marigolds, and other more rounded summer flowers. Use them in containers and window boxes, and in drifts in flower borders. Place near hummingbird feeders to attract the hungry birds with their alluring red trumpets.

Personal Favorites
For a really bright red try 'Splendissima'. The Sizzler and Salsa series offer brilliant reds as well as several other rich colors.

Snapdragon
Antirrhinum majus

When, Where, and How to Plant

Snapdragons perform best in cool weather. Though a long, deep freeze can kill most varieties, plan on planting some in the fall, and the rest in late winter. Snapdragons tolerate full sun, but they like afternoon shade, especially the closer you live to the Gulf Coast where winter sun can bake. They like fluffy, slightly alkaline, well-drained soil. Set plants 8 to 12 inches apart, loosening their potting soil a little at planting time to encourage wider root growth. Transplants are widely available, but you can start seeds in the late summer or midwinter in small pots to set out later.

Growing Tips

In-ground snapdragons usually get enough water from rainfall, but water occasionally during dry spells in the fall and late spring. Do not over-water, especially plants grown in pots, or their roots may rot. Fertilize regularly but very lightly, or they may get top-heavy and flop over.

Care

Pinch young plants back to promote bushiness. Stake tall snaps with short bamboo poles painted green. During severe winter cold, cover fall-planted snaps with pine straw or mulch, but remove as soon as weather moderates. Snaps are subject to rust, so look for rust-resistant selections. Wilt affects them. Fall cleanup of debris and excellent drainage reduce the likelihood of problems, as does planting in containers of fresh potting soil.

Companion Planting and Design

Snapdragons are ideal vertical accents for the back or middle of a cottage garden border, or for blocks of color between shrubs in suburban flower beds. They are almost perfect winter and spring container specimens, especially when combined with pansies, daffodils, grape hyacinth, and dusty miller—and you can drag containers into the carport during nasty winter weather.

Personal Favorites

Medium to tall snaps, such as the Rocket and Topper series, medium-sized 'Liberty', 'Cinderella', and the Princess series, perform well. Popular dwarf selections include 'Floral Showers' and 'Floral Carpet'.

Showing a child where snapdragons get their common name—by squeezing an individual flower between thumb and forefinger and making it open and close its "jaws" in mock menace—is a tradition with gardeners. The flowers are treasured for the spiky drama and Popsicle colors the cool-weather-loving plants add to beds, borders, and flower arrangements in the fall, spring, and warm winter spells in between. Snaps add zest to pots of pansies and bridge the "color gap" between camellias and roses. Though they are popular summer plants in the North and along coastal California, where nights are cool, they burn out in our hot, muggy summers.

Other Common Name
Snaps

Bloom Period and Seasonal Color
White, apricot, orange, yellow, red, pink, rose, purple blooms in spring and fall

Mature Height × Spread
8 to 24 inches × 8 to 12 inches

Wax Begonia

Begonia Semperflorens-Cultorum Hybrids

A popular summer bedding plant, wax begonia forms 8-to 15-inch mounds of squeaky-shiny foliage continuously covered with small single or double red, pink, or white flowers. Dependable foliage color is green (best for shade) or variegated, or more sun-tolerant bronze or red, and can be used to design patterns or even "write" words in a display bed. This fibrous-rooted begonia will freeze to the ground, but in the southern half of our states it may survive a mild winter to come back for another season or two. They are excellent potted plant fillers, surviving even downtown planters.

Other Common Name
Bedding Begonia

Bloom Period and Seasonal Color
Red, pink, white blooms from spring to fall

Mature Height × Spread
8 to 15 inches × 8 to 12 inches

When, Where, and How to Plant

Though easy to grow from seed, save time and trouble by buying a flat or two of small begonia plants from a garden center—their uniformity will make them easier to place in your garden. Set plants out in the spring or early summer, and water only enough to get them established, then only occasionally as needed; too much water is often worse than none at all! Red- or bronze-leaf selections bloom quite well in full sun. Give begonias a well-drained soil, rich in organic matter. Though it seems too far apart at planting time, set transplants at least 12 inches apart for good air circulation, and they will quickly fill in.

Growing Tips

Water only as needed, and avoid evening watering or risk disease. Fertilize regularly but lightly as needed.

Care

Keep flowers pinched back to promote heavier flowering and more compact plants. Begonias are pest tolerant, but slugs can be a problem, as can disease caused by over-watering (especially at night) and too-close spacing.

Companion Planting and Design

Wax begonias are well suited for mass effects where they provide blocks of eye-catching color and dependable bloom in beds, or as a neat edging at the front of a border. Blend red and white begonias with other annuals, such as coleus, for a cooling tropical look. These tough little plants are ideal for containers. Wax begonias are commonly selected for floral bed designs, and can be tucked between clumps of caladiums and sometimes with asparagus fern in a tropical border.

Personal Favorites

The dwarf, bronze-leaf Cocktail series ('Vodka', 'Whiskey', and 'Gin') is good for sunny areas. The Encore series (green or bronze foliage) is taller, with larger flowers and leaves.

Zinnia

Zinnia species

When, Where, and How to Plant

For earliest bloom, sow seeds of zinnia indoors in late winter, but move the seed trays out into the "real" sunshine every warm day to prevent legginess. Transplant into the garden after the danger of frost has passed. Direct-sow seeds onto freshly dug and raked, rich, well-drained soil when the weather really starts to warm up. Keep seeds evenly moist until seedlings emerge. Thin seedlings to 1 to 2 feet apart once they have at least four leaves. Plant tall cut-flower ones behind smaller plants to hide ugly "legs" as older leaves dry and fall.

Growing Tips

Water *Z. elegans* seedlings deeply but infrequently until they are well established, then only when the soil gets really dry (regular irrigation will rot zinnias quickly). Fertilize lightly every month or so to keep them blooming.

Care

It's difficult for novice gardeners to accept, but pinching flowers off new plants is important to promote bushiness and to force the plants into making more flowers faster. Deadhead to promote more constant flowering and to prevent diseases. Tall types may need staking. *Z. elegans* is susceptible to powdery mildew. Choose mildew-resistant selections and avoid watering in the afternoon and wetting foliage. Provide ample space between plants to prevent disease.

Companion Planting and Design

Grow dwarf types in containers or near the front of borders. Tall types go at the back of the border. Zinnias look nice near garden art, even around a birdbath or gazing globe. Good companions include drought-loving dusty miller, daylilies, iris, and sunflower.

Personal Favorites

Though the old State Fair series is still very popular for tall cut flowers, look for mildew-resistant selections of *Z. elegans* such as 'Rose Pinwheel', or proven garden performers such as 'Dreamland Scarlet' and the Zenith hybrids. *Z. angustifolia* comes in several good selections including 'Crystal White', 'Golden Orange', 'Star Gold', and 'Star White'.

Zinnias are outstanding "starter" flowers for kids and new gardeners. These plants love hot, dry weather, sending forth many dozens of single or double flowers in an astounding range of sizes and cheerful colors atop stiff branching stems. Perhaps the best all-purpose butterfly and cut-flower garden flowers, zinnias are available in dwarf forms for edging and planters, mid-size plants for bedding, and long-stemmed giants for cutting. In midsummer, powdery mildew appears and burns the leaves of Z. elegans, disrupting what otherwise could be a glorious fall show. That's when narrowleaf zinnia (Z. angustifolia) comes into its own. The 1-foot plants covered with single, 1-inch flowers never flag. Tough, pretty, and undemanding, narrowleaf zinnia is the perfect summer bedding plant, blooming well into fall.

Other Common Name
Old Maids

Bloom Period and Seasonal Color
Red, orange, pink, purple, white, yellow blooms from summer to fall

Mature Height × Spread
8 to 40 inches × 1 to 2 feet

Bulbs *for Alabama & Mississippi*

A good bulb is like money in the bank. Year after year, it can grow and even multiply with a minimum of care. That's why our grandmothers, who were too busy to fuss over finicky plants, planted daffodils, summer snowflakes, and spider lilies that mark the progress of the seasons across the landscape of the South. These bulbs still prosper around foundations of abandoned houses—a testament to their staying power.

True bulbs, like onions, store energy, immature leaves, and flower buds underground during non-growing (usually dry) seasons, ensuring the plant's survival during adverse conditions. A number of plants are not true bulbs, but are typically grouped with bulbs, because they have underground structures and their planting and maintenance are similar. Bulb-like plants include gladiolus (corm), caladium (tuber), and iris (rhizome).

Many people think bulbs just come and go in the spring, but really there are flower- and foliage-producing bulbs for all seasons, even winter. It isn't unusual to have paper-white *Narcissus* between Thanksgiving and Christmas, the beautiful variegated leaves of painted arum all winter, milk-and-wine lilies in midsummer, red spider lilies in the fall, and dozens of others in between—all "doing their thing" for decades, even around abandoned farmhouses, with no care whatsoever other than the initial planting!

Hardy Gladiolus

Protect Bulbs from Critters

Voles are small, mouse-like rodents that tunnel underground and eat bulbs and the roots of other plants. Not much can control these destructive pests or deter squirrels that dig bulbs. Here are a few tips on protecting new bulb plantings:

• When planting bulbs, surround them with gravel or other coarse material that voles hate digging through, line sides of beds with half-inch "hardware cloth," or plant in buried plastic mesh baskets.

- Place "live" traps nearby (which have a mechanism that closes the door on the trap, without killing the critter), baited with peanut butter and covered up with upside-down pots. You will need to take the animal to another location for release.
- Lay chicken wire over new beds: Bulbs can grow through it, but squirrels and cats have a hard time digging around.
- Surround susceptible bulbs and perennials with daffodils, which repel burrowing pests.

Annual or Perennial?

Tulips are perennial only in the North—very few types get enough cold in the winter in the South, or they rot in our wet springs and hot, muggy summers. Caladiums and gladiolus are perennial in warm climates if they don't freeze or rot from heavy rains in heavy soils. Treat these very showy, highly desirable beauties as one-shot annuals. Yet some bulbs are long-lived perennials, such as lilies and daffodils. There could be a whole chapter on how to handle perennial bulbs—many of them can live for decades with little or no care.

To keep it simple, here are a few things that benefit perennial bulbs, other than planting them where they can show off without hiding or being hidden by other plants. To get the maximum performance, give them a light annual feeding early in their growing season (feed spring bloomers in the fall, and

Crocus

Daffodils

summer and fall bloomers in the spring). And though many perennial bulbs can obviously survive for years around old home sites on little more than sunshine, rainfall, and the good earth, you can get much more out of them by fertilizing them at least every two or three years. But the bone meal of Grandma's garden day is not enough—it contains only phosphorus, and bulbs also need nitrogen and potassium. Use a good-quality bulb food, or an all-purpose garden fertilizer. Broadcast it over the planting area early in the growing season: in the fall for daffodils and other spring bloomers, or spring for summer bloomers. Water perennial bulbs only as needed during extreme dry spells. Cut off faded, dead, or pest-damaged foliage as needed. Either label or be sure to remember where they are planted when they are dormant, so you don't cut them up while adding other plants to the garden.

Advice for Growing Bulbs

Bulbs are easy to grow, if you follow these basic guidelines:

- Pick the right bulb for your site. Most bulbs need full sun to bloom best; however, many spring bulbs grow over the winter, so it is okay to plant them under the south side of deciduous trees where they get winter and early spring sunshine.
- Prepare beds correctly at planting time. This year's bloom is the result of last year's growing season—freshly purchased bulbs will always flower at least once, because the grower gave them the proper sunlight, water, and soil the previous year. For a repeat show, you'll need to do the same.
- Most bulbs require good drainage, meaning they need to be in a site with sandy loam soil, on a slope, in a raised bed, or in a container. Poor drainage can make them prone to disease or to outright rot. Test for drainage in your garden by digging a hole about a foot deep and filling it with water. If the water drains away in two or three hours, the soil is probably sufficiently drained.
- Mix a commercial, slow-release bulb food into the soil before planting and reapply every year or two. Bone meal by itself is not good enough.

- Always remember to plant the bulbs tips up! If you're not sure which end is the top (crocus corms can be confusing), plant them on their sides.
- Buy new bulbs early, as soon as they become available in the fall when the selection is best. Store them in a cool, dry place if you can't plant them right away. Note: Do not store bulbs in the refrigerator with fruit, because gases given off by the fruit can cause bulbs to sprout too quickly.
- In general, plant bulbs with the tips two or three times as deep as the bulbs are big around. There are exceptions, however.
- Prolonged warm spells and sudden cold snaps in late winter can nip spring bulbs in the bud. To lessen the impact, mulch the bulbs in the fall, and the new growth will come up through it in the spring.

Some bulbs are dormant in the winter, others in the summer, which makes it important to have other plants nearby to "carry" the garden through all seasons. The important thing to consider is that all the plants in the area grow well together (with the same soil, sun or shade, and water requirements). For example, spring bulbs that need dry soil in the summer can be planted with drought-tolerant plants like lantana, which hates a lot of water; and summer bulbs can be overplanted with pansies for winter and spring, or even spring bulbs. Garden centers and mail-order companies usually have many different types of bulbs, and often dozens of varieties of some. Always stick with the tried and true, but add a few interesting new types as your garden space and budget allow. Because they are so easy to grow and long lasting, bulbs make great gift or "pass-along" plants. Many gardeners also enjoy "forcing" spring bulbs for winter blooms indoors. The following few are among the most dependable and hardiest for our part of the South, and should be in every garden.

Oriental Lily

Blazing Star
Liatris species

Liatris *is one of our most stunning Southeastern peren-nial wildflowers—which is ironic because it is grown commercially in South America for importing here as a very expensive florist cut flower. Depending on the species, the bulb-like corm, native to moist clearings in woodlands, bottomlands, prairie outcroppings, and even coastal areas, thrives in alkaline and acidic soils and is commonly seen along roadsides. Its tall spikes of electric lavender purple are among the very best butterfly, bee, and bouquet flowers for any garden. Because the clusters of curly flowers open from the top of spikes and move downward—the opposite of gladiolus—flower arrangers cut the tops off as they fade to keep arrangements fresh.*

Other Common Name
Gay Feather

Bloom Period and Seasonal Color
Purple, lavender, or white flowers in summer

Mature Height × Spread
3 to 4 feet × 1 foot

When, Where, and How to Plant
Plant corms or small potted plants a foot or more apart any time during the late winter or spring in sunny or lightly shaded areas in nearly any kind of soil. Sow seed in the late summer or fall. Over-pre-pared soils tend to produce leggy, floppy plants, so do not go to great lengths to add organic matter where blazing star is to be grown. Be very sure to loosen potting soil from roots of container-grown plants, or they may stay wetter or drier than the soil around them, leading to decline. If you have to divide mature plants when they are in full flower, cut the stalks nearly to the ground, using the cut stems in flower arrangements.

Growing Tips
Water new plants thoroughly but don't keep them wet. Feed very lightly in the spring—remember that this native plant thrives on nearly nothing in the wild!

Care
Liatris will multiply readily by seed, usually com-ing up along walkways and other openings in mulch. Some tall varieties may need staking, or you can just let the stems weave in and around one another. Never spray for pests, because the plants are host to many insects, including butterflies, bees, and nectar-feeding flies.

Companion Planting and Design
Liatris is easy to reach as a cut flower when grown in rows along with other perennial cut flowers such as summer phlox and ornamental grasses, or as a perennial companion to annual cut flowers such as sunflowers and zinnias. It is the perfect linear complement to perennial borders, and works especially well along fencerows and wet ditches, and in other naturalistic plantings where it becomes a "nice" flower that brings credibility to weedier-looking natives. Dwarf forms grow very well in containers.

Personal Favorites
'Kobold' stays under 3 feet, and the odd *L. squar-rosa* has rounded tufts of flowers spaced along stems instead of the usual "bottlebrush" habit of other blazing stars.

Caladium
Caladium × *hortulanum*

When, Where, and How to Plant

Plant tubers in the spring after the soil has warmed up; start earlier indoors in pots. Some experts note that caladiums tolerate full sun, but they usually look ratty with burned leaf edges; heavy shade tends to dull the colors, however. Plant in dappled shade under trees, or in a northern or eastern exposure where plants get a little morning sun. Caladiums need very well-drained soil, amended with compost and a little fertilizer mixed in. Plant knobby side up, spaced a foot or so apart, even when planting in groups.

Growing Tips

Water frequently to keep soil moist, but don't rot the tubers. To keep new leaves coming through summer and fall, feed regularly but very lightly.

Care

Snap or cut off the unusual flowers to keep the leaves in top form. Squirrels and other rodents dig these tubers when they are young; outsmart them by growing caladiums in pots. If you want to save caladiums over the winter, dig them ahead of the first frost, shaking off their loose soil but leaving foliage stems on until they dry and shed naturally (pulling them off early causes damage that can lead to decay). Store tubers in dry vermiculite indoors. Pre-sprout them indoors in pots to get a jump on the growing season.

Companion Planting and Design

Caladiums are commonly massed in one color along walkways or in front of shrubs, or interplanted with ferns and liriope. They are even more effective in large repeated groups, so if some plants do poorly they don't leave gaps. They are ideal container plants because of the excellent drainage, especially when combined with impatiens, asparagus fern, and other annuals and tender tropical plants.

Personal Favorites

The easiest approach is to just grab a sackful of whatever strikes your fancy. There are nearly solid whites, reds, and pinks that complement other shade plants. Mix in a few with narrow leaves for contrast. Some good cultivars if you can find them are 'Frieda Hemple', 'Miss Muffet', and 'White Christmas'.

Second only to impatiens for shady gardens and patios, caladiums are grown for their masses of triangular leaves that shimmer in bold white, red, pink, and every imaginable variegated combination, usually with contrasting leaf veins, edging, or marbling of colors. Caladiums almost glow in dappled or high shade, which provides enough sunlight for plants to develop their full color without burning the leaves. Given perfect drainage, ample moisture, and rich soil, they provide a continuous display from summer's first heat until the arrival of frost. They usually produce curious "spathe" flowers (with a finger-like stalk wrapped in a light green cloak) that are very unusual but not interesting enough to enjoy—and they prevent plants from producing new leaves, which is the main show.

Other Common Name
Showy Elephant's Ear

Bloom Period and Seasonal Color
Foliage in green, white, red, rose and combinations, late spring to frost

Mature Height × Spread
1 to 2 feet × 15 to 18 inches

Crinum

Crinum zeylanicum

The "milk and wine" lily was once a common sight in cottage and old gardens across the South, and is making a comeback as its slow-to-grow bulbs find their way into commercial propagation. With its big mass of strappy foliage and upright stems of drooping trumpets of white striped with wine-red, this is one of the largest bulbs you will ever plant, or try to dig—its bulb can get as big as a head! And talk about tough—noted Texas horticulturist William Welch has flatly said that "none have ever died." One clump reportedly was dug from between the sidewalk and street curb, growing in hard clay and broken glass.

Other Common Name
Milk-and-Wine Lily

Bloom Period and Seasonal Color
White, wine-red, or rose flowers from spring to fall

Mature Height × Spread
2 feet × 4 feet

When, Where, and How to Plant

Crinums are hard to come by commercially, but can be planted any time the bulbs are available. Dig and divide old clumps any time, although winter or spring is better; cut off flowers if digging while in bloom. They will thrive in nearly any soil, even heavy clay, but will rot if planted where water stands in the winter or spring. To increase drainage, add generous amounts of coarse sand to heavy soils, or plant on a slope for at least some surface drainage. Crinums, which bloom best in full sun, should be planted so their "necks" are level with or slightly above the surrounding soil level. Space them several feet apart.

Growing Tips

These super-drought-hardy lilies never need water after initial planting. Light feeding every two or three years in the spring will increase number and quality of flowers, but too much will cause floppy foliage. They tend to flower best when the soil is lean, so do not plant in over-prepared soil.

Care

Crinums multiply very slowly, but can be divided every few years. When digging, be aware that the bulbs are nearly always deeper and bigger than you would have imagined, so start well away from the plants and angle downwards to get under the bulbs—they are too precious to waste by slicing in half! After a hard freeze turns the foliage to mush, cut it off and mulch around the plants.

Companion Planting and Design

Crinums make great, bold accents all by themselves, but can be planted in a row almost like a low hedge. Give them a "skirt" of tall spring-blooming daffodils, soapwort, yarrow, or other contrasting foliage plant that withstands severe neglect.

Personal Favorites

There are several lovely hybrid crinums: Solid wine-red 'Ellen Bosanquet' is often available from mail-order nurseries, as are the pink ruffled 'Emma Jones' and 'Carnival' with its pink flowers with white streaks.

Crocus
Crocus species and hybrids

When, Where, and How to Plant
Crocus show up in garden centers in September, but that's too early to plant. Store corms in a cool, dry place and wait until at least mid-October or November to plant. Plant crocus corms where they receive full sun (six hours a day) in the late winter and spring, in a loose, well-drained soil. Planting depth is generally 2 inches, but set large corms 3 inches deep. Crocus bear small flowers close to the ground, so plant in masses. Plant at least ten corms, 3 to 6 inches apart, in one location. For heavy soil add organic matter, such as compost, potting soil, or rotted pine bark. Water thoroughly to settle the soil. When plants emerge, mulch around them to keep weeds at bay.

Growing Tips
During summer and fall, crocus are dormant and have low water requirements. In winter and spring, there is usually enough rainfall to meet their needs. Do not plant where irrigation will rot them.

Care
Crocus multiply readily if left in place. Though it is unlikely that crocus will need dividing, do so if blooms appear minimized by overcrowding. Before the foliage dies back for the season, label crocus so that you don't accidentally dig them up when setting out other plants. Chipmunks will dig every bulb you have, so overlay with chicken wire.

Companion Planting and Design
Plant crocus where you would naturally pass them on the way into or out of the house. They are ideal for small gardens, rock gardens, containers, and other "up close" settings. Interplant with miniature daffodils, which do not compete for show, and under winter-dormant perennials that are drought-tolerant, such as lantana. Naturalize them in the lawn under trees.

Personal Favorites
The giant Dutch crocus (*C. vernus*) is a good choice for viewing crocus from afar; cultivars include 'Pickwick' and 'Remembrance'. *C. tommasinianus* comes in 'Barr's Purple' and 'Whitewell Purple' and naturalizes well.

Crocus corms defy winter cold to boldly display their stemless, cup-shaped blossoms starting in late January or early February, signaling the end of winter. Colors include solids and stripes in a variety of combinations. After flowering, the tufts of foliage expand to become an attractive addition to the garden. The narrow leaves grow as long as 12 inches. In summer, crocus has the grace to go dormant without fuss, its foliage dying back quickly and quietly. Fall-blooming crocus also perform well in the South. Colchicum, a type of lily (the genus Crocus is actually in the iris family), is generally known as autumn crocus and can be planted in the summer (when they are dormant) for pretty fall blooms. Crocus may not spread very well along the coast.

Bloom Period and Seasonal Color
White, yellow, blue, lavender blooms in late winter, early spring, fall

Mature Height × Spread
6 to 12 inches × 3 to 6 inches

Daffodil

Narcissus species and hybrids

Daffodils are the most popular hardy bulb in the South, and often can be found at the site of an abandoned home or across fields. However, some are not reliable perennials, so plant mostly the tried and true varieties, and experiment with others to find those you like. Growing from 8 to 20 inches tall, daffodils vary in form (single or double), color, and bloom time, so you can have a long display with only a few varieties. Many daffodils give off a heady fragrance and make ideal cut flowers. Narcissus, by the way, is the Latin name for all daffodils, and includes multiple-flowering paper-whites as well as fragrant jonquils.

Other Common Names
Buttercup, Jonquil

Bloom Period and Seasonal Color
White, yellow, orange, and blends bloom in late winter, spring

Mature Height × Spread
8 to 20 inches × 6 to 8 inches

When, Where, and How to Plant
Daffodil bulbs show up in garden centers in September, but store them in a cool, dry place until mid-October or November to plant. Plant daffodil bulbs in loose, well-drained soil, spaced 6 to 8 inches apart, depending upon the selection. (Note: Closer spacing looks dramatic, but plants have to be divided sooner.) Daffodils grown as container plants should be planted more deeply than those in the ground. Mulch to keep soil temperatures more uniform over the winter and summer.

Growing Tips
Daffodils need little care, other than light feeding in the fall when new growth begins to emerge. Do not feed in the spring, or risk bulb rot.

Care
A common mistake is cutting or braiding foliage after blooming. Flower buds are formed in the spring after current season flowers fade, so wait until foliage has begun to yellow and flop before cutting or tying. Instead, hide it with leafy companions such as daylilies or summer perennials. Naturalizing types do not need dividing, but showy ones that stop blooming will need dividing and replanting every few years.

Companion Planting and Design
Daffodils are great for spring borders, interplanting with perennials that tolerate summer drought, in containers with pansies and other winter annuals, or mixed with other spring bulbs and wild violets for a naturalistic effect. The spring foliage of yarrow or daylilies will easily hide the fading or flopping foliage of daffodils in the spring.

Personal Favorites
There are many different daffodils—from early blooming paper-whites that flower between Thanksgiving and Christmas, to "twin sisters" that flower in late April or even May. These hardy varieties are wonderful and widely available commercially: 'Accent', 'Tahiti', 'Peeping Tom', 'February Gold', 'Jetfire', 'Ice Follies', 'Mistral', ' 'Geranium', 'Grand Primo', 'Tête-á-Tête' (a very good small one to plant in front of others), 'Mount Hood', 'Thalia', 'Hawera', 'Cheerfulness', 'Unsurpassable', 'Carlton', and the species *N. jonquilla*.

Elephant's Ear
Colocasia esculenta

When, Where, and How to Plant
Plant elephant's ears in the spring to give them time to get established before winter cuts them to the ground, especially north of Interstate 20. Divide plants in late winter or early spring before large leaves sprout, or cut the leaves off to reduce shock—they quickly produce new leaves. They tolerate a wide range of moist soils, and grow in any light, except the densest shade.

Growing Tips
Keep young elephant's ears moist until they get established, then give them a good soaking every week or two—otherwise, leaves may yellow and burn around the edges. For large leaves, feed very lightly two or three times from spring to midsummer, but pushing them too hard at the start of fall may make them more susceptible to winter injury. In high elevations of northern areas, carry them over the winter in pots protected from hard freezes, such as in a greenhouse or cool garage.

Care
Cut off yellowed older leaves during the summer, and cut plants completely down after a frost turns their aboveground parts to mush. Mulch to help protect them over the winter, especially in northern areas, or dig and pot them up to keep them over the winter indoors. Elephant's ears do not have major pest problems.

Companion Planting and Design
Plant elephant's ears against a fence, wall, or backdrop of dark green hedges; at the edge of a pond or water garden; or beside a birdbath or pool where moisture and humidity are high. Combine with canna, banana, pentas, caladium, hibiscus, or other tropical foliage and flowering plants, especially in large containers. A "hard" feature (birdbath, urn, and so forth) will provide something to look at when elephant's ears are winter dormant.

Personal Favorite
'Black Magic' has beautiful, dark wine-colored leaves.

Elephant's ear is one of the most aptly named bulbs around—and is the boldest foliage plant this side of Ecuador. No tropical garden should be without the strikingly coarse contrast provided by these half-hardy bulbs. Some places along the Gulf Coast consider this Asian native an invasive exotic plant that runs along waterways with little to control its spread. Its love of moisture makes it ideal as a water garden specimen, and it can tolerate temperatures to near zero, maybe lower with mulch. New variegated, chartreuse, purple, or near-black forms continue to gain in popularity in all but the most formal gardens. A very similar genus of plants, also called elephant's ear, is Alocasia.

Other Common Names
Taro, Dasheen

Bloom Period and Seasonal Color
Foliage from spring to frost

Mature Height × Spread
3 to 6 feet × 2 to 5 feet

Gladiolus
Gladiolus species and hybrids

One of the easiest cut flowers to grow in any garden setting is the inexpensive South African corm called gladiolus. The narrow, sword-like leaves and tall flower stalks complement everything around. The flowers, which come in nearly every color of the rainbow, bloom from the bottom up, usually on just one side of the stalk, providing sometimes over two weeks of flowers per stem. Few other flowers are as striking; it is common to see country gardens with long rows of only gladiolus. Most gardeners find gladiolus—especially florist types—to be fickle as perennials, and usually grow them as inexpensive annuals; however, they are very easy to dig, store, and save for replanting the next year.

Other Common Names
Glad, Sword Lily, Corn Lily

Bloom Period and Seasonal Color
White, red, yellow, orange, lavender, apricot, and purple all summer

Mature Height × Spread
18 inches to 3 feet or more × 6 to 12 inches

When, Where, and How to Plant
Wait until the soil has warmed in mid-spring before planting the corms, unless you prefer to get a late winter head start in pots. Plant in full sun if possible, toward the back of borders (the plants get tall), in well-drained soil of medium fertility. To have a continuous supply of flowers, plant a few corms every two or three weeks until midsummer. Buy new corms every year, even if you save some, to refresh your stock.

Growing Tips
Fertilize lightly when stems get a few inches tall, but don't overdo it or the plants will be more likely to flop over. To prevent flopping (especially after heavy rains), insert a thin, 2-foot bamboo stake beside each plant shortly after the corms come up, and tie in two places: a few inches above the ground, and farther up when the plants get a little taller than the stake.

Care
While there is no need to keep them wet, water during summer drought. Thrips (tiny cigar-shaped insects) can cause streaking on foliage and some flower distortion—use neem oil or insecticidal soap for control.

Companion Planting and Design
Glads are stunning in small groups, or in rows to make cutting easier, or in mixed plantings of other flowers or even herbs. Smaller types are suitable for container gardens. Plant lower-growing flowers such as melampodium or small zinnias in front to hide the leggy lower parts of the gladiolus plants.

Personal Favorites
There are many choices of regular garden glads, including small ones under 18 inches and tall ones up to 4 feet. For an unusual treat, look for the shockingly magenta red or white "hardy" gladiolus (*G. byzantinus*) that naturalizes throughout the South, or Abyssinian sword lily (*G. callianthus*, sometimes named *Acidanthera bicolor*), which has large white flowers with a purple blotch.

Grape Hyacinth
Muscari botryoides

When, Where, and How to Plant

Plant these small, inexpensive bulbs as soon as you can in the fall, 4 to 8 inches apart in well-drained soil and where they can get full sun all winter (avoid north sides of walls or the house, where the winter sun never shines). Just push them into the ground and their multiplying habit will help them "find" the right depth for future generations. Feed lightly at planting time with an all-purpose or special bulb food, and they will do fine for years.

Growing Tips

During summer and fall, Mediterranean-native grape hyacinths are dormant and have no water requirements. In winter and spring, usually enough rain falls to meet their needs. Do not plant where irrigation will rot them. Avoid the use of herbicides on the lawn where these and other bulbs are planted.

Care

Grape hyacinth multiplies readily if left alone in the spring until their seedpods mature and turn tan and papery. After that, mowers simply spread the seeds. Though it is not necessary to divide this little bulb, they can get so crowded they almost choke themselves out. If rodents are a problem, overlay the area with chicken wire, which the bulb foliage and mulch will cover up.

Companion Planting and Design

Catch their delicate fragrance by planting where you would naturally pass them on the way into or out of the house. They are perfect—foliage, flowers, and all—for border edges, rock gardens, containers, and other "up close" settings. Interplant with miniature daffodils (which do not compete for show) and low-growing Johnny jump-ups, and around drought-tolerant winter-dormant perennials such as lantana and the taller sedums. Naturalize them as a "river of blue" in the lawn, since they are dormant in the summer when grass is actively growing.

Personal Favorites

M. latifolium has much larger flowers and is better suited for mixed-flower plantings, where it is less likely to get lost under the foliage of other plants. *M. armeniacum* 'Blue Spike' has double flowers.

Every spring, old cemeteries and small-town home lawns across the South are covered with masses of the deep hazy-blue flowers of thousands of these small, old-fashioned bulbs. The short grassy leaves of this late winter bloomer come up very early in the fall, making them useful as "markers" for the gardener, so they aren't accidentally dug during soil preparation for pansies and other fall-planted flowers. The short stalks of tightly packed, juicy, urn-shaped flowers usually have enough time before the first mowing of the spring to set and mature seed, helping the bulbs spread easily, almost weed-like, into the lawn and beyond.

Bloom Period and Seasonal Color

Blue, white, or pinkish flowers in late winter and early spring

Mature Height × Spread

6 to 8 inches × 4 to 8 inches

Lily

Lilium species and hybrids

Considered the most regal bulb—and arguably the fussiest to get started by novice gardeners in new settings because of the need for rich, deep, moist soil—the true lily and its many species and varieties are the "tall boys" of the spring and summer garden. Their stately, straight stems with narrow leaves are topped with—what else?—lily-shaped trumpets of white, pink, red, orange, yellow, mauve, and many variations, including stripes, spots, and contrasting throats. Native to deep, rich leafy woodland soils and light shade, they require excellent drainage, regular moisture, and light shade to thrive in most of the middle and lower South. Grown as fragrant, long-lasting florist flowers, they last for many years once you get them established in the garden.

Other Common Name
Garden Lily

Bloom Period and Seasonal Color
Many colors and variations from spring to midsummer

Mature Height × Spread
2 to 6 feet or more × 8 to 12 inches

When, Where, and How to Plant
Garden lilies should be planted quickly in late winter or spring, and can die if bulbs are allowed to dry out; keep cool and moist and plant as soon as a location with good soil is ready. Most lilies flower best in afternoon or light shade, and need staking or protection from wind in very deep, moist but well-drained soils high in organic matter, with lots of mulch. Set scaly bulbs pointy ends up, and deep—the roots that anchor the tall plants grow off new stems that sprout above the bulbs. Water deeply at planting time and cover with a mulch of leaf mould.

Growing Tips
Water regularly, especially during windy or dry periods, and fertilize lightly in the spring and again when flower buds begin to form. Divide by separating bulblets from the outside of freshly dug bulbs. Keep mulched.

Care
When stems are a foot or so tall, loosely tie stems to sturdy plastic or bamboo stakes. Maintain a loose layer of leaf mulch over lilies at all times to keep soil cool and moist in the summer. Thrips, aphids, and beetles can feed on lilies; use a natural spray such as neem oil. Rust, fungus, and viral diseases affect lilies, but the only good control is replanting new, disease-free bulbs.

Companion Planting and Design
Plant lilies at the back of borders with lower-growing sedum, daylily, iris, and full-bodied perennials to hide leggy lower stems and to help shade lily roots. Interplant with Siberian iris and hibiscus that tolerate moist soils. Short varieties are outstanding container plants for cool patios or porches.

Personal Favorites
Asiatic hybrids are very easy to grow. Some of the best species lilies are the ancient orange-spotted tiger lily (*L. lancifolium*); short, native pine lily (*L. catesbaei*); and summer-flowering Formosa (*L. formosanum*), Philippine (*L. philippinense*), and turk's cap lilies (*L. canadense, L. martagonum, L. superbum*). Other standards include Madonna (*L. candidum*) and regal (*L. regale*) lilies.

Lycoris

Lycoris species

When, Where, and How to Plant

Plant in the fall when bulbs are most readily available, or transplant immediately after flowering when foliage is dormant, or immediately after foliage begins to die down in the spring. Plant where they get winter and early spring sunshine in well-drained soil rich in organic matter. Plant bulbs 12 to 18 inches apart.

Growing Tips

These bulbs, which grow most actively in late winter and spring, are extremely drought tolerant, growing on rainfall alone. Fertilize at planting with a slow-release bulb food and again at least every three or four years when foliage emerges in the fall.

Care

Leave bulbs undisturbed to multiply for years, as they resent being bothered. Do not cut or mow the foliage over the winter, but allow it to ripen fully. Divide only when you want to share bulbs or spread them into other areas of the garden.

Companion Planting and Design

Because they bloom without foliage, interplant lycoris with a groundcover such as Asiatic jasmine, English ivy, or liriope. The flowers are stunning in massed plantings, or when bordering a bed or path. They naturalize well in summer-shaded but winter-sunny gardens. When naturalizing in the lawn, be aware that they can be bothersome to mow between in the summer.

Personal Favorites

Different colored varieties of *L. radiata* are hard to come by. It is best to stick with the very satisfying red form, and the species *L. squamigera*.

Two highly popular but very different bulbs are the late summer and fall, red spider lily (Lycoris radiata, sometimes called "hurricane" lily), and the larger, mid-summer-flowering pink "naked ladies" (L. squamigera, often called magic, resurrection, or surprise lily). Both have winter foliage that dies down in mid-spring heat, then flower suddenly, seemingly overnight, in hot weather on leafless stems topped with a cluster of flowers. Red spider lily (which has a white form also) has lots of airy flowers on stems up to nearly 2 feet tall; pink naked ladies have large trumpet-shaped flowers on stems up to 3 feet tall. Other species of spider lily (somewhat less hardy) are yellow or peach colored.

Other Common Names

Hurricane Lily, Resurrection Lily, Spider Lily, Magic Lily, Surprise Lily

Bloom Period and Seasonal Color

Red, pink blooms midsummer to late summer

Mature Height × Spread

15 to 36 inches × 12 to 18 inches

Painted Arum
Arum italicum

This antique surprise is one of the best winter foliage plants around! In the northern parts of our country it is a summer bulb, but here in the Deep South its foliage emerges in late fall and persists with upright-pointing arrowheads of deep green, usually with pale cream veins in the leaves. Its unusual flower, produced in the spring, is a spathe shaped like (and about the size of) a slightly cupped hand, and the center spike produces bright orange-red berries that persist well into summer. The plant is often found in older gardens where people have swapped plants for a long time, and fills a huge gap in the winter garden when summer hostas are dormant.

Other Common Name
Italian Arum

Bloom Period and Seasonal Color
Winter foliage, spring flowers, and summer berries

Mature Height × Spread
1 foot × 1 foot

When, Where, and How to Plant
Plant bulbs any time you can get them, but fall is best for winter show; arum may take a year or two to reach mature size, so don't forget where you planted them when it comes time to set out summer plants. It is a Southern European native that tolerates a good bit of shade, but for the best flowers and berries, place it where winter sunshine can hit it, avoiding north sides of buildings or evergreen shrubs. Set the drought-tolerant bulbs in a well-drained soil, or work in generous amounts of organic matter and coarse sand to build up the drainage capacity. You can space each bulb 12 inches apart, or create ready-made clumps by putting several in larger holes, allowing 4 or more inches between. Feed lightly at planting time and cover the area with leaf mulch.

Growing Tips
There is no need to water this bulb in the summer, because it is dormant like daffodils. Feed in the fall when foliage begins to emerge, using a thick layer of compost or leaf mulch that feeds both the bulbs and the soil around them.

Care
When cutting off faded foliage in the late spring, be careful to leave the stalks of green berries, which will turn red and remain well into summer. Arum has no major pests other than voles, which can be controlled by planting arum (and other bulbs) in plastic baskets buried in the ground.

Companion Planting and Design
Painted arum can be used as a winter "skirt" around shrubs, especially in gardens that have summer shade but are winter-sunny, and also just outside the base of evergreen cast-iron plant. Perhaps its best effect is when planted in small groups as winter companions between liriope and mondo grass, and dormant clumps of hosta and ferns. In the spring its foliage helps hide the fading leaves of daffodils.

Personal Favorite
Arum italicum 'Pictum' has very attractive white-veined leaves that make a great accent in the lightly shaded winter garden.

Rain Lily
Zephyranthes species

When, Where, and How to Plant
When you can buy them commercially, plant bulbs in the fall or late winter in full sun or partial shade in rich, well-drained soil. When you are "rescuing" them from old home sites, mark the best bloomers and make a note to come back in the fall—however tempting, it is rarely good to move bulbs that are in bloom. To create mature looking clumps, set bulbs 2 or 3 inches apart, or in small groups of bulbs 6 or 8 inches apart, with a little compost or other organic material and a pinch of slow-release bulb food. Plant small rain lily bulbs fairly close to the surface, with tips up. Firm the soil around the bulbs and water thoroughly. For naturalizing, plant where their reedy foliage will not be cut too close by mowers.

Growing Tips
Water this drought-tolerant bulb when needed, and fertilize lightly in the spring or early summer with a slow-release bulb food.

Care
No need to cut the foliage of this bulb, but you can increase your bulbs by dividing clumps in the fall every couple of years or whenever they get too thick. Potted bulbs flower best when a little rootbound.

Companion Planting and Design
Perfect for small gardens and rock gardens, and naturalizing in large mulched areas of the landscape. Plant at the front of a border as an edging, or between clumps of dwarf daylily, or another low-growing perennial. Plant several thick clumps as an accent in a small area near an entryway where you can enjoy the blooms and fragrance up close.

Personal Favorites
Pink rain lily (*Z. grandiflora*) has flowers up to 4 inches wide on 8-inch stems. White rain lily (*Z. candida*) opens into pure white flowers, as do the pink-striped buds of native atamasco lily (*Z. atamasco*) that blooms naturally along our streams and rivers in the spring. Yellow rain lily (*Z. citrina*) is fragrant.

This genus of low-growing, clump-forming, grassy-leaved bulbs provides a lush, green edging in spring and summer, and produces masses of flowers on short stems in the summer and fall after stimulating rains or waterings. Their fresh, open, lily-like flowers or nearly closed crocus-like funnels can be white, yellow, or pink, and some are fragrant. Winter hardy in all parts of Alabama and Mississippi, rain lilies need very little care to bloom and even multiply across the garden when left alone. They can pop up after summer showers in overgrown lawns of abandoned old home sites; mark a few clumps so you can come back in the fall to collect them for your own garden (with landowner permission, of course).

Other Common Names
Zephyr Lily, Fairy Lily

Bloom Period and Seasonal Color
White, pale pink, yellow blooms in summer

Mature Height × Spread
6 to 12 inches × 8 to 10 inches

Summer Snowflake
Leucojum aestivum

This European native, a close relative of the flattened-flower "snowdrops" (Galanthus nivalis) that Northern and high-elevation Southern gardeners love, is one of the most taken-for-granted heirloom bulbs in the South—even along our Gulf Coast. So named because of its summer-flowering habit in Europe, it is commonly found in small towns and cottage gardens where it has been passed along by gardeners for generations. Its bright green foliage (shaped like a butter knife) pops up bravely in late fall and is topped in late February and March with foot-tall stems holding one, two, or sometimes three nodding bells of white with green spots on the tip of each petal. It multiplies rapidly, even into ditches and summer-shaded gardens with winter sunshine.

Bloom Period and Seasonal Color
White blooms in late winter, early spring

Mature Height × Spread
10 to 18 inches × 6 to 8 inches

When, Where, and How to Plant
Plant snowflake—or *Galanthus*, if you live in northern areas or high elevations—in November in a rich soil for a good show the following spring. It will grow but not flourish in heavy clay or wet soil, and requires at least some sunshine in the late winter so it can form flower buds for the following year. Plant bulbs 3 or 4 inches deep with their tips up, 6 to 8 inches apart. Firm the soil around newly planted bulbs and water thoroughly to settle the soil. Mulch around them to keep summer soil cool and weeds at bay.

Growing Tips
No need to ever water this hardy bulb, but a little all-purpose or specialty bulb food every few years will help form more flowers on sturdier stems. Feed by broadcasting fertilizer over the general area in the fall.

Care
Do not cut foliage until after it starts to turn yellow or flop over, or risk losing the following year's flowers. No need to ever divide clumps unless they just get too thick or you need more for other parts of the landscape. Because they bloom in the winter, and tolerate a wide range of growing conditions, these plants seem to have no pests or diseases.

Companion Planting and Design
Snowflake complements plantings of early- to mid-spring bulbs and is lovely with crocus and early daffodils in a winter garden. Its tall leaves usually flop badly after flowering, so put it toward the back of a bed, or interplant with yarrow or hosta to hide the fading foliage. Snowflake naturalizes easily, growing well with Asiatic jasmine, English ivy, or other groundcovers, or as random plantings under trees and toward the front of shrub borders.

Personal Favorites
There really are no improved varieties of this centuries-old bulb. The somewhat hard-to-find, single-flowering "spring snowflake" (*L. vernum*) will grow in northern areas but does not flower as well on the coast.

Tulip
Tulipa hybrids

When, Where, and How to Plant

Refrigerate new bulbs for at least six weeks before planting in late October or November (December or even January on the coast). Do not store with ripe fruit, which gives off a natural gas that causes bulbs to sprout. Tulips require perfect drainage or they will rot. Because their flower bud is already formed from the year before, you do not need to fertilize tulips—unless you insist on trying to get them to rebloom for more than one season. Plant pointed end up, 8 to 12 inches apart. If you plan to pull them up and discard after flowering there's no need to plant them any deeper than a trowel's depth. Smaller species tulips can be planted more shallowly.

Growing Tips

Mulch with pine straw or evergreen boughs once soil has cooled to maintain even temperatures during warm spells in winter. Tulips usually get sufficient water from winter and spring rains, even in containers.

Care

After flowering, deadhead tulips and enjoy the blue-green foliage as long as you can. If you want to try getting them to rebloom, fertilize when you plant them in the fall, and dig in the spring as soon as foliage yellows. Store cool and dry indoors over the summer, and chill in the refrigerator for at least six weeks before planting in the fall. Good luck!

Companion Planting and Design

Unless you can afford knockout, one-shot mass plantings, tulips are best used in repeated groups, or in complementary drifts with one another; mix them not only according to color and height, but also blooming periods. Interplant with other, hardier bulbs. They are perfect for beds and containers that are normally bare in the winter. Interplant with daffodils, grape hyacinth, violas, and solid-color dianthus that don't compete for attention.

Personal Favorites

There are too many great one-shot tulips for anyone to have a favorite. Early-blooming tulips to try to perennialize include *T. fosteriana* or small-flowering species tulips such as lady or candystick tulip (*T. clusiana*)—which are not only perennial, but actually reseed themselves into summer-dry spots.

Showy as they are, most of the incredibly beautiful tulip species and varieties are not perennial in our part of the South. The winter temperatures are too fickle, rarely with enough cold "chilling hours" for them to set flower buds after their first winter. Plus, the heavy rains and hot, humid summer nights usually cause bulbs to rot. On top of that, the bulbs are very slow to reproduce in the South, so they dwindle away—the main reason "saving" them is difficult at best, even with digging and pre-chilling the following fall. It is best to treat them as annuals, buying only as many as you can bear to compost the next spring.

Bloom Period and Seasonal Color

Yellow, red, pink, white, near-black blooms in spring

Mature Height × Spread

8 to 30 inches × 8 to 12 inches

Groundcovers
for Alabama & Mississippi

What do you do when your treasured shade trees finally mature into woodland giants—and the lawn beneath dies from lack of sunlight? How do you handle a slope so steep you have to tie a rope to your lawn mower to mow? How do you increase the beauty and texture of your landscape while reducing your chores?

The answer to all these twenty-first century questions is simple: groundcovers. Smaller than shrubs, but able to cover large areas with little or no maintenance, low-growing, spreading groundcovers make sense to busy homeowners who want their gardens to look good without eating up their weekends and requiring a lot of "artificial life support" (fertilizers, weed killers, pesticides, irrigation, equipment). These groundcovers offer a lush carpet in areas where grass or flowers would be difficult (or impossible) to grow, such as banks or deep shade. As with any plant, there are pros and cons, but the rewards are worth the consideration.

Keep these things in mind to ensure success with groundcovers:

- Light requirements: Choose plants that are adapted to your conditions, rather than try to change the conditions to please a plant. While Asiatic jasmine and liriope can grow in either sun or shade, some groundcovers do better in one light situation or the other. Ivy and mondo grass usually scorch in full sun, and junipers thin out in heavy shade. It is far better to choose a plant to suit the site (even if you don't like the plant as much as others), than to put something you love where it simply won't grow—or where it will look bad most of the time!

- Growth habits: Some groundcovers, such as English ivy and periwinkle, are so vigorous that they can become invasive. Choose and plant them with this   in mind, so your low-maintenance dream doesn't turn into a nightmare.

- Site preparation: Do this right the first time, because it is difficult to do after the plants are in the ground. It is important to completely eliminate any old turfgrass or weeds before planting a groundcover, and to prepare the soil so roots can penetrate and begin spreading quickly.

- Plant spacing: This varies based on what type of groundcover you choose, how fast it will spread, and what your budget is. Sometimes it is easier to do a small area at a time, and let the plants spread from there, or take cuttings or divisions to use in other areas.

Variegated Lily Turf

Creeping Juniper

- Mulch: Until your new plants get established and begin to spread on their own, cover the soil to prevent it from being compacted by alternating baking sun and pounding rain, to keep your soil from washing away, and to help reduce the number of weed seeds that sprout.
- Water and fertilizer: Water weekly during the first summer and prolonged dry spells. To encourage plants to grow together faster, fertilize very lightly with a slow-acting fertilizer.
- Weed control: Do whatever is necessary to keep weed seeds from sprouting and taking over your groundcover, until it gets thick enough to shade the ground. Mulches, hand weeding, and even selected chemical herbicides all have their uses, but a balance between the three usually works best. Remember, what will kill weeds will often kill groundcovers as well. Check with your County Extension agent for recommendations on effective, safe herbicides.

To get groundcovers started on steep slopes, do not do a lot of deep cultivating, or your soil may wash away during heavy rains (especially over the winter). Instead, do a good job of planting individual plants, and then mulch heavily between them. The mulch will keep the soil cool and moist in the summer, help prevent many of the annual weeds that sprout from seed, and loosen and even "feed" the soil as earthworms carry bits of the mulch deep underground. Synthetic mulches and "weed barrier" fabrics do not have these benefits, by the way.

In addition to the groundcover selections listed here, many small shrubs, ornamental grasses, and perennials can be grouped, massed, or combined to cover a lot of ground. Your landscape can be more beautiful and lower maintenance (and safer, when you reduce the use of power equipment over tree roots or on steep slopes) through the generous use of groundcovers.

Ajuga
Ajuga reptans

Ajuga is one of the easiest mat-forming groundcovers you can plant, and it is fast growing. This low, wide-leaved member of the mint family has no fragrance to its foliage, but comes in a wide array of foliage colors and variegations. The plant colony spreads quickly during warm weather from short runners that constantly sprout both roots and new rosettes of leaves as they grow. The overall effect is lush, even without the flowers, which are produced in the spring and early summer on 6-inch stalks. Each stalk is covered with small lavender, pink, or blue tubular flowers that attract bees and hummingbirds. Ajuga will tolerate a lot of sun but is at its best in light shade.

Other Common Name
Bugleweed

Bloom Period and Seasonal Color
Blue or pink flowers in spring

Mature Height × Spread
3 to 6 inches × 1 to 2 feet

When, Where, and How to Plant
Ajuga can be planted from container-grown stock or transplanted all year, or rooted from runners in the summer and fall. Plant ajuga in soil amended with organic matter (especially under trees). Established ajuga can recover from considerable drought, but quickly rots in wet or poorly drained soils, so choose a site where soil can be amended easily. Plant small runners a foot apart, with stems in the soil but crowns with rosettes of leaves on top of the soil surface. Mulch to prevent soil compaction, and keep plants moist until they begin to "run."

Growing Tips
Water lightly but regularly to keep plants spreading, but do not keep them wet, which can quickly rot crowns. Feed lightly in the spring and again in midsummer if ample moisture is present—don't feed the second time if you can't support the new growth with watering. Because ajuga is a dense groundcover, mulching after the first year is not necessary.

Care
Use a small sharp hoe to keep the site weeded and soil worked up during establishment. There is no advantage to deadheading flowers, but mow or cut old stalks back for neatness. Do not allow tree leaves to pack down over ajuga. In years of heavy rain, plants are susceptible to fungal diseases, but usually rebound with runners from remaining plants.

Companion Planting and Design
While it spreads easily, ajuga's root system is not very dense, so it works best as a groundcover under shrubs and perennials such as salvia, phlox, hosta, lilies, and surprise lilies. It is a great plant to cascade from the edges of raised beds, and can be contained easily as an edger between liriope, and even between large stepping stones.

Personal Favorites
'Atropurpurea' has bronze-tinted green leaves and 'Variegata' has leaves edged and splotched with creamy yellow. 'Burgundy Lace' has reddish purple foliage variegated with white and pink. *Ajuga pyramidalis* 'Metallica Crispa' has shiny, crinkled, very dark burgundy leaves.

Asiatic Jasmine
Trachelospermum asiaticum

When, Where, and How to Plant

Set out container-grown plants any time, in any amount of sun or shade, in well-prepared soil to help get them started. They will grow but not thrive in low, wet areas, preferring a hot or dry site that drains well in the rainy seasons of spring and fall. Prepare a wide bed or generous individual planting holes, and use the potting soil from each container as the only source of organic matter. Set plants 18 to 24 inches apart. Poke long runners into the ground with just the tip sticking out, and the buried parts will root. Cover the planting area with mulch to help control weeds the first season or two.

Growing Tips

For fast establishment, keep weeded, feed lightly with a slow-acting fertilizer, and water deeply every two or three weeks. Root new cuttings by wrapping long vines around your hand into a small doughnut-sized circle, and sticking it halfway in the ground. Keep moist for a month, and the part in the ground will be rooted and the aboveground part will be sprouting new shoots.

Care

Trim edges of Asiatic jasmine beds to keep them neat and within bounds, and to thicken the groundcover. If it gets too tall or thick, simply cut it close to the ground and it will start all over again, very quickly. There are no major insect or disease pests.

Companion Planting and Design

When using Asiatic jasmine as a groundcover, leave it either unpruned and naturalistic, or keep it sheared tightly into contemporary or even whimsical designs. Few plants other than trees make good companions without getting swallowed up.

Personal Favorites

'Bronze Green' has very shiny bronze new growth that matures to dark green. Climbing confederate or star jasmine (*T. jasminoides*) can also be used as a groundcover; 'Variegatum' has white borders and blotches.

This easy-to-propagate vine, grown by the tens of thousands by area wholesale plant producers every year, is a mainstay of low-maintenance commercial landscapes. Banks, offices, hospitals, and other large buildings are surrounded with acres of Asiatic jasmine because it is such a versatile, durable, fast-growing groundcover, and cheap to buy. Fragrant, starry spring flowers add to its value. Though it can be trained as a vine, it is most often planted as a thick groundcover, in sun or shade. Though it is usually kept clipped into foot-tall masses, it still cuts down dramatically on mowing, fertilizing, spraying, and other landscape maintenance chores. It is so common that it has now been accepted as a major element of low-maintenance home landscapes.

Bloom Period and Seasonal Color
Lilac-blue blooms in spring, evergreen foliage

Mature Height × Spread
6 to 12 inches × 2 to 4 feet

Creeping Juniper
Juniperus horizontalis

Creeping juniper is a good choice for banks and tough sites for mowing. It's also heat tolerant and can take the sun—even in parking lot dividers. This native plant grows naturally on sea cliffs, gravelly slopes, and in swamps with sandy soils; it is even tolerant of salt spray, making it a good pick for beach homes. The medium-fast grower has blue-green foliage that develops a plum-colored cast in cool winter weather. There are many selections of creeping juniper, each with different growth habits and hues of green, whose performance varies in different areas and uses; any good garden center will have several from which to choose.

Other Common Name
Groundcover Juniper

Bloom Period and Seasonal Color
Evergreen needles

Mature Height × Spread
4 to 12 inches × 4 to 6 feet or more

When, Where, and How to Plant
Plant creeping juniper as you would a small shrub, in the fall if possible. Plant in loose, sandy or rocky, well-drained soils—when these plants die, it is usually from heavy soil that stays too wet. Amend heavy or clay soils with sand and organic material, and be sure the site has excellent drainage (on a slope or in a raised bed). Mix in a slow-release, all-purpose fertilizer, and set the plants 4 to 6 feet apart with roots loosened and spread over a slightly raised mound of earth to facilitate good drainage. (Do not set the plants too deep.) Water thoroughly. Mulch around plants to prevent weeds.

Growing Tips
Water during extreme dry spells, at least every two or three weeks in sandy soil or hot sites. Fertilize in the spring with compost or a slow-release fertilizer; once plants reach maturity, cut back on fertilizing.

Care
Hand weed to keep weeds from competing with the plants, especially the first year. Prune to remove any dead wood, and shear new growth to thicken it—but never prune heavily or below the foliage on the branch, or the entire branch will die back to its point of origin. In years of unseasonably heavy rains, creeping juniper may show signs of root rot. Watch for yellowing, and prepare to prune off branches if they show serious signs of decline. Treat spider mites with horticultural oil spray.

Companion Planting and Design
Use creeping juniper in hot dry areas, on slopes or banks, and between other foundation shrubs as a unifying element. It contrasts well with ornamental grasses, yucca, sumac, and other small trees. Junipers also make super-hardy, handsome container plants, especially when combined with bulbs and summer annuals.

Personal Favorites
Some very popular choices include blue rug juniper (*J. horizontalis* 'Wiltonii'), Andorra creeping juniper (*J. horizontalis* 'Plumosa'), and 'Bar Harbour'. Other good groundcover junipers include shore juniper (*J. conferta*) and parson's juniper (*J. davurica* 'Parsonii').

Creeping Lily Turf
Liriope spicata

When, Where, and How to Plant

Plant or dig and divide lily turf any time of the year. Plant in shade or part shade with morning sun only, in soil that is well drained. If planted under shallow-rooted shrubs such as azaleas, monkey grass will compete for moisture and nutrients to the detriment of the shrubs. Loosen the soil thoroughly; if planting under shade trees or shrubs, dig individual planting holes to minimize root damage to existing plants. Soil amendment is generally not needed for this tough plant. Divide clumps (even container-grown clumps) at planting time, and replant from 6 to 12 inches apart with the crown level with the soil around it. Cover the area deeply with natural leaf mulch to keep the soil loose and cool, and lily turf will quickly send out rhizomes to colonize the entire area.

Growing Tips

Water deeply but not too often, as the drought-tolerant plant will send runners only into moist areas, not wet. After plants have been in the ground for a summer, watering is rarely necessary. Fertilizing is also optional, but if you want to hasten growth, fertilize in spring with a slow-release or natural fertilizer.

Care

To keep the plants attractive, cut down the previous season's foliage in January or February before new growth begins to emerge, being careful to not damage newly emerging growth, or the plants will look ragged the rest of the year. Use sharp shears or a highly revved string trimmer, not a mower with a dull blade. Liriope has no major pests; even deer tend to step over it if other food is available.

Companion Planting and Design

Use monkey grass as a lawn replacement for large shaded areas; once established it provides evergreen color with almost no maintenance. Cast-iron plant will grow up through the dense foliage as a texture companion.

Personal Favorite

'Silver Dragon' has thin green leaves with silvery white stripes.

There are two distinct types of "big" monkey grass—the clump-forming Liriope muscari (including variegated forms), which spreads very slowly into mounds and is used for specimen plants and for edging flower beds and sidewalks, and the solid green but rapidly spreading creeping lily turf (Liriope spicata) that grows so fast it often comes out of the drainage holes in the bottom of its container. Both are effective, with creeping lily turf spreading so quickly and steadily that it will form a good groundcover even under the dense foliage of Southern magnolia trees! As a bonus, its thick foliage is sturdy enough to absorb and help compost the thick oval leaves of the magnolia.

Other Common Names
Running Monkey Grass, Liriope

Bloom Period and Seasonal Color
Evergreen foliage with white, lavender blooms in midsummer

Mature Height × Spread
10 to 12 inches × 1 foot

English Ivy

Hedera helix

With its strong ties to tradition, English ivy creates a sense of history in a garden after only a couple of growing seasons. To some gardeners, its ability to grow several feet in a season makes the glossy-leaved vine almost too aggressive, but usually it is merely an outstanding solution for dry shady areas where few other plants will grow. Still, it is wise to contain the vine where possible, by planting it beside paving, buildings, or open ground. If it seems to grow too well after a few years, simply prune it back and let it quickly start again. By the way, ivy does not kill large trees (though allowing ivy to grow upward into the trees encourages it to flower, set seed, and create seedlings where you might not want them), but it can overtop and overwhelm small trees and shrubs. Choose from dozens of interesting varieties.

Other Common Name
Ivy

Bloom Period and Seasonal Color
Evergreen foliage

Mature Height × Spread
4 to 8 inches × 6 to 10 feet or more

When, Where, and How to Plant
Set out container-grown English ivy any time during the year, as long as the ground is not frozen. During the first summer, late spring and summer transplants require regular (at least weekly) watering. Plant cuttings from mature growth directly in the ground or in pots when the soil is warm. Ivy tolerates almost any soil except soggy locations, but a loose soil that is rich in organic material is ideal. Loosen the soil in the entire planting area, or dig individual planting holes amended with organic matter, and set plants or rooted cuttings 12 to 18 inches apart, mulch the area, and drench the soil with water.

Growing Tips
Water young ivy at least once a week, but mature plants can go for months even without rain. Leaf mulch will decompose and feed both the soil and ivy, and tree roots as well, but an occasional application of an all-purpose tree fertilizer will help—at least every three or four years.

Care
Prune vigorous vines in the spring to help slow them down and thicken them. Ivy sometimes develops a bacterial leaf spot that causes dieback. The disease is difficult to control, but with pruning and treatment with recommended fungicides, you can get ivy to start over again. Avoid overhead irrigation and high rates of fertilization.

Companion Planting and Design
Ivy goes beyond being a groundcover for use under trees; it also prevents erosion in shaded areas, and can be used to soften the look of brick or stone walls (though its aerial roots will destroy wooden walls). Tall perennials and bulbs such as surprise lily, hosta, and ferns can grow up through thick ivy groundcovers.

Personal Favorites
'Thorndale' is extremely cold hardy and has light green veins. 'Congesta' (also called 'Minima') is also cold hardy and has small leaves just an inch across. 'Glacier' has creamy white variegation. Algerian ivy (*H. canariensis*) has very large leaves widely spaced on the vines.

Japanese Pachysandra
Pachysandra terminalis

When, Where, and How to Plant
Plant in the fall, winter, or early spring to avoid having to water a lot the first summer. Pachysandra, which will not tolerate sun in the South, grows best in moist, well-drained soil enriched with compost or organic material; amend clay soils by adding sand and organic materials. Set plants 6 to 12 inches apart in soil that has been dug deeply so runners can spread quickly, mulch heavily, and water deeply every week or so until plants get established and begin to run.

Growing Tips
Water every few weeks to keep plants lush and vigorous, and to help them cope with our hot, dry summers. Avoid over-watering or risk foliar diseases. In early spring, fertilize very lightly with a slow-release, all-purpose fertilizer, and spread chipped leaves over the area in the fall to help enrich the soil and protect roots from winter sunshine.

Care
Prune pachysandra in the late winter for height control and to reduce leaf spot disease problems caused by over-watering or rainy spells in our hot, humid climate. If disease occurs, cut the plants down, rake up the debris, and spray new growth with a recommended fungicide.

Companion Planting and Design
Japanese pachysandra makes a handsome groundcover for the shade, and can be contained easily as a border plant. It is well adapted for rock gardens and large containers in the shade, combining well with hosta; ferns; and taller shade shrubs such as camellia, azalea, and even magnolia.

Personal Favorites
Good cultivars include 'Green Carpet', 'Green Sheen' with especially shiny leaves, and the less vigorous but variegated 'Silver Edge'. Allegheny spurge (*P. procumbens*), native to the Southeast, has wider leaves with a purplish-brown cast, and lightly fragrant white or pinkish flowers.

Where it's happy, Japanese pachysandra is an almost ideal groundcover for a difficult situation—deep shade under trees where grass will not grow, even in competition with tree roots. The plants have shiny, dark green leaves that glimmer and gleam through winter, clustered at the tops of short stems. And unlike English ivy, slow-to-spread pachysandra, which increases by underground runners, is not likely to take over the woods. It also has fairly attractive tufts of white flowers in the late winter and spring. The downside to pachysandra is that it has trouble coping with the summer heat and humidity of the Gulf Coast, except on the north side of buildings in very well-drained soils.

Other Common Name
Spurge

Bloom Period and Seasonal Color
Small white blooms in spring, evergreen foliage

Mature Height × Spread
6 to 12 inches × 1 to 2 feet

Mondo Grass
Ophiopogon japonicus

Mondo grass, or "little monkey grass," is perhaps the easiest shade groundcover of all. It spreads steadily by short runners, but not as fast as a vine, and it will grow between mature tree roots, pavers, and other plants without taking over. It can be planted high to grow as a solid border, or mowed just like turfgrass, making it a deep evergreen lawn substitute where grass won't grow (as a bonus, mowing helps uncover the short stalks of pinkish white flowers and blue berries normally hidden in the foliage). The plant's delicate leaves—thin, curving, and a deep, clean green—lend a sense of timelessness to gardens. From its first season, mondo grass gets busy filling in space with dense, turf-like clumps.

Other Common Name
Little Monkey Grass

Bloom Period and Seasonal Color
Evergreen foliage

Mature Height × Spread
3 to 10 inches × 5 to 12 inches

When, Where, and How to Plant
Plant container-grown or divided mondo grass any time of the year. Divide plants in the fall or spring by simply cutting into established plants and separating individual plants, each with leaves and roots. Mondo requires shade or morning sun in fertile, well-drained soil. Loosen the soil thoroughly, but soil amending is unnecessary unless you have very heavy clay or nearly pure sand, both of which are improved with generous amounts of organic material. While loosening container-grown plant roots, divide plants into smaller pieces and set plants 5 to 12 inches apart. Fertilize lightly, mulch deeply, and soak the planting area.

Growing Tips
Water every week or two to get plants established, but mature mondo grass needs little or no water. Feed lightly in the spring every two or three years with an all-purpose or natural fertilizer, which feeds nearby trees at the same time.

Care
An annual grooming keeps the plants attractive. Using very sharp shears or a highly revved string trimmer, remove the previous season's foliage in January or February, before new growth begins to emerge. There are no major pests.

Companion Planting and Design
Mondo grass can increase steadily, so plant it where it can either spread without causing problems, or contain it with buried edging or pavement. Use it as a shaded lawn replacement; to frame color beds; or to fill in under flowering trees such as crape myrtles, with their cinnamon-colored bark. Interplant with dwarf daffodils, surprise lilies, small hosta, and ferns.

Personal Favorites
Dwarf mondo grass (*O. japonicus* 'Nanus') is ideal for use between stones in a walkway or patio, or in a rock garden. Black mondo grass (*O. planiscapus* 'Nigrescens') is almost jet black, a perfect companion for yellow sedum. Aztec grass (*O. intermedius* 'Argenteomarginatus' is a rapidly spreading mondo grass with yellowish white margins on green leaves, and bright blue berries.

Southern Shield Fern

Thelypteris kunthii

When, Where, and How to Plant

Divide Southern shield fern in the fall as it goes dormant, or in spring when fiddleheads emerge. Plant container-grown ferns any time, even summer, but be prepared to cut off broken fronds and to water regularly to get the plants through their first summer. When planted in good soil that is high in organic matter and kept moist, this fern tolerates heat, drought, and some sun. Water (or soak) containerized ferns before planting 1 to 2 feet apart, loosen rhizomes, and plant level with the soil around it. Mulch with rotted leaf mould or rotten pine bark, and water deeply.

Growing Tips

In the first year, water every week or two to get it established, and help it develop a good root system. Water established ferns monthly during prolonged drought, and fertilize with cottonseed meal or fish emulsion, both good, slow-release forms of natural nitrogen.

Care

The plant spreads steadily but is fairly easy to control. Divide Southern shield fern every few years in the winter or early spring for replanting in other areas of the landscape and to share with others. There are no major pests or diseases, but brittle fronds are easily broken when planted in high-traffic or windy areas.

Companion Planting and Design

Plant Southern shield where it can spread to its heart's content, as a groundcover under deciduous trees, with liriope to have a winter evergreen in its place, in rock gardens and along fences and walls where its beautiful form and bright green hue are displayed best. Plant under camellia, deciduous azalea, crape myrtle, vitex, and other small trees, interplanted with bulbs that benefit from the winter sunshine.

Personal Favorites

There is only the species Southern shield fern available in the market. Other hardy, nearly foolproof groundcover ferns include autumn fern (*Dryopteris erythrosora*) and Christmas fern (*Polystichum acrostichoides*).

This tough, deciduous fern is no doubt the easiest and most common fern passed around between garden club members and cottage gardeners. The hardy native loves our hot weather, wet winters, and summer drought; it will even tolerate a good bit of sun, especially in moist areas with no reflected heat. Growing 2 to 3 feet tall, it is an impressive fern with upright, narrowly triangular fronds that remain a light, bright green color all season until turning a rich brown at first frost. This fern spreads aggressively by rhizomes into fertile soil, forming dense colonies that tend to overstep their bounds, often requiring digging excess plants from around the edges of colonies—hence it has become a popular "pass-along plant."

Other Common Name
Wood Fern

Bloom Period and Seasonal Color
Deciduous foliage

Mature Height × **Spread**
2 to 3 feet × 12 to 18 inches

Vinca
Vinca minor

This lovely evergreen groundcover is native to Europe and hardy in almost every state in the union—and is commonly found planted in old cemeteries in our own states. It is an aggressive evergreen spreader, but not a good competitor; it grows best alone and not with other plants. Vinca creates a low blanket of shiny green, oval leaves that contrasts well in autumn with fallen tree leaves, which only melt into the vinca to compost and recycle nutrients. In early spring, five-petaled flowers of lilac blue (a rare flower color) open. Vinca is happy in full to partial shade and tolerates drought. So many gardeners are willing to give vinca away that it's surprising that anyone buys it.

Other Common Name
Periwinkle

Bloom Period and Seasonal Color
Lilac-blue blooms in spring, evergreen foliage

Mature Height × Spread
4 to 6 inches × 3 to 4 feet

When, Where, and How to Plant
Plant container-grown vinca any time, but be prepared to water spring-planted plants through the first summer. Plant in shade, in well-drained soils that do not have standing water in the winter. Set plants 1 to 2 feet apart and cut the stems back to encourage thicker growth. Some gardeners help the vines spread more quickly by bending the long, arching stems over and poking them into the ground at a leaf joint, so they will root. Set vinca plants so the top of the rootball is level with the top of the soil. Firm the soil around the roots, then water thoroughly to remove air pockets. Mulch to prevent weeds from encroaching the first season.

Growing Tips
Established vinca does not need watering even in extended dry spells. Vinca wilts in drought, but this is not a real problem, just a way to conserve moisture; the plants perk up when rains come again as if a drought never occurred. Vinca will be adequately fertilized by autumn leaves.

Care
Regular pruning is the only real maintenance for vinca. To keep it in its place, just cut back the trailing stems or pull up excess plants, which come up easily after a rain. Vinca will not climb trees or buildings, so it is not as invasive as English ivy. It can easily be increased by division or rooted cuttings.

Companion Planting and Design
Plant vinca under trees or shrubs, or on banks or slopes, where grass is difficult to maintain. Its root system does not compete with shallow-rooted trees, so vinca is good under dogwoods and redbuds. Daffodils can be interplanted with vinca—the periwinkle flowers fill a difficult color gap when most bulbs are dormant.

Personal Favorites
Some tempting selections are available, such as 'Alba', which is white flowered, and 'Bowles's Variety', which has larger flowers. 'Sterling Silver' has green leaves edged and speckled with pale green.

Wintercreeper

Euonymus fortunei

When, Where, and How to Plant

This vine is hardy to below freezing, and completely heat and drought tolerant, so it can be planted any time you can dig a hole. Young plants spread quickly and root as they go; you can also stick unrooted cuttings directly in the ground, keep them moist for two or three weeks, and they will take root. Wintercreeper grows in full sun or light shade, and will tolerate a wide range of growing conditions. Loosen the soil enough to get the plants in the ground, cover with leaf mulch, and water to get started.

Growing Tips

This vine has no real needs with water or fertilizer, just an occasional soaking during dry spells and fertilizer every two or three years. Tip-prune new plants to thicken them more quickly.

Care

Prune wintercreeper only to keep it compact and close to the ground, and to head it in the direction you want it to grow (or not grow). Keep it from growing up into trees, because once it is vertical it flowers and sets many seeds, sometimes causing a weed problem with its seedlings. Mildew on leaves can simply be pruned out. Scale insect can be troublesome, but can be treated with an oil spray in the late winter or early spring.

Companion Planting and Design

The dense, readily rooting evergreen vine is an excellent choice for the type of poor soil found beside steep hillside steps and walkways where erosion is a problem. It combines with iris and hosta, but is most often used on its own where the foliage and its seasonal color change can be appreciated.

Personal Favorites

Most varieties of wintercreeper can grow into small shrubs or thick, vining groundcovers if left alone. 'Coloratus', or purple wintercreeper, sprawls to several feet high and up to 8 feet wide, and its leaves turn dark purple in the fall and winter. Common wintercreeper (*E. fortunei* var. *radicans*) is lower growing at only a foot high over open ground, but will climb anything in its path.

If there is one plant that sends shivers up the spines of horticulturists and landscapers, it is euonymus (pronounced you-AH-ne-mus), not because it is necessarily a "bad" plant, but because it is so commonly planted and has a couple of pest problems. (As if roses don't!) People typically plant this shrubby vine simply because they like it, and because it works. It is unkillable with cold, heat, drought, or rain, and grows for decades with almost no maintenance. Given a chance, it can become a small shrub or climber, but can easily be kept low and spreading, growing in the toughest soils to prevent erosion.

Other Common Name
Wintercreeper Euonymus

Bloom Period and Seasonal Color
Evergreen vine with fall fruits

Mature Height × Spread
2 feet × 4 to 8 feet or more

Herbs *for Alabama & Mississippi*

The plants we call "herbs" are fascinating to have in the garden for many reasons. Besides being attractive in flower, foliage, and form, they have uses other than mere beauty. Most herbs have been grown for centuries for flavoring food or tea, for their fragrance, or as home-remedy medications. But many are grown simply as great garden plants, never to be used for a practical purpose. And herbs don't have to be grown in "herb gardens"—you can also use them in the vegetable garden or with "regular" landscape plants. They can be grown nearly anywhere, in average soil in a vegetable or flower garden, raised beds, pots (both singly and in combinations), or hanging baskets. Some are hardy outdoors, while others need to be brought indoors in the winter.

There are many good examples of this multiple-use approach to growing herbs. A fall planting of pansies or violas (with their edible flowers) in front of a bright green mound of parsley is lovely in

Golden Oregano and Bronze Fennel

midwinter. Chives have beautiful flowers, basil is great for attracting bees and butterflies, and oregano and mint make fragrant groundcovers. Hot peppers, known for the fiery zest of their edible pods, are tough garden annuals. And bee balm, a Southeastern native perennial, is beautiful to behold and attracts bees, butterflies, and hummingbirds; its flowers are spicy when eaten and its leaves make a soothing tea. Who could ask for more from a garden plant?

Either way you want to say it—"erb" or "herb"—is correct! The French drop the "h" but the English pronounce it. The only wrong thing to do is make others uncomfortable about how they say it!

Growing Herbs

Because of our dramatic geographical ranges and unusual weather (wild temperature swings, heavy spring rains, and high summer humidity), some herbs are difficult for even experts to grow. If you want to grow lavender, for example, try selections that have been tested in Deep South gardens to increase your chances of success.

When it comes to growing herbs, keep these basics in mind:

- Many Mediterranean herbs don't like our climate—don't feel like a failure if you can't grow them all!
- Most herbs need at least half a day of sun, ideally morning sun with partial afternoon shade.

Rosemary

- Herbs need excellent drainage. Plant on a terraced site or in a raised bed or container. Amend soil with generous amounts of compost, sand (for drainage), and lime (if necessary to lower the soil's acidity) before planting.
- Herb oils will be diluted in overfertilized plants. Feed soil annually with compost, or small amounts of slow-acting natural fertilizers.
- Water herbs as needed, but don't keep them wet—many originate near the Mediterranean, a naturally dry region.
- Mulch around herbs to keep roots cool and moist in summer and to protect them from wildly fluctuating temperatures in late winter.
- Culinary herbs should never be sprayed with anything that is not approved for food crops.
- Mix herb plants in garden designs according to size, contrasting shapes, and complementary foliage colors.
- Try to plant culinary herbs near the kitchen door so you will be tempted to cook with them more often. Some herbs are tasty, healthful salt substitutes, so an accessible garden has long-term benefits.
- Harvest herbs regularly—or at least cut them back from time to time—to promote new growth and bushier plants. Harvest in the morning after the dew has dried, when herbs' natural oils are most concentrated. Herbs are best used fresh, but you can freeze or dry them, or preserve them in vinegars.

Using Herbs

The "essential oils" in herb leaves concentrate as leaves dry. To get the same general effect in cooking, use about three times as much of a fresh herb as you would the dried form. For example, if a recipe calls for a teaspoon of dried oregano, use three teaspoons (a tablespoon) of fresh oregano leaves. Note: Before using herbs for medicinal purposes, research dependable references. Keep in mind that dosage is important, and be aware of potential side effects or interactions with other medications (even nonprescription ones) that you are taking.

The relatively few herb plants chosen for this book serve at least double duty—they are useful as herbs, but are also great garden plants even if you don't use them for another purpose. There are many, many others—some easier or harder to grow in our climate than others—from which you can choose.

Basil
Ocimum basilicum

Lush and leafy, basil fills the air with a clove-like aroma when you brush against it on a warm summer day. Basil makes a great summer foliage plant, and comes in selections with different forms and scents such as lemon, clove, and cinnamon. Some have attractive flowers that bees and hummingbirds love. Although this cuts down on leaf production, it might be worth sacrificing a few leaves for the clusters of tiny lavender or white flowers. A favorite culinary herb, this fast-growing annual is harvested in summer and fall for pesto; refrigerated herb butters; salad toppings; tomato-based dishes (even sprinkled on fresh-sliced tomatoes right in the garden!); along with meats, soups, and sauces. Enjoy it fresh, frozen, refrigerated in oil, or preserved in vinegar.

Harvest and Bloom Period
Edible foliage from spring to frost

Mature Height × Spread
1 to 3 feet × 1 to 3 feet

When, Where, and How to Plant
Sow seeds directly into the ground after the last frost, keeping the soil evenly moist while seeds germinate; thin the seedlings to a foot apart. Or set out transplants a foot or more apart in spring after danger of frost is past, when the ground warms up, in rich, loose, well-drained soil in full sun (although plants in coastal areas benefit from afternoon shade). Dig a hole at least 8 inches deep, and mix in an organic or time-release fertilizer with compost. Set the plant at the same level it grew in the container and backfill. Mulch and water thoroughly. One or two basil plants will be more than enough for most families.

Growing Tips
Basil needs frequent thirst quenchings to support its rapid growth. Water deeply as needed, without letting the soil dry out completely between soakings. Water basil in containers more frequently. After heavy harvesting, or in midsummer, apply a little more fertilizer.

Care
Harvest frequently to encourage branching new growth. Do not harvest more than one-third of the plant at a time or risk sunburn to stems. Remove flowers to keep basil from going to seed. Basil is susceptible to aphids, spider mites, and other minor insect damage on its leaves, but nothing really serious; smaller-leaved selections seem more resistant. Make a final harvest in early fall.

Companion Planting and Design
Plant the compact, mounding 'Spicy Globe' basil as a pretty border with tomatoes and peppers, or plant 'Purple Ruffles' alongside pink petunias or dianthus for a flower border. Use dwarf selections for edging and in containers. For an ornamental, plant basil in groups of three to five plants.

Personal Favorites
A good collection of basils would include 'Purple Ruffles', lemon basil, cinnamon basil, and the basketball-size 'Spicy Globe'. The large, spicy 'African Blue' hybrid basil has purple stems and large butterfly-attracting flower spikes.

Bay
Laurus nobilis

When, Where, and How to Plant
Plant bay or move potted specimens to a protected area outdoors in spring after the threat of frost is well past. In the north and central areas, bring bay indoors sometime after a light frost slows growth, but expect a few older leaves to shed. Bay benefits from some shade during the summer, so choose an eastern exposure (morning sun), or a southern one with afternoon shade. Water before planting. Dig a hole three to five times the width of the rootball and the same depth. Mix compost, plus an organic or time-release fertilizer, with your native soil. Set bay at the same depth it grew in the container and backfill. Mulch around it and water thoroughly. Repot containers every two years. Use a quality potting mix plus a time-release fertilizer, if the mix does not contain it.

Growing Tips
Water bay only as needed, which should be rarely if it's in the ground, and do not keep a potted specimen too wet. If planted in the ground, fertilize with compost or an organic or time-release fertilizer in spring and late summer; feed container plants once a month with a balanced liquid fertilizer, according to the directions.

Care
Bay can get pretty big, so be prepared to cut on it fairly often (especially if you train it as a topiary), and thin out long branches annually. In the winter, place a potted bay in a cool, sunny room. Do not over-water. If the tree is attacked by scale, thoroughly spray the entire plant with nontoxic insecticidal soap.

Companion Planting and Design
A potted bay serves as a classical sculpture in a formal herb or kitchen garden, a specimen plant on a patio or deck, or, in southern parts of the state, as a background screen or hedge. Underplant with durable groundcovers such as liriope or needle-point ivy.

Personal Favorite
'Saratoga' is a hybrid *Laurus* that has broader leaves and is more tree-like than the species *L. nobilis*.

Bay is prized by herb gardeners today as both a culinary and ornamental treasure. The evergreen tree or small shrub can be planted outdoors in the lower half of our states, but farther north or in higher elevations keep your bay tree in a pot and bring it indoors in winter. Bay is easy to grow, as long as it is not over-watered or damaged by cold. Its glossy green leaves—each plant has more than the average cook will ever use—can be harvested any time for soups, stews, and herb and spice blends, or just crumbled into potpourri. Because it is as long-lived as it is beautiful, a bay tree makes a thoughtful gift for any occasion.

Harvest and Bloom Period
Evergreen edible foliage all year

Mature Height × Spread
4 to 6 feet indoors / 20 to 30 feet outdoors × 2 to 4 feet

Chives
Allium schoenoprasum

Grassy-looking, onion-flavored chives is an ideal herbal topping for foods and perfect in a perennial border or container garden. Tough and hardy, chives relish the cool season. It has hollow round leaves of deep green and round, purple, spring flowers (which are also edible). Its multiplying growth makes it easy to divide for new plantings or as a pass-along gift to new gardeners. Garlic chives (Allium tuberosum) has flat, dull-green leaves with a very strong garlic fragrance and white flowers in summer and fall. Both are evergreen, even in pots left outdoors all winter. Use chives fresh, frozen, or preserved in vinegar or refrigerated herb butters. It makes a savory, colorful garnish for potatoes, rice, pasta, salad, vinaigrette, pizza, and meat dishes.

Harvest and Bloom Period
Edible foliage from spring to frost, lavender blooms in spring and summer

Mature Height × Spread
8 to 12 inches × 1 foot

When, Where, and How to Plant
Plant chives in early fall or spring (as soon as the ground warms up). Chives enjoys the cool of spring, survives summer, and flourishes until late fall, when the leaves yellow and wane with freezing temperatures. Plant chives in rich, well-drained soil in full sun. It languishes in the shade. Water transplants before setting out 1 foot apart. Set transplants at the same depth they grew in the container and backfill with slightly amended soil. Mulch and water thoroughly. Sow seeds (according to directions on the package) in spring after the threat of frost is past. When seedlings are 3 inches tall, thin to 1 foot apart. It takes a year to harvest seed-grown chives.

Growing Tips
Water only as needed, because this is a very drought-hardy plant! After a heavy harvest, water with a balanced liquid fertilizer. Feed with compost or organic or slow-release fertilizer every spring.

Care
Pinch off faded blossoms to prevent chives from reseeding and to stimulate thick, grassy foliage. Harvest chives regularly to encourage new growth. Clip leaves about half an inch from the ground, harvesting from the outside of the clump. Do not harvest more than one-third of the foliage at one time. In early fall, clean up dead foliage and divide clumps to avoid overcrowding. There are no major pests to chives, other than foliage or root problems from being kept too wet.

Companion Planting and Design
In the landscape, chives makes an excellent edging plant; adds low vertical interest to a flowerbed; and is fantastic in containers, even all winter during the most severe freezes. Plant with pansies, parsley, oregano, and spring bulbs. Its strong linear foliage provides a nice backdrop to a small garden sculpture.

Personal Favorite
Improved varieties are hard to come by. For a tall spring-blooming extra treat, throw in some cloves of real garlic, planted in the fall.

Cilantro
Coriandrum sativum

When, Where, and How to Plant

Plant cilantro in well-drained soil. In coastal areas, it tolerates light shade. Plant cilantro in early fall, sowing seeds directly into the ground (fall-sown seedlings are winter hardy). When the seedlings are 3 inches tall, thin to 15 inches apart. In the spring after last frost, set out small transplants. They develop deep taproots and suffer if kept in the pot too long and planted at a larger size. Water transplants before planting. Set plants 15 inches apart. Dig a hole from 8 to 12 inches deep, and mix the soil with compost and organic or time-release fertilizer. Partially backfill with amended soil, leaving room for the rootball of the plant. Set the transplant at the same depth it grew in the container and backfill. Mulch and water thoroughly.

Growing Tips

Water cilantro as needed, but do not over-water. After heavy harvesting, apply balanced liquid fertilizer. Cilantro flowers as soon as the weather warms in early summer, and the foliage becomes sparse. If you are growing plants for coriander seeds, watch for flowers to turn light brown, then harvest seedheads and dry in a paper bag for a week before storing in the refrigerator.

Care

Harvest cilantro leaves regularly, never harvesting more than one-third of the plant at a time. Whiteflies are a minor problem in the late spring, as are slugs and snails. Other than insecticidal soap for whiteflies, no controls are usually needed.

Companion Planting and Design

Use it as a back-of-the-border plant, or as a filler with other annual herbs and flowers that reseed and return every year. It can be planted in rows in the vegetable garden, but it is actually a nice companion to other plants.

Personal Favorites

"Slow bolting" selections such as 'Santo' and 'Long Standing' are slow to flower and go to seed in our early summer heat, and produce foliage over a long period of time.

A cool-season annual, cilantro creates a wild, wispy presence in the garden with its parsley-like leaves and gossamer white flowers. It is primarily a culinary herb, and both its leaves and fragrant, spicy seeds (called coriander) are used. The foliage of cilantro puts the vida (Spanish for life) into homemade salsa and most Mexican cooking. Native to Europe, the Middle East, and Far East, cilantro is also popular in other international cuisines. When cooking, use cilantro sparingly at first (it is one of the bitter herbs of the Bible). Enjoy cilantro's leaves fresh or frozen. They do not retain their flavor when dried. Store coriander seeds in a jar in the refrigerator.

Other Common Names
Chinese Parsley, Coriander

Harvest and Bloom Period
Edible foliage from winter to late spring, white blooms and seeds in summer

Mature Height × Spread
2 to 3 feet × 15 inches

Dill
Anethum graveolens

A cool-season annual, fern-like dill is a culinary herb that has made its way out of the kitchen garden into the flower garden. Its feathery blue-green foliage brings unusual color and texture to a border, and is a very important "host" food for swallowtail butterfly caterpillars. Its roundish umbels of delicate chartreuse spring flowers (resembling Queen Anne's lace) are fabulous in floral arrangements. Dill flowers, leaves, and seeds are all edible, and are used in international cuisines as well as pickling recipes. Dill is increasingly popular as a salt substitute—sprinkle some fresh dill on steamed green beans and you'll understand why. Dill is best enjoyed fresh, but can be dried, frozen, preserved in vinegar, or refrigerated in oil or butter.

Harvest and Bloom Period
Edible foliage from winter to spring, blooms and seeds in late spring and summer

Mature Height × Spread
4 feet × 15 inches

When, Where, and How to Plant
Sow seeds in early fall, two months before frost. Or sow seeds in spring one month before the last anticipated frost, and continue sowing every couple of weeks to prolong the harvest. Thin seedlings to 15 inches apart. Set out small transplants in spring. Water transplants before planting. Mix compost into the soil before planting, along with organic or time-release fertilizer. Set the transplant at the same depth it grew in the container and cover with soil. Mulch and water thoroughly.

Growing Tips
Water drought-tolerant dill only as needed during dry spells, especially dill planted in highly amended soils or pots. Plants benefit from being planted near a fence for support. Stake plants when they reach 18 inches tall. After heavy harvesting, apply balanced liquid fertilizer.

Care
Harvest dill leaves regularly, never clipping more than one-third of the plant at a time. Dill flowers in late spring or early summer. At this time, harvest the entire plant. If you are growing plants for seeds, harvest stalks with seedheads and dry upside down in a paper bag. Store seeds in an airtight container. Leave a few seedheads on the plants for reseeding. The "parsley worm" larvae of black swallowtail butterflies can eat quite a bit of dill, so plant several plants—some for the caterpillars and some for yourself. Few other pests bother dill, which usually dies before pests can build up in the summer.

Companion Planting and Design
Grow it as a back-of-the-border plant, in a cutting garden, or with other annuals where it will reseed and return next year. Because it is such a good "filler" plant, use it as a companion to other drought-tolerant flowers such as daylilies, iris, and coneflowers.

Personal Favorites
Dwarf selections such as 'Bouquet' are useful in containers, small gardens, or areas where you do not want to stake plants.

Lavender
Lavandula species

When, Where, and How to Plant
Plant in the fall or spring, depending on species. Lavender requires very well-drained soil, and little or no fertilizer. Add coarse sand and even gravel to your soil, and plant on the "high" side to give better drainage during wet seasons. Loosen roots of transplants to get them growing outward into well-drained soil, instead of planting them in the tightly packed balls of potting soil they come in. Give plants ample room to grow and spread without crowding—-at least 3 feet between plants. Only cutting-grown plants are dependably true to type; seed-grown varieties can vary wildly in form.

Growing Tips
Do not water a lot, and do not fertilize more than once a year (and very lightly at that!). Lavenders used in containers are as tricky as garden-grown ones. Mulch with gravel to further reduce humidity around plants. If some plants die, try other varieties until you find the one that works best for you and your garden.

Care
Deadheading or light pruning will keep new flowers coming on. After flowering, prune plants by a third or a half—or thin overcrowded older stems—to stimulate strong, healthy new growth and help prevent fungal diseases. Lavender usually doesn't live long enough to develop major insect problems.

Companion Planting and Design
Use lavender in airy borders, away from reflected heat of walks or walls, in containers or raised beds, or as accents in rock gardens where drainage is excellent. Companions would include anything that does not require a lot of water or fertilizer, and does not create humid conditions—especially spring bulbs such as crocus, small daffodils, and grape hyacinth.

Personal Favorites
Hedge lavender (*L. × intermedia*) is the best for sweet-smelling flowers, especially the 'Provence' and 'Grosso' selections. Spanish lavender (*L. stoechas*) is easy to grow and long-lived, though not as fragrant. Farther south grow French lavender (*L. dentata*) as an annual and container plant.

*Prized for spikes of narrow, blue- or gray-green foliage and fragrant purple flowers, lavender is used for perfume, soap, sachets, medicine, and flavoring. This nearly too-popular herb is generally difficult to grow in areas with heavy soils, wet winters, and hot, humid summers—many great gardeners fail at growing it, while others find some types relatively easy. English lavender (*L. angustifolia*, sometimes sold as* L. officinalis *or* L. spica*) is cold hardy, but dies in heat and humidity; French lavender (*L. dentata*) and Spanish lavender (*L. stoechas*) tolerate more heat and humidity, but not cold weather. Hedge lavender (*L. × intermedia*) is a hybrid that tolerates a little of everything. Choosing the right species—and variety—can make a difference in whether it is annual or perennial.*

Harvest and Bloom Period
Evergreen foliage, summer flowers

Mature Height × Spread
18 to 36 inches × 2 to 3 feet

Lemon Balm

Melissa officinalis

There are many lemon-flavored herbs, but one of the best is lemon balm—a mint relative that is very hardy in all parts of the South. Not as "lemony" as lemon verbena (Aloysia triphylla, a tender perennial), lemon balm is a many-stemmed perennial with light green, heavily veined, crinkled leaves that are lemon scented. Pink and lavender flowers appear beside leaves near the tops of the plant, and are very attractive to butterflies and bees (the Latin genus name is an old Greek name for "bee"). Leaves are used in fruit cups, salads, and fish dishes, and give perfume to potpourris and sachets. A refreshing tea made from its leaves produces a subtle calming effect.

Other Common Names
Balm Mint, Melissa, Sweet Balm

Harvest and Bloom Period
Edible foliage from spring to frost

Mature Height × Spread
18 inches × 18 inches

When, Where, and How to Plant

Set transplants out in the late winter or early spring, loosening potting soil to get roots started outward quickly into loose, very well-drained soil in full sun, with perhaps light shade in midsummer. Water deeply every week or two until plants get established. Divide root masses of old plants in the fall or late winter. Sow seed in the spring when the soil warms up, and thin out as needed (lemon balm can become weedy with self-sown seed).

Growing Tips

Water lemon balm deeply during dry spells, but there is no need to keep the drought-tolerant plants wet. Feed very lightly in the spring and again in midsummer. Divide every few years to keep centers from getting too woody. Mulch to keep roots from drying out too quickly in the summer and to prevent rapid changes in soil temperature in the winter.

Care

Prune plants near the ground after a frost. Deadheading or light shearing by cutting plants back a fourth to a third after flowering will keep them looking fresh into the fall. There are no major pests to worry about, which is good because pest controls would damage the butterflies and bees that constantly work the flowers. White flies and a few aphids are rarely a serious concern, and leaves may brown around the edges from excess fertilizer, rainfall, or watering.

Companion Planting and Design

Grow it at the back of the border, close enough where you can enjoy its fragrance and harvest it easily, but not so close to walkways that all the bees on the flowers will make visitors feel threatened. Compact daylilies such as 'Stella d'Oro' and tall perennials such as summer phlox make good companions, as do spring bulbs that provide interest when lemon balm is dormant.

Personal Favorites

The contrast between foliage and flowers on the regular species is nice. 'All Gold' has solid yellow leaves and 'Aurea' (same as 'Variegata') has green and yellow foliage.

Mint
Mentha species

When, Where, and How to Plant

Propagate by dividing in spring or fall or by stem cuttings taken in summer. Plant mint in the fall or in the spring after the last frost, in rich, moist soil. Mint is an aggressive spreader. Make a "mint bed" to keep mints from covering everything in their path. Plant them in a bottomless container and sink it in the ground (to prevent runners from creeping). Start with transplants and water them before planting. Set plants 1 foot apart. Dig a hole that is 8 inches to 1 foot deep, and mix compost plus an organic or time-release fertilizer with top-soil. Partially backfill with amended soil. Set the plant at the same depth it grew in the container, and backfill. Mulch around the base of the plant (but keep the mulch from piling up on the stems) and water it thoroughly. Leave about 1 foot between each plant and about 4 feet or some kind of barrier between different types of mints.

Growing Tips

Water mint deeply but not frequently. It recovers quickly from wilting, but leaves or leaf tips may be burned in full sun during prolonged dry spells with no water. After heavy harvest, feed with a balanced liquid fertilizer.

Care

As mint begins to flower, cut the plants to within a couple of inches of the ground to rejuvenate faded foliage. Do not make heavy harvests right before the first frost, as plants need time to reestablish themselves before winter. After four to five years, a mint patch begins to lose its flavor. Dig and replant small divisions.

Companion Planting and Design

Use it as an aggressive groundcover, as raised bed edging, or in a container. Hardy bulbs will come up through mint in the winter and spring, and mint will quickly cover their withering foliage by summer.

Personal Favorites

Try peppermint (*M.* × *piperita*), spearmint (*M. spicata*), apple mint (*M. suaveolens*), pineapple mint (*M. suaveolens* 'Variegata'), and chocolate mint (*M.* × *piperita* 'Chocolate').

Mint makes an excellent perennial groundcover, not to mention a refreshing addition to everything from tea and wine to lamb and ice cream. It comes in as many flavors as candy: spearmint, peppermint, chocolate mint, apple mint, lemon mint. Mint doesn't require much care and spreads on its own into cracks and crevices, and among other plants. It is often invasive in damp areas in the garden and is one of the few herbs that tolerates some shade. Some mints, such as variegated pineapple mint, are evergreen in southern areas. Most die back in winter, but any time leaves are present they can be enjoyed fresh, or frozen in ice cubes, preserved in vinegar, or dried for herb sachets.

Harvest and Bloom Period
Semi-evergreen edible foliage from spring to frost

Mature Height × Spread
1 foot × 3 to 5 feet

Oregano

Origanum vulgare

In ancient Greece and Rome, newlywed couples wore wreaths of oregano to banish sadness. This classic culinary herb is a mainstay of Italian, Greek, Asian, and Mexican cuisine. The several species of Origanum include very close relatives of oregano called marjoram; O. majoricum is so similar to oregano it is difficult to tell the difference. Both the shrub and sprawling oreganos are attractive foliage plants, and their bee- and butterfly-laden flowers are a bonus. You can enjoy oregano fresh, frozen, refrigerated in oil, dried, or preserved in vinegar.

Other Common Name
Marjoram

Harvest and Bloom Period
Evergreen edible foliage from spring to frost, purplish pink flowers in summer

Mature Height × Spread
1 to 3 feet × 2 to 4 feet

When, Where, and How to Plant
Plant oregano in fall, or early in the spring after the last frost, in a rich but well-drained soil in full sun or part shade. It is best to start with transplants, or to take root cuttings in the summer from hardy varieties whose flavor you like. Water oregano before planting. Set plants 2 feet apart and expect them to grow together.

Growing Tips
Water drought-tolerant oregano only during extreme dry spells, and then deeply but not frequently. After a heavy harvest, feed lightly with a balanced liquid fertilizer.

Care
Keep flowers cut back to conserve the plant's energy. Harvest leaves regularly, to promote branching and foliage growth. Make major harvests before oregano begins to flower, cutting back plants to within a couple of inches of the ground. Do not make heavy harvests right before the first frost, as plants need time to reestablish themselves before winter. Oregano, which has no major insect pests, will suffer from foliage and root fungus if it is not planted in a well-drained soil. From time to time pick plants clean of dead leaves. Mulch plants in winter to protect them against cold weather.

Companion Planting and Design
Use dwarf selections as edging plants or in containers. Because it is drought tolerant, it makes a good container plant. Some gardeners find that oregano, like mint, is an aggressive spreader. They plant it in a special bed, or in a bottomless container they sink in the ground (to prevent runners from creeping). Plant with taller herbs, or between clumps of daylilies or variegated liriope.

Personal Favorites
The two best hardy perennial selections for culinary use are *O. majoricum* and *O. vulgare* ssp. *hirtum.* Golden oregano (*O. vulgare* 'Aureum') makes a fragrant and attractive groundcover, but is not suitable for cooking. Sweet marjoram (*O. majorana*) is similar to oregano but is not frost hardy except on the coast.

Parsley
Petroselinum crispum

When, Where, and How to Plant
Sow parsley seeds from late summer to late winter; they are difficult to sprout unless you soak them overnight (or freeze them, three or four at a time, in ice cubes, then plant the ice cubes). Keep soil moist until seeds germinate, and thin plants to a foot apart. Parsley will rot if not planted in a well-drained soil in full or nearly full sun. Mulch around the base of the plant (but do not pile the mulch against the stems) and water thoroughly. Space 1 to 2 feet apart.

Growing Tips
Water parsley once a week, though the plants will recover from wilted conditions. Water plants in containers more frequently. Feed regularly but lightly with a balanced liquid fertilizer. Tall flower stalks may flop after a heavy rain in the spring, so be prepared to stake them.

Care
Harvest leaves as needed, clipping stalks from the outside of the plant (about 1 inch above the soil); do not harvest more than one-third of the plant at a time. Keep flowers cut back at first to prevent parsley from going to seed prematurely. Parsley is prone to sudden wilting and dying in hot weather, usually from a combination of heat, drought, and other factors. A striking caterpillar, the parsley worm, is the larvae of the beautiful black swallowtail butterfly, so plant enough parsley (or dill) nearby to have a place to relocate caterpillars from your culinary patch.

Companion Planting and Design
Nothing is as stunning in late winter and spring as parsley used as a companion to pansies, violas, snapdragons, and other cool-season flowers, or with late-blooming marigolds and salvias in the fall. You can also place pots of parsley, chives, daffodils, grape hyacinth, and short varieties of tulips around the winter garden for color repetition.

Personal Favorites
Italian flat-leaf parsley has a much better flavor than the curly-leaf species, but the curly types are prettier as garden plants. 'Triple Curled' is especially ruffled.

Although it is a true biennial—meaning it lives for two years, flowering in the second, then dies—parsley is usually treated like a winter annual, planted in the fall and pulled up the next summer. Its use as a "garnish" on the side of a plate comes from an almost magical ability to cleanse the breath even after a meal laden with garlic. Its mound of bright green ferny leaves makes it a fantastic winter foliage plant, tolerating extreme weather, even in a pot outdoors. Both the frilly, curly-leaf French parsley (P. crispum) and the more heat-tolerant flat-leaf Italian parsley (P. neapolitanum) require little care. But when they flower (flower stalks can be peeled and steamed like asparagus), they die. Swallowtail butterfly larvae love parsley.

Other Common Name
Breath Fresh

Harvest and Bloom Period
Edible foliage in fall, winter, and early spring

Mature Height × Spread
1 to 2 feet × 18 to 24 inches

Pepper
Capsicum species

Unlike true pepper, which is from the dried black fruit of a tropical vine (Piper nigrum), *hot garden peppers include a wide variety of tough little woody shrubs that produce fiery-hot fruits all summer and fall—or year-round if kept in a pot in a sunny, warm greenhouse. Even ornamental peppers can be used as spice, though they have little flesh and flavor. Foliage can be green or variegated, and small white flowers yield a constant supply of colorful seedpods that are at first green, then usually ripen to red, orange, yellow, or purple. Dried and crushed, hot peppers are a staple of Italian, Cajun, and Mexican dishes. The capsicum oil in hot peppers actually stimulates digestion and causes an overall cooling effect on the body.*

Other Common Names
Cayenne, Jalapeno, Habanero, Tabasco Peppers

Harvest and Bloom Period
Continuous harvest from late spring to fall

Mature Height × Spread
2 to 3 feet × 1 to 2 feet

When, Where, and How to Plant
Hot peppers need warmth to grow, so wait until mid-spring before sowing seed or setting out transplants 1 to 2 feet apart in sunny, well-drained garden soils or rich potting soils. They do not like extreme heat—flowers and small fruit often shed when temperatures stay in the upper 90s, but resume production in the cooler nights of fall—so keep them away from heat-retaining walls or pavement.

Growing Tips
Peppers produce best with regular, even watering and light feedings, particularly when in fruit, so water regularly and feed monthly with a very light or dilute fertilizer (too much fertilizer results in lots of leafy growth, not more fruit production). Mulch to keep roots cool and moist.

Care
Harvest regularly—the more you pick, the more they bear. Use snippers to remove pods from plants, as oil on the outside of peppers can cause intense eye irritation if you happen to touch your eyes while harvesting. Few pests bother peppers enough to warrant sprays, but whiteflies can be fairly aggressive; treat with insecticidal soap or neem oil sprayed on the undersides of leaves where adult insects hide.

Companion Planting and Design
Peppers are handsome foliage plants even when not in fruit. Grow them in groups throughout a vegetable garden where their shiny foliage provides a contrast to boring rows of other vegetables, or as colorful centerpieces to herb gardens. Use container-grown plants as filler beside bolder tropical plants. They are appealing in combination with spreading herbs such as mint, oregano, and thyme, but work well with any flower garden.

Personal Favorites
The tabasco pepper (*C. frutescens*) is a huge plant with very showy long red fruits; *chile pequin* is sometimes called 'Birdseye' for its many small, round fruit used as "poppers" or hot snacks. The habanero pepper (*C. chinense*), perhaps the hottest of them all, has flattened orange fruits and superb flavor—once you get past the feeling that you are on fire!

Rosemary
Rosmarinus officinalis

When, Where, and How to Plant

Plant rosemary any time you can work the soil, preferably in the spring, or in the fall, in an airy spot that is protected from harsh winter winds. Rosemary needs well-drained soil, so add sharp, coarse builder's sand and a little organic matter to your existing soil. Add lime if your soil is very acidic, at the rate of half a cup to an area 3 feet by 3 feet. Plant in part sun. Water transplants before planting so you do not over-water afterwards. Set the transplant in the hole at the same depth it grew in the container and cover the roots with soil. Mulch around the base of the plant but keep mulch from touching the plant. If you plant more than one rosemary plant, allow enough space between plants—at least 2 to 3 feet—to accommodate full-grown plants.

Growing Tips

Water rosemary only as needed, but deeply—it tolerates drought very well, even in large containers. When possible, avoid wetting the foliage, and sprinkle a ring of builder's sand around the base of the plant for further protection against stem-rotting fungus.

Care

Harvest stems regularly to increase branching, clipping every third stem. Herbal oils are strongest just before flowering. In spring, prune dead wood and feed rosemary with compost or organic or slow-release fertilizer. Mulch to protect roots from cold in winter and moisture loss in summer. Good drainage and air circulation help rosemary fend off fungal attacks.

Companion Planting and Design

Rosemary is often planted as a specimen shrub beside steps leading to the kitchen door. It is also easily interplanted with low-growing spring bulbs, pansies, and oregano in raised beds, large containers, or rock gardens. Rosemary can also be used as a lavender substitute, at least visually.

Personal Favorites

Prostrate rosemary makes an excellent container plant or groundcover, but is not as hardy as the upright forms. 'Arp' is the cold-hardiest rosemary of all, but is not as flavorful as 'Tuscan Blue' or 'Blue Spires' ('Athens Blue Spires').

A delightful Mediterranean shrub, rosemary has the happy distinction of smelling like holiday meals—all year round. Evergreen and exotic, rosemary comes in both upright and prostrate forms that make valuable contributions to the landscape as hedges or in containers or the rock garden, all with bright blue winter and spring flowers. A "half-hardy" perennial, rosemary is typically long-lived in the garden—some varieties tolerate even temperatures below freezing—except for sudden freezes that catch plants off guard. The popular culinary herb is used to flavor meats, vegetables, stews, and other foods. It is enjoyed fresh; preserved in refrigerated butters, oils, and vinegars; or dried (in which case its flavor is twice as strong).

Harvest and Bloom Period

Edible foliage year-round, blue or pink blooms in winter or spring

Mature Height × Spread

2 to 5 feet × 2 to 3 feet

Sage
Salvia officinalis

Like many other furry, gray-green leaved plants, this culinary favorite, long used to season chicken, turkey, and pork, has trouble tolerating our rainy winters and humid summers. Even with perfect drainage, it often collapses and dies, usually in midsummer after being over-watered. Lesser-grown varieties such as variegated or golden sage handle the weather much better than common garden sage, and are just as aromatic in the kitchen. Still, most gardeners grow sage with a carpe diem outlook, as if it were an annual: enjoying the frosty green foliage and spicy scent while it's here, but not mourning its passing. Sage is used fresh, dried, or frozen, but unless stored in the refrigerator or freezer its oils can become rancid.

Other Common Name
Garden Sage

Harvest and Bloom Period
Edible foliage year-round, lavender flowers in summer

Mature Height × Spread
1 to 2 feet × 1 to 2 feet

When, Where, and How to Plant
Propagate sage by divisions in fall or spring, softwood cuttings in late spring, or layering through the summer (covering small portions of stems with soil, so roots will grow even while the cutting is still attached to the "mother" plant). Seeds sprout readily, but are very difficult to find. Sage planted in the fall will be better established before hot, humid summer sets in. Plant in perfectly well-drained soils amended with coarse sand and organic matter, or grow in containers in light shade where watering is not as big an issue. Allow enough space between plants—a foot or two—to provide the "elbow room" mature plants will need to spread out.

Growing Tips
Water sage only as needed, keeping in mind that root and stem rot are likely even in dry seasons. Avoid wetting the entire plant by watering only at the base. As further protection against fungus, sprinkle a ring of builder's sand around the base of the plant to speed drainage and keep the soil surface dry. In spring, fertilize with compost or organic or slow-release fertilizer.

Care
Harvest year-round, cutting new growth rather than older growth (stems cut back to bare wood usually die all the way back). Replace with new plants rooted from new growth every few years. Few pests are serious enough to warrant spraying, but slugs, snails, and white flies can be troublesome.

Companion Planting and Design
Sage works perhaps the very best in containers, and ones that are especially cute or ornate add to the fun. Rock gardens are perfect spots for dwarf or colorful sages. Companions would include sedums, dwarf daffodils, chives, or other drought-tolerant herbs with contrasting foliage.

Personal Favorites
'Tricolor' has gray-green leaves with a creamy border tinged with purple; golden sage (*S. officinalis* 'Aurea') and purple sage (*S. officinalis* 'Purpurascens') have purplish new growth that fades to green with age.

Thyme
Thymus species

When, Where, and How to Plant

Well-rooted plants can be set out nearly any time but midsummer is the most stressful. Divide plants in the fall or late winter, or root small stem cuttings taken in late spring or early fall. Plant thyme in rich, well-drained soil, or keep in containers or raised beds. To ensure good drainage, add builder's sand plus a little compost to your soil. Set the transplant in the hole at the same depth it grew in the container and cover the roots with soil. Mulch around the plant but don't pile it up on stems. Thyme can be used as a groundcover if planted 8 or 10 inches apart.

Growing Tips

Water thyme when dry, but don't keep it wet! As further protection against fungus, sprinkle a ring of builder's sand around the base of the plant. In spring, fertilize with compost or an organic or slow-release fertilizer.

Care

Harvest lightly and regularly so plants do not get woody. Avoid harvesting heavily in hot weather. In the spring, prune back upright selections that have lost their shape. If creeping types look scraggly, cut them back as well. Weeding can be a problem, so pull weeds as soon as you see them. Thyme is susceptible to fungus where drainage and air circulation are poor. Regular harvesting keeps disease at bay. In northern areas of our states, cover thyme lightly in the winter with pine straw that does not "smother" the little plants. There are no major pests other than the occasional whitefly, snail, or slug.

Companion Planting and Design

Thyme is a good choice for containers (but give it partial afternoon shade, especially in summer). Upright selections work as small shrubs or borders. Creeping selections make colorful, full-sun groundcovers and lovely container plants. It likes the good drainage provided by raised beds and terraces.

Personal Favorites

Lemon thyme (*T.* × *citriodorus*) is excellent for cooking. Mother-of-thyme (*T. praecox* ssp. *arcticus*) is a lovely creeping thyme with purplish pink flowers in early summer.

Most thymes are hardy perennials throughout the South, but they can also be kept in pots and brought indoors or rooted to carry over the winter for new plants the next year. Thyme comes in an intriguing variety of shapes and scents, with upright, shrubby selections for culinary use and creeping selections for landscaping. Flowers are usually white or lavender in spring or summer. A native of Europe, thyme is an ancient culinary classic that immigrated to this country with the colonists. Thyme is enjoyed fresh, frozen, dried, refrigerated in butters and oils, or preserved in vinegar. Garden thyme (T. vulgaris) is the most popular thyme for culinary use.

Harvest and Bloom Period

Evergreen edible foliage year-round; white, pink, lavender blooms in summer

Mature Height × Spread

3 to 12 inches × 6 to 18 inches

Ornamental Grasses
for Alabama & Mississippi

To serve as a "plant bridge" between shrubs and perennials there is an entire class of plants known collectively as ornamental grasses. The plants are neither woody like shrubs, nor do they fit neatly with herbaceous flowering perennials. They are, in effect, a different category of plants. Even though the Bamboo Farm and Coastal Gardens near Savannah, Georgia, has evaluated nearly every imaginable variety of grass for horticultural use and to monitor its invasive tendencies, until fairly recently very few ornamental grasses have been used in our gardens (other than the long overused trio of pampas grass, bamboo, and striped cane). But with more grasses showing up every year in botanical gardens, in high-end "designer" landscapes, and even around fast-food restaurants and other public displays, "garden variety" gardeners have finally been exposed to exciting grasses for home use.

Designing with Ornamental Grasses

Cottage gardeners and botanical garden curators have used shrub-like and groundcover grasses for centuries, for their forms, textures, and seasonal effects. The plants run the gamut from tall, woody

bamboos (which are in the grass family, as is corn) to fast-growing groundcovers, with a lot of mid-size clumps in between. Instead of colorful flowers, they have "panicles" and plumes; their foliage, which sways in every breeze, changes from greens and variegations to light browns and taupe in the fall and winter.

Designing with grasses is easy. They can be used as shrub substitutes or as contrasts to long rows of evergreen shrubs or trees. They stand out when planted in front of wooden, brick, or stone walls, and lend a naturalistic effect to wildflower meadows and informal-style gardens. Groundcover types give alternatives to the "same old, same old" monkey grass and ivy, and tall varieties create a soft, Southern "sense of place"

Burgundy Fountain Grass

Miscanthus

that makes us feel at home. Ornamental grasses are grown mainly for the wonderful texture they bring to the garden, but they also add lovely muted colors, which are perfect backdrops and interplanted companions for bright flowered annuals and perennials. They also add movement and sound as they sway and rustle in the wind.

Growing Grasses

To plant container-grown grasses, position so the roots are well underground and the crown is slightly above ground level. If roots are in a tight mass, loosen them as much as you can before planting by teasing them apart or scoring along the sides in a few places with a sharp knife or pruning shears. Most ornamental grasses grow best in full sun (exceptions are noted in the plant descriptions that follow), in ordinary garden soil. Though some grasses are perfectly well suited for use in wet areas or bog gardens, most grow well without being watered, even in dry summers. The only real maintenance for grasses is cutting them back in late winter to 6 inches to 1 foot above ground to keep them looking tidy as new leaves emerge in spring. Leaving the foliage in place during winter protects the crown from freeze damage.

Dividing mature clumps to get more plants for your garden or to share with others sounds and looks easy, but can be daunting because of the spongy nature of the clumps, which resist even the sharpest spade. Cutting new plants out of mature clumps, each with a piece of the crown and roots, is best done with a pruning saw or even a chain saw that cuts down through the crown and into the roots. Late winter to early spring is better for most grasses in cooler regions; fall transplants might not have time to get established before winter chills.

Giant Reed Grass

Be Aware of Invasive Grasses

While a few grasses can be aggressive, most are not. When you mention bamboo, many gardeners think of the tall "running" type (*Phyllostachys* species) that is nearly impossible to keep in bounds; others are best planted with some sort of barrier—trenches, deep edging, concrete walks—to check the spread of their woody underground stems. Yet many excellent clump-forming types (mostly *Bambusa* species) remain in slow- or non-spreading mounds. Other grasses can be invasive, depending on your location and the type of grass. The species form of *Miscanthus sinensis* has become very invasive in some parts of the South, but the many beautiful cultivars thus far are well behaved. Most *Pennisetum* species and cultivars are great additions to gardens, but the cultivar 'Moudry' can reseed itself to the point of being obnoxious (if you want to grow this beautiful grass, just be sure to clip off the flowers before they go to seed). In a moist area river oats can also reseed, sometimes aggressively, but in drier locations it will stay in bounds. Be aware of potential problems in your region, and avoid invasive species if you live near a natural area.

Getting Started with Grasses

In general the planting and maintenance of grasses is the same no matter what the species. To best use and enjoy ornamental grasses, keep these tips in mind:

- There is an ornamental grass to suit every garden style or situation.
- Some grasses "run" with underground rhizomes; others are slow-spreading clump formers (there are bamboos in both groups).
- The foliage of grasses (including bamboo) generally lasts only one gardening year, dying in the winter and being replaced the next spring.
- Cutting the old foliage of grasses is not necessary, but can be done for neatness. Foliage can be cut nearly to the ground in late winter. Do not burn grasses, or you risk killing the crowns.

- Propagate grasses by dividing clumps or runners when they are dormant. Some form seedlings in the garden that can be moved to new locations.
- Few pests bother ornamental grasses enough to warrant pesticide use.

There are many types of ornamental grasses, most with several distinct cultivars from which to choose. Here are some of the most commonly grown, many of which are sure to whet your appetite for new possibilities.

Blue Lyme Grass (*Elymus arenarius* 'Glaucus' or *Leymus arenarius* 'Glaucus') is a showy ground-cover of stiff, blue-colored leaves up to 2 feet tall. This aggressive spreader can be weedy in moist soils, but is much more manageable in dry or clay soil. Use it as a texture contrast to yucca, juniper, or chaste tree.

Broomsedge (*Andropogon* species) is the common native grass you see along roadsides or in abandoned fields (and in the past was often cut, tied into bundles, and used as a broom). The 2-foot clump-forming grass is topped in late summer and fall with 3- or 4-foot, upright, feathery flower stalks that fade into a rich blend of browns that give a very naturalistic effect. This aggressive self-seeder is perhaps most effective in wildflower or informal plantings.

Dwarf Bamboo (*Pleioblastus pygmaeus* or *Arundinaria pygmaea*) is a rapidly spreading ground-cover up to 18 inches tall, which grows thick even in dense shade. It must be contained by walkways or deep edging.

Feather Grass (*Stipa* species) grows most of the spring and summer as a fine-textured, knee-high clump, but in the summer and fall shoots up a billowy cloud of yellowish flowers on stems up to 3 feet tall. It really stands out when planted in groups on a slope, against a dark green backdrop of shrubs, or with meadow type plants such as purple coneflower; where possible, plant it where it can be backlit by the setting sun.

Feather Reed Grass (*Calamagrostis acutiflora* 'Stricta'), an upright clump of stiff but arching foliage, is topped in early- and midsummer with starkly erect flowering stems to 5 or 6 feet tall that persist through the winter. This mainstay of northern grass plantings flowers poorly in the lower and coastal South.

Broomsedge

Fountain Grass (*Pennisetum alopecuroides*) is a fuzzy, knee-high clump of fine-textured foliage with many long, narrow, cylindrical "fox tail" flower heads. This small grass is very easy to work into a sunny flower border as a contrast to black-eyed Susan, purple coneflower, blazing star, goldenrods, asters, and other untidy summer and fall perennials. Note: the very popular and showy purple fountain grass (*P. setaceum* 'Rubrum') is strictly an annual, best used as an accent or container specimen.

Maiden Grass (*Miscanthus sinensis*) is perhaps the most-used ornamental grass in America. Most of the many cultivars of this versatile clump-forming grass reach only 4 to 6 feet tall and nearly as wide, with very narrow foliage that turns completely tan at first frost. Each clump produces dozens of taller flowers that open as tassels and gradually expand into soft feathery plumes in late summer and fall. It is vastly superior to pampas grass in most gardens because it is a smaller size and is not so razor-sharp. Favorite cultivars include 'Cosmopolitan' (erect habit and broad leaves striped with white), 'Gracillimus' (slender weeping foliage with reddish flowers), 'Morning Light' (5-foot clump with white narrow stripes along the leaf edges, an overall silver effect, and bronzy flowers), 'Strictus' ("porcupine" grass with narrow, erect foliage with creamy stripes that run across leaves). Use as single specimens, groups, hedges, or companions to tall perennials such as Mexican sage, sunflowers, and hibiscus.

Pampas Grass (*Cortaderia selloana*) is a commonly planted large grass, up to 6 or 8 feet tall and wide, which grows in a round, billowy, cascading clump. It produces many stiffly upright stems topped with showy, dense, cotton-candy flower plumes of white or pink in the late summer. Its foliage is razor sharp, making the plant difficult to cut back in the winter. 'Pumila' is a more practical compact form that reaches 5 to 6 feet tall. Use as specimens, masses on a hillside, or a dense hedge-like barrier.

Purple Muhly Grass (*Muhlenbergia* species) is a fairly new plant on the market, a 3-foot tall and wide clump that in the late summer and fall becomes a stunning, billowy mass of pinkish red. Particularly effective when backlit by the sun, it makes a good companion to roses, salvia, butterfly bush, and other airy shrubs and perennials, and a stunning contrast to bold-leaved plants such as canna.

Dwarf Pampas Grass

River Oats

River Oats (*Chasmanthium latifolium*) is the most widely used native grass, which tolerates a good bit of shade as well as full sun. It grows as a stiff clump up to 18 inches tall, with bamboo-like foliage and stems. By early summer it is topped with dozens of arching flowering stems up to 3 feet tall, each dangling two dozen or more florets that have been compared to "flattened armadillos" or fish on a fishing line, and hold up very well in dried arrangements. River oats can self-seed to the point of being invasive, but makes a superb filler or edger, or companion in naturalistic gardens. Because it tolerates both drought and long wet spells, it works well in both rock and bog gardens.

Striped Cane (*Arundo donax variegata*) was introduced by Spanish colonists for its many uses, but today it is used mostly as a large accent or mass planting. Its very tall bamboo-like stems are festooned with wide, coarse, corn-like foliage that starts out variegated with white and green stripes, but turns to all-green by late summer; flowering stems may reach 12 or more feet tall. Striped cane is usually too aggressive a spreader for small gardens, so use it in large areas, along ditches, or beside a barn or other outbuilding where its size can be appreciated, not cussed.

Variegated Ribbon Grass (*Phalaris arundinacea* 'Picta') is a fairly aggressive creeping groundcover to 2 or more feet high, variegated with clean white stripes. It is a great border plant, but can also be used as a "skirt" for leggy shrubbery and small trees. It turns brown at frost.

Variegated Ribbon Grass

Perennials *for Alabama & Mississippi*

With perennials, just as with friends, you end up liking some more and keeping them longer than others. Some come your way naturally as referrals, while others find you with their attractions and charms. Technically called "herbaceous perennials," they usually lack the permanent woody stems of shrubs and vines. Perennials partially or completely "die down" part of the year but return from their base or underground parts with new foliage and flowers the following year. Some, such as columbine and hollyhock, are short-lived, returning for only two or three years. Others, such as iris and artemisia, can be friends for life. Still others are so vigorous you end up having to thin them out lest they overtake your garden. It is up to the gardener to discover which of these friends will be "fair weather" or loyal.

This chapter profiles a sampling of very popular herbaceous perennials for our Deep South gardens, some for sun and some for shade. They include native perennial wildflowers, old-fashioned "passalong" favorites, ornamental herbs, flowering beauties, and easy-to-grow foliage plants. If your garden is small, look for plants that serve double- or triple-duty by having more than one attribute: good flowers, interesting foliage, attraction for butterflies, good cutting flowers, fragrance, long bloom period, and tolerance of neglect. Or all of these.

Tatarian Aster

Designing with Perennials

Unlike simply setting out a lot of annuals that will be discarded in a few months, placing long-lived perennials can be a little scary at first. It's like painting a moving canvas that changes every few weeks over the entire year. The best approach is to not take on more than you can handle. Though most perennials are grown almost exactly alike (with minor adjustments for some), start with just a few. Plant two or three different new perennials at a time, and you will quickly gain the confidence to try even more.

You will also learn which ones you like and which ones are adapted to your garden conditions. Before you know it, you will have a great collection that gives pleasure and good looks throughout all the seasons. The main thing is to not be in a big rush. Combine perennials with small shrubs to give you something to look at during "off" times, and fill in the gaps with annuals until you have arranged the perennials where you like them. Use them as flower bed accents, in long borders, in containers, and in combination with every other type of plant in this book—the possibilities are endless! Remember that, in spite of our elaborate dreams and designs, the plants call the shots. Learn to let some of them go if either they or you aren't happy.

Planting and Propagation

Timing is the key to success with perennials in the Deep South. Plant hardy perennials in the fall so they have time to get well established during the winter rains. This is especially important for any spring-blooming plants, yet all perennials need a head start before weathering a long, hot summer.

Hibiscus

Most perennials grow best in loose, moist, well-drained soils that are high in organic matter and neither too acidic nor too alkaline. Prepare beds or individual holes by digging your native soil a shovel's depth and twice that wide. Mix in a shovel or two of organic matter such as peat moss, manure, compost, or finely ground bark, blending it well with your native soil. If your soil is too acidic, add lime; if it is too alkaline, add sulfur. If you think you might have a soil problem, take a soil sample to the Extension office for analysis. Most plants are adaptable to a range of pH, as long as it is not too extreme one way or the other—acidity or alkalinity. When planting, spread roots of perennials out, and plant level with or slightly higher than the soil around them to allow for settling. Water to settle the soil around the roots, and add mulch.

Grow your own new plants from established ones. Many perennials can be grown from seed, but can take a year or more to reach flowering size. The two most common methods of propagating perennials are

Hosta, Ferns, and Solomon's Seal

division and rooting cuttings. Divide multi-stem perennials by digging up their clump and pulling or cutting them apart into smaller plants, each with roots and leaves; this is best done in the season opposite of when the plants bloom. Stick stem sections in moist potting soil or well-drained garden soil to form roots, covered with a plastic cola bottle with the bottom cut off and the cap thrown away to let out excess heat (we want humidity, not steam!). Water as needed, and most cuttings will be rooted within six or eight weeks.

Perennial Basics

While it takes more time to establish, a well-planned perennial garden can be low maintenance. Here are some keys to growing them:

- Location, location! A perennial garden is long lasting and too much trouble to move, so choose perennials carefully to suit your garden's sun or shade, drainage during wet spells, and average winter temperatures in your part of the state.
- Plan for year-round interest. Many perennials show up well with a backdrop of a wall, fence, or evergreen shrubs. Don't worry about always having perennials in bloom—many have out-standing foliage.
- If planting in a bed, make sure you can reach from either side to weed, divide, or deadhead—4 or 5 feet total bed width is plenty.
- Prepare the soil well the first time for long-lived perennials.
- Natural leaf or bark mulches help control weeds, keep the soil loose and moist, and feed the soil as they decompose.

- Fertilize perennials at the beginning of their growing season, but also feed the soil by applying compost or manure in the spring.
- Water perennials deeply but only as needed.

Heat and Cold

Gardener Beware: There are quite a few perennials on the market that may be perfectly fine in one part of the state, but not in another. For example, many varieties of hosta that can tolerate winter temperatures well below 0 degrees Fahrenheit, can suffer along the Gulf Coast from hot summer nights; lantana and ginger are wonderful "Florida perennials" that can grow well in the southern half of our states, and even "come back" from winter damage in central areas, but will often freeze completely in higher elevations or northern counties.

This is not to suggest that you should avoid unknown plants altogether; many gardeners experiment and find thrilling additions to their gardens that the "experts" say should not grow there. If you are unsure of a plant's cold hardiness or heat tolerance, research it in a thorough reference book (or several), then try it on a limited basis. Plant tender summer perennials on the south or east side of your home for winter protection, and more cold-hardy plants on the north side where they will not be exposed to afternoon sun and sunny winter days that can keep them too warm.

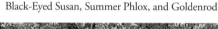

Black-Eyed Susan, Summer Phlox, and Goldenrod

Artemisia
Artemisia species

Artemisia is one of the grand dames of the garden—and one of the toughest perennials of all time, grown for many centuries as a "wound wort" or Band-Aid plant for wrapping bad cuts and wounds. Its musty aroma reputedly repels insects (another common name is "wormwood"). Artemisia is very important for its attractive cloud-like companion effect in flower beds, especially where reflected heat and drought can cause stress to everything else. Hardy and long-lived, some types of artemisia can be invasive; 'Silver King' can be a hard-to-rid spreading plant, but if it finds a home in a dry bed, it can be a perfect, low-maintenance companion.

Other Common Name
Wormwood

Bloom Period and Seasonal Color
Evergreen silver-gray foliage

Mature Height × Spread
2 to 4 feet × 3 to 5 feet

When, Where, and How to Plant
Plant artemisia any time of the year, or divide in the late winter, cutting excess growth back; it will quickly resprout in the spring. Artemisia grows best in full sun or part shade, in a perfectly well-drained or dry soil with low to moderate fertility. Plant where it can get plenty of good air circulation, leaving 3 feet or more between plants (they will quickly fill in).

Growing Tips
Artemisia is one of the most drought-tolerant perennials you can plant; regular watering can cause it to rot. In spring, pull mulch away from new growth at the base of the plant to reduce chances of stem rot. Fertilize plants each spring with a slow- or time-release fertilizer or compost.

Care
If artemisia begins to look scraggly in summer heat and humidity, cut it back and it will return with healthy new growth. Trim mounding types back in the late winter or early spring. Divide every couple of years in the fall. Artemisia has no major pests, but is prone to rot in areas of high humidity, especially when irrigated.

Companion Planting and Design
Low-growing selections are good choices for raised beds and container gardens, as edging, and as a "skirt" for upright, airy trees such as crape myrtle, althea, or chaste tree. Taller selections make excellent filler and contrast plants for iris, summer phlox, perennial salvias, and canna. The light color of artemisia draws attention in the summer, and can also be used for repetition in long flower borders.

Personal Favorites
'Powis Castle' remains an all-time favorite for its silvery foliage and aromatic scent year-round. The stems, which spread over a wide area, are easy to prune when out of bounds, making it one of the best gray foliage plants for perennial gardens and herb beds. Southernwood (*A. abrotanum*) is ferny green, mounding, and reaches 2 feet tall. Also try *A. ludoviciana* 'Silver King'.

Aster
Aster species

When, Where, and How to Plant
Set out container-grown plants any time of the year, divide existing plants in the fall or spring, or sow seeds in the late summer or fall and keep moist until seedlings appear. Plant in full sun and well drained soils of average fertility. Don't over-water—if young plants wilt, cut them back and they will quickly put out new growth that is better balanced with their roots. These are very tough plants that tolerate a wide range of conditions. Leave 2 feet or more between plants in a border.

Growing Tips
Once established, asters are very hardy and need little or no water; over-watering causes rot. Feed lightly in the spring. Mulch helps control weeds, but these plants are pretty competitive by themselves.

Care
Regular deadheading can encourage longer bloom-ing on summer flowering asters, but leave fall flowering kinds in place until seeds have been self-sown or birds have eaten their share. After a hard freeze, cut dead stems back to keep them looking neat. Divide clumps every few years to keep them vigorous. Mildew can be a problem on foliage.

Companion Planting and Design
Asters generally spread easily, but are fortunately easy to transplant at any stage. In an area where it can naturalize, it multiplies happily to become a companion for summer perennials like bee balm, salvia, and summer phlox, and complements fall goldenrods and sunflowers. It also looks great along a fence or with a wall for backdrop. Interplant with spring bulbs so the bulbs will bloom when the asters are still emerging from dor-mancy, and the asters will come up to hide the fading bulb foliage.

Personal Favorites
Aromatic aster (*A. oblongifolius*) is a spreading mass topped with brilliant yellow-centered purple flowers—it grows in rock rubble and pure clay! Frikart aster (*A.* × *frikartii* 'Wonder of Staffa' and 'Monch') is lavender-blue. New England aster (*A. novae-angliae* 'Purple Dome') has brilliant purple blossoms. Tatarian aster (*A. tataricus*) is a 5- to 6-foot-tall, wide-leaved, almost invasive summer bloomer.

There are more than 500 species of true asters, from small kinds suitable for rock gardens to bushy plants over 6 feet tall. Some flower in the spring or summer, many are mainstays of the fall border or meadow. All are out-standing butterfly plants and provide endless amounts of material for sprays of cut flowers; some species also have very aromatic foliage. Asters, many of which are native to the Southeast (even the so-called "New England" aster is from here as well), are invaluable for masses of blue, pink, purple, lavender, or red color in sunny beds and borders, or, because they tend to spread readily from underground runners and seed, for naturalizing in wild-flower meadows.

Bloom Period and Seasonal Color
Purple, pink, red, white, blue flowers in spring, summer, and fall

Mature Height × Spread
2 to 6 feet × 2 to 4 feet

Balloon Flower
Platycodon grandiflorus

Tough and long-lived, balloon flower hails from China and Japan, where it is well loved. It completely disappears in winter, emerging in mid- to late spring—making it easy to accidentally dig up during regular spring chores. The shrubby plant has slender stems covered with oval leaves up to 3 inches long. The plant often starts to sprawl in the summer under the weight of its dozens of puffy, inflated buds—which give balloon flower its name—that open into 2-inch, star-shaped, blue flowers with purple veins. Balloon flower is easy to grow, but may take two or even three years to get completely established.

Bloom Period and Seasonal Color
Blue, pink, white blooms from June to August

Mature Height × Spread
18 inches to 3 feet × 1 to 2 feet

When, Where, and How to Plant
Set out transplants in the fall or early spring, and water to keep moist until established. Sow seeds outdoors in the spring, keeping them evenly moist until they sprout. Plant in sandy or loose, well-drained soil, in full sun, preferably out of hot afternoon sun, leaving 1 to 2 feet between plants. If the soil is poor or compacted, loosen it with organic matter. Add a slow- or time-release fertilizer to the soil.

Growing Tips
Water deeply but not frequently—no more than once a week, or it may get floppy or deep roots may rot. Balloon flower is slow to emerge in the spring, so be careful to mark where it is planted to avoid cutting it up when planting something else. Fertilize balloon flower each spring with a slow- or time-release fertilizer or compost.

Care
Deadhead or cut plants back to promote repeat blooms, and cut plants back in the fall after they have quit blooming to keep them looking neat until they completely disappear in the winter. There are no major insect pests, though whiteflies can be troublesome.

Companion Planting and Design
Balloon flower works beautifully in a perennial bed or border; use plants in the middle or front of the border as they sprawl somewhat. For a cool combination, use with pink or gray plants, such as artemisia, garden phlox, iris, yarrow, or 'The Fairy' rose.

Personal Favorites
The species has single, deep blue flowers on 30- to 40-inch stems. *P. grandiflorus* 'Albus' has lovely white blooms and looks beautiful with blue companions. 'Fuji' is tall, 25 to 30 inches, with single blooms in blue, white, or pink. 'Shell Pink' is best grown in partial shade. 'Sentimental Blue' and 'Mariesii' are dwarf selections whose stems reach a foot or so tall. 'Hakone Double Blue' has double flowers.

Bluestar
Amsonia species

When, Where, and How to Plant

Dig and divide mature plants in the fall or winter, or plant container-grown plants any time of the year. Amsonia grows best in full sun or light shade, but will tolerate moderate shade with fewer flowers. It grows naturally in low, moist boggy areas, but will grow well in any well-drained soil that is kept moist in the hottest part of the summer and fall. Plant clumps 3 feet apart for a solid mass, adding a little slow-release fertilizer in the planting hole and keeping the plant moist through the first summer.

Growing Tips

Bluestar has a willowy growth habit, so pruning is generally not necessary except to remove stray or floppy outer stems. Entire plants can be cut down in midwinter after its fall foliage effect has been enjoyed. Deadheading to prevent seed formation can encourage more flowers, but is rarely worth the effort. Propagate by division any time in the fall, winter, or spring.

Care

Keep clumps well watered in the hot summer, or fall color will arrive surprisingly early. Feed very lightly with slow release or natural fertilizer in the spring. Bluestar has no major pests.

Companion Planting and Design

Bluestar spreads slowly in clumps, making it easy to plant with other perennials and shrubs without being invasive. Use in groups as mass plantings, or place where its narrow foliage contrasts with bolder plants such as sedum, hibiscus, canna, daylily, iris, and blazing star. Its flowers complement iris and shrub roses.

Personal Favorites

The species *A. tabernaemontana* has willow-like leaves and slate blue flowers. It is widely available, but is rapidly being replaced in the landscaping trade by narrowleaf bluestar (*A. ciliata*) and the almost needle-leaved Hubricht's bluestar (*A. hubrichtii*) with sky blue flowers and bright, clear, gold fall color.

Roadside ditches in the spring are often filled with willowy clumps of grassy leaves topped with airy clusters of pale or sky blue, star-shaped flowers. Bluestar, tough enough to grow in "blue mud" beside railroad tracks, is one of our most dependable native cut flowers for spring, and its fine-textured foliage has golden fall color to boot. The elegant native grows quite well in wet soils and drought, making it a versatile companion to many of our treasured flower border perennials. It is becoming more available in the nursery trade—any garden center can get it through their perennial grower channels, if you ask, and you will end up with a plant that can easily outlive you and your garden.

Other Common Name
Amsonia

Bloom Period and Seasonal Color
Blue flowers in spring, golden fall color

Mature Height × Spread
3 to 4 feet × 3 to 4 feet

Cardinal Flower
Lobelia cardinalis

Blooming from July to September, few native plants have a color so intense. A native of the Eastern United States, cardinal flower produces tall spikes and is a favorite of the ruby-throated hummingbird. In the wild, it grows along sunny stream banks, in swamps, and low, wet places. Cardinal flower is a wonderful boost to shade gardens in summer and fall. Once established, cardinal flower reseeds. The key to success is fall and winter cleanup. Don't let leaves accumulate on the plants in the winter. That's when cardinal flower makes its rosettes. A heavy winter mulch kills them. Another wonderful lobelia is a sister plant, called L. siphilitica, which has superb blue flowers and tolerates more sun and needs less moisture than L. cardinalis.

Other Common Name
Lobelia

Bloom Period and Seasonal Color
Scarlet blooms in late summer

Mature Height × Spread
2 to 4 feet × 12 to 15 inches

When, Where, and How to Plant
Set lobelia plants out any time of the year, but be prepared to keep young plants moist through the first summer. Divide plants after they finish flowering in the fall. Cardinal flower seeds scatter freely and help the plant spread naturally into a ragged colony, especially in moist soils. Plant in morning sun or light shade, with filtered light being the best. It likes rich, moist, slightly acid soil, like that found in moist woods and along stream banks. Set plants 1 foot apart for fast effect, spreading their roots out and keeping the tops of the plants level with the surrounding soil. Water deeply to settle soil around roots.

Growing Tips
Cardinal flower, being a natural bog plant, grows and flowers best with a good soaking every week or so. Fertilize in the spring with compost or a very small amount of slow-release fertilizer; too much causes floppy growth. Do not mulch.

Care
The rosettes of leaves stay green through mild Southern winters, and can rot if kept covered with thick mulch. Cut—don't pull or tear—tall stems close to the ground after frost has turned them brown and seeds have had a chance to scatter. There are no major pests of this outstanding native perennial.

Companion Planting and Design
It's an excellent bog garden plant that naturalizes along stream banks, edges of ponds, and other damp areas, but it also flourishes in a perennial bed with regular watering. Excellent companions include blazing star, bee balm, and Louisiana and Siberian irises.

Personal Favorites
The species is sold simply as *Lobelia cardinalis*. 'Summit Snow' is a white form, and a warm pink selection known as 'Heather Pink' originated in a North Carolina garden. The hybrid 'Ruby Slippers' is another good hummingbird plant. Blue lobelia (*L. siphilitica*) is leafy, 3 feet tall, and has a white 'Alba' form.

Cast-iron Plant
Aspidistra elatior

When, Where, and How to Plant
Set out potted specimens any time of the year, or divide established clumps in the fall or winter when plants are dormant, cutting back old foliage to keep plants from flopping over until new growth emerges. Plant very shallowly in shady areas (including in the winter), in soil that has been amended with organic matter to help roots get established quickly. Set plants 2 feet apart, and water only as needed the first summer.

Growing Tips
Aspidistra needs little or no extra water in the summer, but may burn during long, dry, windy spells without an occasional soaking. Fertilize very lightly in the spring with a slow-acting fertilizer or nitrogen-rich cottonseed meal, and top dress with compost once or twice a year.

Care
Cut out individual leaves that get burned in the sun or tattered in the wind, leaving the good ones to give structure through the year. Plants can be cut completely down in the winter to allow new growth to come up clean and neat, but do this before new leaves emerge or risk snipping and disfiguring the new growth—which is all there is for the entire year. Voles eat the roots of aspidistra, but are difficult or impossible to control except with underground wire barriers.

Companion Planting and Design
Use cast-iron plant as a foundation planting; as accents under old trees; in other difficult, densely shaded sites; or as a skirt for shade shrubs such as mahonia. Good companions include holly fern, liriope, Lenten rose, and Asiatic jasmine. Use as a container specimen in low-light homes where humidity is not too low.

Personal Favorites
Many people prefer the standard green species, but two variegated ones—'Okame' with vertical stripes and 'Asahi', whose top third of each leaf turns nearly white by midsummer—really stand out in the shade. The standard 'Variegata' can turn solid green in rich soil.

This old-garden favorite is not called "cast-iron" plant for nothing—it is commonly seen growing in dense shade around old homes, still thriving after decades of complete neglect. This asparagus and monkey grass relative has no main plant body, just masses of knee-high leaves, broad and spear-like, of forest green. New leaves emerge in the spring and replace older ones from the year before, which may take several weeks to disappear. The plant, which is often grown in pots even indoors, requires shade all year, or its foliage will yellow and burn. Sometimes a harsh winter will kill the foliage, but its new growth will appear faithfully in the spring. The plant can spread to become a tall groundcover.

Other Common Name
Aspidistra

Bloom Period and Seasonal Color
Evergreen foliage

Mature Height × Spread
2 to 3 feet × 2 feet

Chrysanthemum
Dendranthema hybrids

Names come and go, but the mum remains the queen of autumn. Old-time florist mums are not as tidy and compact as the "cushion" mums sold as annuals for fall color, but they return year after year with little fuss other than an occasional tip-pruning to tidy them up and make them more compact. They are impervious to heat, cold, drought, and humidity, and, in spite of minor cosmetic pests, they flower well without a lot of pesticides. Most have survived fickle garden tastes in country and cottage gardens, and are making comebacks as soft, natural, easy fall color where people feel free to garden "outside the lines."

Other Common Name
Mum

Bloom Period and Seasonal Color
White, pink, burgundy, other colors in late fall

Mature Height × Spread
2 to 4 feet × 2 to 3 feet

When, Where, and How to Plant
Mums are rarely available in garden centers except in midsummer and fall, which means they need a lot of water to stay alive. But stem cuttings taken from new growth on old plants root quickly in the spring and summer, and plants can be divided after flowering. Set mums in full or nearly full sun, beside other supporting plants or where they can be staked, in well-drained soil that is somewhat moist and moderately fertile. Set level or slightly above the surrounding soil to prevent crown rot in wet seasons.

Growing Tips
Pinch the growing tips from new shoots to force more compact growth with many more flowers; do this again in the early summer but not after mid-July or the plants may not have time to set fall flower buds. Stake plants early to prevent flopping and limb breakage; hoop and staking kits (used for supporting peonies) work also.

Care
Fertilize very lightly in the spring and again in midsummer, and water deeply but only when needed. Mums have a few minor pests, including whiteflies, thrips (tiny bud-eating insects), leaf miners, and caterpillars, but few sprays other then insecticidal soap are effective. It is better to enjoy the floppy old plants and flowers from afar.

Companion Planting and Design
Use toward the back of flower borders where their foliage will not be a distraction and they can sprawl over other supporting plants, or in the middle of beds (but where they can be reached for pinching). Allow them to cascade down rock walls or along the edge of a raised bed. Interplant with spring bulbs, sedum, yarrow, elephant's ear, and fall-blooming perennials.

Personal Favorites
"Country girls" (*C.* × *rubellum* 'Clara Curtis', sometimes sold as 'Ryan's Pink') is an old standard pale pink; 'Mary Stoker' is soft yellow touched with apricot. There are many others to be rooted from area cottage gardens. Other good fall mums to try include a new compact series sold as "My Favorite Perennial Mums."

Columbine
Aquilegia species

When, Where, and How to Plant
For best spring flowering, set out transplants in the fall or winter so they can experience winter temperatures and get established before summer stress starts. Divide in the fall. Seeds sprout only after being exposed to winter chill; sow them in the fall where they won't be buried under a lot of leaf mulch, or in pots left outside all winter. Plant columbine in average to rich, well-drained soil, 12 to 18 inches apart, where they will be protected from hot sun and drying summer breezes.

Growing Tips
Columbines planted in a shade garden need watering only during very dry periods, more often if planted where they receive sun. The plants need very little fertilizer, just compost or a rich leaf mulch, which also helps keep roots cool and moist in the summer.

Care
Unless you are planning on collecting seed to sow in other areas or to self-sow nearby, cut plants back after they flower to promote fresh new leaves that will last longer in the summer; columbines cut back may rebloom. Leaf miners, which are the larvae of tiny flies, burrow inside leaves making light-colored "trails," but are easily gotten rid of by cutting off infested leaves. There are no other major pests.

Companion Planting and Design
Use columbine for naturalizing in a shade garden with hostas and ferns, or in a spring perennial border that gets only morning or filtered light. Columbine blooms about the same time as blue phlox, making a pleasing color combination. Grow the showier columbine cultivars that bloom in mid-April and May along with foxglove and perennial geraniums.

Personal Favorites
The Music series includes a "symphony" of colors in blue, red, pink, and white. 'Beidermeier Blue' columbine grows only 1 foot tall. 'Hensol Harebell' is a deep blue selection growing 2 to 3 feet tall. Longspur columbine (*A. longissima*) is a Texas native with yellow flowers that grows well along the Gulf Coast.

Columbines hail from both the United States and Europe, inhabiting open woodlands; the red and yellow A. canadensis is the one most commonly seen in the eastern U.S. Most columbines, being native to mountain areas, are short-lived in the Deep South, especially in the heat and humidity and brief winters along the Gulf Coast (with one notable exception, see Personal Favorites below). However, in well-drained shaded gardens they often reseed and naturalize into nearby areas near their original plantings, in effect "acting" like perennials (though seedlings of hybrids may not come true to the parent's color). Arching stems are covered with lacy, maidenhair fern-like leaves of green, blue-green, or gray green. They are topped with open, fairy-like flowers, with long, back-facing spurs laden with nectar. Flowers also come in pastels of blue, pink, yellow, or white in early to mid-spring.

Bloom Period and Seasonal Color
Yellow-red, pink, lavender, blue, yellow, white blooms in spring, early summer

Mature Height × Spread
1 to 2 feet × 12 to 18 inches

Coreopsis
Coreopsis species

If you love these sunny, yellow country flowers—the official state wildflower of Mississippi—consider planting several different coreopsis selections to ensure blooms from April to July. The earliest to bloom is the dwarf eared coreopsis (Coreopsis auriculata), flowering from April to June. The native lanceleaf coreopsis (C. lanceolata) grows in sprawling clumps, about 2 to 3 feet tall, forming colonies of yellow, disk-shaped flowers. Bigflower coreopsis (C. grandiflora) is a short-lived perennial that grows up to 3 feet tall, with flower heads 1 to 2 inches across. Both lanceleaf and bigflower types are summer bloomers. Threadleaf coreopsis (C. verticillata) is a delicate, ferny plant with golden or yellow flowers that works best in sunny, well-drained sites or containers and blooms through the summer.

Other Common Name
Tickseed

Bloom Period and Seasonal Color
Yellow blooms in spring or summer

Mature Height × Spread
6 inches to 3 feet × 12 to 18 inches

When, Where, and How to Plant
Set out transplants in the fall (October and November), so roots benefit from winter rains and plants are exposed to winter cold. If set out in the spring, water regularly but do not over-water or you will rot the plants. Divide crowns of mature plants in the fall or late winter. Sow seeds in fall at least six weeks before the first freeze and keep seeds evenly moist until they sprout. Thin seedlings to 1 foot apart or more. Plant dwarf eared coreopsis in the shade of deciduous trees because it blooms in the spring as the trees are leafing out; plant other coreopsis in full or nearly full sun.

Growing Tips
These native prairie and woodland edge plants are fairly drought tolerant, and need watering only during extreme dry spells. Coreopsis needs little fertilizer, other than what decomposes from natural mulch. Mulches help control weeds, but also reduce the important seed-to-soil contact needed for coreopsis seeds to sprout.

Care
Divide clumps every year or so in spring or fall. Regularly deadhead coreopsis to keep plants looking neat and to promote longer flowering; cut plants back by a half after flowering to promote another flush of growth and flowers. Coreopsis has no major insects or diseases, except mildew and leaf spots when planted in heavy or wet soils.

Companion Planting and Design
Plant lanceleaf and bigflower coreopsis in sunny borders, toward the front of perennial beds, with daffodils, daylilies, iris, black-eyed Susan, and grasses, and in herb gardens to brighten the greens and grays. Dwarf eared coreopsis is great for naturalizing in a light shade garden with ferns, hostas, and river oats. Interplant threadleaf coreopsis with daylilies, blazing star, and yarrow.

Personal Favorites
C. auriculata 'Nana' is a compact form. *C. grandiflora* includes compact, 18-inch selections such as 'Early Sunrise' and 'Sunray'. For *C. verticillata*, try 'Zagreb' and the lemon yellow 'Moonbeam'.

When, Where, and How to Plant

Plant or divide daylilies any time of the year, even when in full bloom—they are that tough! Daylilies flower in light shade, but are best in full sun in a well-drained soil lightly amended with organic matter. Loosen potting soil of container-grown plants or the roots of garden divisions, then spread the fleshy roots out over a small "cone" of soil before backfilling with good soil. Plant level with or slightly higher than the soil around the plant, cover the area with mulch, and do not over-water or plants will wilt or rot.

Growing Tips

Water deeply but not too often, as daylilies are very drought tolerant. Fertilize lightly in the spring with an all-purpose fertilizer, and again in mid-summer with a little slow-acting, nitrogen-rich fertilizer such as alfalfa meal or cottonseed meal. Maintain mulch to help control weeds.

Care

Unless you are saving seed, pick off wilted blooms to keep plants looking fresh. Cut off (do not pull) old flower stems, or risk crown rot diseases. Daylilies are subject to an incurable "rust" disease, which is considerably worse on overfed, over-watered hybrids. Thrips can distort flowers, but are very difficult to control with spraying.

Companion Planting and Design

Add daylilies to sunny flower borders with ornamental grasses, frilly yarrow, sedum, blazing star, salvia, and Siberian iris. Use as a groundcover on a bank to control erosion, or include small varieties in an herb or kitchen garden (the buds and blossoms are edible). Use one color, mass-plant a wild combination, or intersperse in a perennial border to complement flower colors of other plants.

Personal Favorites

Hundreds of hybrids are readily available from local growers who welcome garden visitors, but easy, common, all-summer-flowering choices are 'Happy Returns' (lemon yellow, miniature, fragrant), 'Stella d'Oro' (golden yellow, slightly ruffled), the old, lemon-yellow 'Hyperion', and the antique double-orange 'Kwanzo'.

Daylilies are among the world's favorite perennials for their ease of growth and large flowers that pop open from fat, edible buds in the spring and summer. Hybrid varieties have much to offer in color, flower shape and size, and foliage over the hardier, widely popular orange "ugly duckling" ones you see in ditches and cottage gardens. Each clump-forming plant has several (sometimes branched) flower stems with up to a dozen or more wide-open flowers that range from 1 to 6 or more inches across. Though a plant can flower for many weeks (there are even some great repeat bloomers), each flower lasts no more than a day. Lush, grass-like foliage adds a nice texture to the garden even when not in bloom.

Bloom Period and Seasonal Color
Yellow, peach, lavender, red, orange, pink blooms in summer

Mature Height × Spread
1 to 4 feet × 2 to 3 feet

Dianthus
Dianthus species

When, Where, and How to Plant
Set out transplants in the fall or spring, or divide plants in the fall or summer right after flowering. Root cuttings in the summer. Plant dianthus in perfectly well-drained soils high in sand content, in mostly full sun with protection from hot afternoon sun in humid areas. Set plants 1 to 2 feet apart, with a slow-release fertilizer and light mulch (too much can cause stem rot). Mulch with gravel or grit, not organic mulch, and do not over-water when planting.

Growing Tips
Pinks can tolerate dry spells, but grow well when watered deeply every week or two in the heat of summer (water in the morning, not evening, to reduce rot). Fertilize lightly each spring with a slow- or time-release fertilizer or compost.

Care
Trim plants back after they bloom to keep foliage thick. Dianthus is susceptible to stem rot in our heat and humidity, which can be aggravated by heavy organic mulch and over-irrigation. Water only to keep plants alive. Pinks have no major insect pests, though slugs may be attracted to the musky fragrance of the flowers.

Companion Planting and Design
Raised beds, containers, and rock gardens, all with perfect drainage, are great for cascading dianthus. Use as a border or edging to an herb or rose garden. Because of the fragrance, plant a patch of pinks in a large container near a door or entryway. Interplant with drought-hardy plants such as iris, winter bulbs, rosemary, and peonies.

Personal Favorites
Cottage pinks (*D. plumarius*) come in many selections, including the fragrant, humidity-tolerant 'Itsaul White'. 'Musgrave's Pink' is a foot-tall heirloom classic with white flowers, each with a green eye. For cheddar pinks (*D. gratianopolitanus*), try the fragrant, humidity-tolerant 'Bath's Pink'. Carnations (*D. caryophyllus*) are recommended only for cool, mountainous northern counties, but maiden pinks (*D. deltoides*) are also good perennial dianthus.

Unlike annual dianthus, which grows best in cool weather and usually dies out quickly in our hot summers, varieties of perennial dianthus have been beloved "pass-along plants" for generations. The plants form grassy tufts that spread into dense, evergreen mats (often with blue-green foliage color), especially in well-drained soils. The stiff-looking foliage alone is a terrific contrast to other plants. Masses of spring or early summer flowers, which include single, semi-double, and double forms, usually with nipped or "pinked" and often color-contrasted edges, are bright, with a spicy fragrance. Easy to root from stem tips, easy to grow with neglect, these age-old flowers create an old-fashioned effect wherever they are planted.

Other Common Names
Cottage Pinks, Pinks

Bloom Period and Seasonal Color
Pink, rose, red, yellow, and white blooms in spring and summer

Mature Height × Spread
6 to 12 inches × 1 to 2 feet

Ginger Lily
Hedychium coronarium

When, Where, and How to Plant
Plant ginger lily any time you can find it, but early spring is best. Divide in the fall or late winter, and replant rhizomes quickly and cover with lots of leaf mulch. Ginger lily grows well in light shade, but flowers best in the sun if planted in a moist area or if provided with ample moisture. Gardeners in northern counties should plant in a protected area with lots of mulch for winter protection. Amend the soil with lots of organic matter, plant rhizomes shallowly, and water newly planted rhizomes well for several weeks. Plant 3 feet or more apart.

Growing Tips
Ginger lilies will tolerate drought but grow much more thickly and flower better in the late summer when given a good soaking every week without rain. Fertilize each spring with a slow- or time-release fertilizer or compost.

Care
Cut floppy plants back after flowering to rejuvenate them, and cut to the ground after a fall freeze browns the foliage, then pile a heavy leaf mulch over the roots for winter protection. Divide when needed (fall or spring) to prevent overcrowding and for continuous bloom. Plants grown in small spaces may need propping or staking to keep them from flopping after heavy rains. There are no major pests for this old-fashioned perennial.

Companion Planting and Design
Plant ginger lily near a walkway or in a container on a deck where you can enjoy its evening fragrance. It's also nice near a pool or other water feature, and will naturalize along the moist edges of a pond or bog garden. Good companions include coleus, Louisiana iris, aspidistra, and ferns.

Personal Favorites
Besides *H. coronarium*, gardeners in the lower half of our states can enjoy golden butterfly ginger (*H. flavum*) with rich yellow-orange flowers, and quite a few hybrids with various flower colors and plant sizes; those farther north can grow them as container plants to protect over the winter.

There is a huge moth that hovers like a hummingbird at dusk as it pollinates light-colored flowers in the evening, and anyone with ginger lily has seen it. Though not as "zesty" as true ginger, the root-like rhizomes of this hardy perennial can be used for cooking. Its narrow, canna-like leaves are produced on stalks up to 5 feet tall and topped in the late summer and fall with clusters of pure white, butterfly-like flowers with one of the richest, honeysuckle-like aromas of any perennial. Ginger lily dies completely down in the winter and needs a thick leaf mulch to protect it over the winter in northern counties. The shade-tolerant plant grows and spreads best in moist areas.

Other Common Name
Butterfly Ginger

Bloom Period and Seasonal Color
White blooms in late summer

Mature Height × Spread
4 to 5 feet × 3 to 4 feet

Goldenrod
Solidago species

European gardens and our own roadsides come ablaze in the fall with tall "field" goldenrod—a native perennial which, by the way, does not cause allergies, but gets blamed for ragweed-induced sneezes. Goldenrod supports a great variety of wildlife, from butterflies and bees to seed-eating songbirds, and makes an outstanding cut flower for arrangements. Out of unjustified fear that they will take over our gardens, we too often overlook the many great compact, non-spreading types of goldenrod that could otherwise light up our late summer and fall flower gardens. Truth is, even the most rampant species are very easy to pull up to thin out, leaving just enough to bring a "sense of place" to our gardens.

Bloom Period and Seasonal Color
Golden yellow blooms in fall

Mature Height × Spread
2 to 6 feet × 1 to 4 feet

When, Where, and How to Plant

Transplant clump divisions of goldenrod in the fall so they take advantage of winter rains, or set out container-grown plants in the spring. When transplanting, cut stems back to a few inches tall to avoid flopping and stress in the summer. Plant in full sun or at the edge of a woodland garden where it gets plenty of sunshine, in soil that is very lightly amended with organic matter. Mulch, if plants are in a border, to reduce weeds. Water thoroughly.

Growing Tips

Most goldenrods are drought tolerant, but can benefit from a slow soaking every few weeks you go without rain. The plants require little fertilizer. Pinch the growing tips from tall-flowering species in midsummer to encourage compact growth and more flowering in the fall.

Care

Goldenrods multiply easily by clump division in the fall. There are no major pest problems on goldenrod, though a few leaf diseases can be caused by heavy rains and humidity. Bees and many other insects visit the flowers, so avoid planting too close to a walkway.

Companion Planting and Design

Goldenrod lights up sunny meadows or perennial borders, bringing much-needed color into the fall garden when other flowers are dwindling. Its graceful, willowy form and feathery, rich sprays contrast nicely with other fall bloomers, including narrowleaf sunflower, wild ageratum, and asters. It makes a graceful cut flower and dries well, retaining its golden yellow color.

Personal Favorites

'Golden Baby', 'Cloth of Gold', and 'Peter Pan' are excellent dwarf hybrids, reaching only 1 to 2 feet tall; rough-leaved goldenrod (*S. rugosa* 'Fireworks') grows 3 to 4 feet tall with long, thin, arching flower stems. Sweet goldenrod (*S. odora*) grows 3 to 4 feet tall and has anise-scented foliage. Seaside goldenrod (*S. sempervirens*) grows 5 to 6 feet tall and is good for coastal gardens. None of these are aggressive spreaders.

When, Where, and How to Plant

Plant container-grown hibiscus any time of the year, typically in the spring or summer when they are in flower. Root cuttings all summer, or divide mature clumps in the fall after frost. Plant where they can get plenty of sun, but away from strong winds that can tear leaves and flowers. Most prefer a moist soil, and even tolerate wet conditions most of the year. Loosen the potting soil of container-grown plants at planting, fertilize lightly, and water deeply.

Growing Tips

Even the hardiest perennial hibiscus freeze to the ground in the winter, and should be neatened up accordingly. Pinch growing tips to encourage bushiness.

Care

Water frequently during dry spells, and provide moderate amounts of slow-release fertilizer in the spring and again in midsummer to promote fast flowering growth. Pests include whiteflies and aphids, which can be controlled with insecticidal soaps, and a "skeletonizer" caterpillar that eats all but the veins of leaves of some varieties. There is no good control for this caterpillar; just feed the plants to encourage more growth.

Companion Planting and Design

These bold plants make stunning masses, especially against dark backdrops or as accents near pools and water gardens. They grow well in large containers, and contrast beautifully with cannas, ornamental grasses, coleus, elephant's ear, and other tropical-effect perennials and shrubs.

Personal Favorites

Texas star (*H. coccineus*) has handsome, glossy, deeply divided (marijuana-like) leaves and incredibly intense, shimmery red flowers. Rose mallow (*H. moscheutos*) has huge flowers up to a foot across, and is available in many varieties as members of series such as Disco Belle, Frisbee, and Carnival. Halberd-leaf mallow (*H. militaris*) is the large type you see in wet ditches with pinkish white flowers, which does well in bog gardens. Cotton-leaf mallow (*H. mutabilis*, commonly called the "Confederate rose") is hardy only in counties in the lower half of each state, with large, double pink flowers late in the fall.

Hardy hibiscus, most of them native to our region, are indispensable to Southern gardens for their large, bold-colored, tropical looking flowers. Closely related to althea, okra, and cotton, the plants are upright and shrubby, usually with large leaves (with at least one major exception; see Personal Favorites) and an astonishing range of flower colors and sizes—some flowers are as large as dinner plates. Most bloom over a very long period, and all love our warm, humid climate and survive our mild winters. All are very easy to root and share with others, though a few have insect pests that annoy gardeners more than they damage the plants. Note that the slick-leaf Chinese hibiscus (H. rosa-sinensis) is not cold hardy except on the Gulf Coast.

Other Common Name
Rose Mallow

Bloom Period and Seasonal Color
White, red, pink flowers from late spring to fall

Mature Height × Spread
3 to 8 feet × 2 to 6 feet

Holly Fern
Cyrtomium falcatum

The leathery fronds of evergreen holly fern, named for its large, deep green leaflets, are so glossy they have a way of catching sunlight and brightening dark areas of the garden. The bushel-basket-size ferns, which grow in compact but loose, slow-to-spread clumps, will grow in almost utter darkness—such as on the north side of a house under cedar trees. The reliably hardy plant remains evergreen in all but the coldest upland counties, and can be used indoors as a potted plant where humidity is not too low.

Bloom Period and Seasonal Color
Evergreen fronds

Mature Height × Spread
1 to 2 feet × 1 to 2 feet

When, Where, and How to Plant
Plant container-grown holly fern any time, or divide in the spring when fiddleheads begin to emerge. Plant holly fern in the shade—even winter sunshine can burn the dark green leaves—in rich, acidic soil that is moist to slightly dry. Water (or soak) containerized ferns before planting, and space 1 to 2 feet apart. No need to plant deeply, because ferns don't have a deep root system. Mulch to keep roots moist and prevent weeds from cropping up until the ferns get established enough to shade other plants out.

Growing Tips
Water every week or two the first summer to get shallow-rooted holly fern completely established. In the fall add fresh mulch (well-rotted leaf mold or pine bark) that will decompose slowly and feed the soil around the fern. No other fertilizer is necessary unless ferns begin to yellow, in which case add a very light application of slow-release, nitrogen-rich fertilizer or compost. Divide every few years to have more plants to set around the landscape.

Care
In central and southern counties, holly fern has no needs at all other than occasionally pruning out burned leaves after a severe winter. In northern counties or when plants are exposed to winter sunshine, prune dead foliage close to the ground in late winter and it will come back out in the spring. There are no major pests or diseases.

Companion Planting and Design
Use holly fern as a foundation plant for shady landscapes or the north side of a home, massed almost like a deep groundcover, or in a border with shade-loving flowering shrubs. Holly fern also makes a handsome accent plant among other perennials, and is especially good when contrasted with cast-iron plant, variegated liriope, hosta, Lenten rose, and mondo grass.

Personal Favorites
Fortune's holly fern (*C. fortunei*) has narrower, more erect fronds. Hard-to-find *C. falcatum* 'Rochfordianum' has fringed leaflets.

Hosta
Hosta species and hybrids

When, Where, and How to Plant
Plant hosta any time, but divide in the fall or winter. Plant in summer-shaded areas (golden varieties tolerate more sun than green). Hosta flourishes in rich, moist, well-drained soil; set hostas 1 to 6 feet apart, depending upon the mature size of the plant (some are quite small, and others are huge). Keep spring-planted hosta regularly watered until plants are well established.

Growing Tips
In the summer in the South, there is a fine line between keeping hostas alive and killing them with kindness. Hosta needs an occasional deep soaking in the summer to help it cope with our hot, drying winds; still, expect blue-leaf varieties to turn green by midsummer. Lightly feed hostas in the spring. Divide as needed to keep plants vigorous and for new "starts" to transplant to other areas.

Care
When hosta dies down at frost, cut off the old foliage and mulch lightly; don't pile it on, or risk crown rot and encouraging overwintering slugs. Slugs and snails munch on hosta leaves at night; try trapping them in beer poured into lids or saucers sunk in the ground near the hosta. Voles also love the roots of hosta, so plant in buried wire baskets.

Companion Planting and Design
Use small hostas to edge shady borders or large types as either specimens or for mass plantings. Group hostas with ferns, liriope, ivy, and spring bulbs that "do their thing" before hosta comes up in the spring. Hosta works well also with shade-loving summer annuals such as impatiens or caladiums.

Personal Favorites
The classic beginner hosta is 'Francis Williams' with large, seersucker, bluish-gray leaves edged with golden yellow. *H. sieboldiana elegans* is another old standard among blue-leaf hostas and tolerates dry shade. Golden yellow 'Sum and Substance' and 'Gold Standard' tolerate a good bit of sun. There are many, many more!

Hosta, one of the most dependable bold-foliage perennials for the shade, grows well in all but the most humid, subtropical gardens. It tolerates the deep freezes of Canadian winters better than the mild ones of our Gulf Coast, but it can still flourish with protection from hot sun and wet soils. There are many species and hundreds of hybrids from which to choose, all grown for their spectacular foliage, which can be big and bold, or miniature and strap-shaped. Hosta leaves can be solid green, blue-green, golden yellow, or variegated. Some are smooth, others crinkled. Most send up sturdy stems of fragrant, drooping, lily-like blooms in the summer.

Other Common Names
Plantain Lily, Funkia

Bloom Period and Seasonal Color
White, lavender blooms in summer

Mature Height × Spread
1 to 4 feet × 1 to 6 feet

Iris

Iris species and hybrids

The rainbow hues of these beloved perennials herald the progress of spring. The iris show begins in late February or March with the historic "sweet flags" white iris you see in old towns, cemeteries, and country gardens, continues with the native woodland groundcover dwarf crested iris, and finishes with the flourish of Louisiana, Siberian, and bearded iris in late April and May (some bearded iris, called "remontant," rebloom later). The exotic flowers, made of three upright and three drooping petals, range in height from miniature (8 inches tall) blooming in late March with daffodils; to the intermediates (15 to 18 inches), blooming in April; and the tall (3 to 4 feet), blooming in late May. The prominent blue-green, sword-like leaves are a bonus that gives contrasting texture and form to gardens throughout the rest of the summer.

Other Common Name
Flags

Bloom Period and Seasonal Color
Purple, lavender, burgundy, yellow, white, other colors, blooms in spring

Mature Height × Spread
8 inches to 4 feet × 12 to 18 inches

When, Where, and How To Plant

Plant iris any time of the year, in full sun or part shade, in a rich, loamy soil with excellent drainage. Lighten clay soils by adding sand and compost and improve sandy soil by adding compost. Space rhizomes 12 to 18 inches apart in groups, but don't bury or mulch them—plant so the top part of the rhizome is on top of the soil—or they may rot, or simply not flower.

Growing Tips

Iris are drought tolerant, and need little or no watering. Feed very lightly in the spring with a slow-release or bulb food.

Care

After flowering, remove seedpods to keep the plant's energy focused on the next year's flower buds. Cut yellow or dead leaves to reduce disease. Divide every few years, soon after flowering, to keep plants blooming. Discard soft or insect-riddled old rhizomes and replant good pieces, with points facing outward to encourage faster spread. Diseases include soft rot from being planted too deep or over-watering, and borers, for which there is very little control other than removing infested rhizomes.

Companion Planting and Design

Plant iris as a "skirt" in front of azaleas and other shrubs. Interplant freely with drought-tolerant yarrow, phlox, daylily, sedum, artemisia, grasses, and reseeding annuals such as larkspur. Some iris are excellent bog or shallow water garden plants that complement canna and bluestar.

Personal Favorites

Native *I. cristata* and *I. verna* are low growing and spreading even in shaded gardens. Taller "bearded" iris (*I. germanica* hybrids) come in too many great cultivars to even begin listing, but one that has very stubby leaves and blooms very early in either sun or dense shade is the old white "flags" (*I. germanica florentina*), with blue or yellow relatives. Louisiana (*I. fulva* and others), Siberian (*I. sibirica*), and yellow flag (*I. pseudacorus*) have tall, narrow leaves and tolerate very wet or boggy soils.

Japanese Painted Fern
Athyrium nipponicum

When, Where, and How to Plant
Plant Japanese painted fern in the fall or late winter when possible, to allow plants to get established before it gets too hot the following summer. Divide in the spring when the fiddleheads (unfurled fronds) emerge. Painted ferns tolerate a fair amount of sunlight, but do best in light shade. The soil should be moist, moderately acidic, and full of composted material. Space ferns 12 to 18 inches apart. Water or soak container-grown ferns before planting, and plant so that crowns are at or slightly above the surrounding soil.

Growing Tips
Water this shallow-rooted perennial deeply and fairly regularly during the summer and dry fall, paying special attention to plants getting more sunlight. Each fall add a fresh layer of mulch to ferns in open sites, which feeds the soil as it decomposes. In spring, feed soil around ferns with a layer of compost or a very light application of slow-release fertilizer or nitrogen-rich cottonseed meal or fish emulsion. No other fertilizer is necessary unless ferns begin to yellow.

Care
Japanese painted fern does not compete well for moisture with tree roots, so work in plenty of organic matter and leaf mould every spring. Slugs and other shade insects can be bothersome, but because sprays can burn the foliage, use traps instead.

Companion Planting and Design
Use in groups to highlight shaded spots, or interplant with mondo grass for accent. Japanese painted fern is at its best when combined with the spiky blue-green foliage of iris, the coarse foliage of blue or golden hostas, or purple-leaved alumroot.

Personal Favorites
'Pictum' is the most widely available cultivar, but also look for 'Silver Falls' with arching silver and green fronds, or 'Ursula's Red' with foliage that is silver tinged with wine red. Hybrids between Japanese painted and lady ferns include the standout 'Ghost' with silvery gray fronds, and 'Branford Beauty' with gray fronds with red stalks.

Few ferns are as elegant as the Japanese painted fern. The green fronds of this hardy, deciduous fern are frosted with silver and gray, with deep purple stems. The fronds of this small fern are upright and very lacy, but grow only half as tall as its 4-foot North American native cousin, the lady fern (A. filix-femina). Unlike the invasive lady fern, the painted fern grows in a tight, slow-to-spread clump, and is best planted in groups for effect. There are many hybrids between the two ferns. During harsh winters, the tips of some fronds may turn brown, but leave them to protect tender new fronds as they appear the next spring.

Bloom Period and Seasonal Color
Deciduous fronds

Mature Height × Spread
12 to 20 inches × 12 to 18 inches

Lamb's Ears
Stachys byzantina

A well-loved cottage flower, this velvety-soft, gray-green foliage plant has been cultivated for centuries. Most of the season, lamb's ears keeps a low, spreading profile, forming an excellent edging. But in the summer, it shoots up fuzzy spikes—a foot or more tall—with soft lavender blooms that are good as cut flowers and dry beautifully as well. Lamb's ears, which hails from the dry climate of Turkey, has specific growing requirements—it thrives in cooler, drier weather, and requires dry soils—but once they are met, this plant is easy to grow. Normally long-lived, lamb's ears might "melt" in heat and humidity, particularly if over-watered or after heavy rains, but can be divided and rooted easily.

Bloom Period and Seasonal Color
Lavender blooms in summer

Mature Height × Spread
8 to 12 inches × 18 to 24 inches

When, Where, and How to Plant
Set out lamb's ears any time, or dig and divide mature plants in the spring. Plant in sun or light shade, in perfectly well-drained soils such as in raised beds or rock gardens. Space plants about 2 feet apart to give them room to spread. Fertilize lightly at planting time, and mulch lightly around the base of the plants with coarse sand or gravel, which reduces the chance of crown rot. Do not over-water at planting time.

Growing Tips
Water lamb's ears only when absolutely necessary, and then only in the very early morning before it gets hot, or late afternoon with time for foliage to dry before dusk; water at the base of the plant to avoid wetting foliage any more than necessary. Feed each spring with a slow- or time-release fertilizer or compost.

Care
In late spring and early summer, remove any dead leaves that may otherwise promote rot in the hot, humid season. Some gardeners cut off the flower stems after they fade. Divide plants regularly to keep centers from dying out and encourage strong new growth. Few pests bother the furry-leaf plants.

Companion Planting and Design
In the landscape, lamb's ears contrasts nicely with pink or white polyantha roses, and with the foliage of iris and sedums. Use as an edging, spreading groundcover, or in a rock or herb garden for a cascading effect. The foliage color and texture are valuable additions to the winter garden, and bring out colors of other perennials in the summer. Lamb's ears is also an excellent container companion to pentas, ornamental peppers, gladiolus, and other drought-tolerant annuals and bulbs.

Personal Favorites
'Silver Carpet' does not produce flowers, and 'Countess Helene von Stein' (also called 'Big Ears') has larger leaves than the species. 'Primrose Heron' has furry leaves that start out yellow and mature to chartreuse, then gray green.

Lenten Rose
Helleborus orientalis

When, Where, and How to Plant

Plant or transplant in the fall for the best chance of blooms in late winter. Spring planting is fine, too, but plants will need watering through the first summer. Plant in rich, moist, well-drained soil high in organic matter, in the shade. Once established, plants are drought tolerant, but they thrive in moist conditions. Set plants 2 to 3 feet apart. Set the plant level with the top of the soil and firm the soil to ensure contact with moisture and to eliminate air pockets. Mulch around the base of the plant to keep roots moist and to prevent the growth of weeds.

Growing Tips

Feed very lightly in the late winter with a slow-release fertilizer, and water during dry spells; otherwise, the plants are very easy to grow for decades with little encouragement. Mulch well with leaves that feed the soil as they decompose.

Care

Keep dead foliage cut back. Divide plants every few years for increase, in the fall. Watch for seedlings in the spring, and thin them to give plenty of growing room. There are no major pests—deer will step over them to get to other plants.

Companion Planting and Design

Plant hellebore in masses under trees on shady slopes and it will fairly quickly spread by seed into a dense groundcover. Plant in raised beds where the flowers can more likely be seen. Interplant with blue phlox, cast-iron plant, liriope, Japanese painted fern, bleeding heart, and wild ginger.

Personal Favorites

There are many hybrid varieties available, but most will cross-pollinate with highly variable results. The Royal Heritage series comes in a range of flower colors—purple, red, white, green, and pink—plus a variety of leaf sizes. The white Christmas rose (*H. niger*) blooms earlier and fades to pinkish. Narrow-leaved or bear's foot hellebore (*H. foetidus*) has striking foliage and bud-like, pale green blooms in late winter, and the foliage has a musty, smelly scent when crushed.

Lenten rose is one of the finest early-blooming perennials for shade gardens—sometimes it is the only plant in bloom in midwinter. The clump-forming plants, some of which can live a hundred years or more, are handsome year-round, with leathery foliage that has leaflets that look like an outstretched hand. However, they are at their best when topped with loose clusters of silky, single or double cup-shaped blooms made of long-lasting sepals; it can be difficult to appreciate the colors because the blooms hang downward. Most are creamy white, but hybrids can be pink, rosy-red, or burgundy, often with purple spots. The dried sepals persist for many weeks, fading to green in the heat of late spring. Deer simply will not eat hellebores, making them an ideal plant for woodland gardens.

Other Common Name

Hellebore

Bloom Period and Seasonal Color

White, pink, or burgundy blooms in winter, evergreen foliage

Mature Height × Spread

1 to 2 feet × 2 to 3 feet

Monarda
Monarda species

This showy native mint relative could be included in the chapter on herbs, because its very fragrant leaves have long been made into a stimulating tea (hence one of its common names, Oswego tea, named after the Native American Oswego tribe). The tubular flowers, which are produced in large, tight clusters atop tall, sprawling stems, are much loved not only by hummingbirds, butterflies, and bees, but also by people who enjoy their zesty, peppery flavor. Though fairly short-lived as individual plants, all the native monardas spread fairly aggressively, especially in cool, moist, "woodsy" soils, rooting as they go until they make large masses of foliage and flowers.

Other Common Names
Bee Balm, Oswego Tea

Bloom Period and Seasonal Color
Red, pink, white, purple flowers in summer

Mature Height × Spread
3 to 4 feet × 2 to 4 feet

When, Where, and How to Plant
Leafy plants are difficult to get established in the summer because new plants need a lot of water, which can rot their stems and cause leaf problems. It is better to plant in the early spring, or divide fast-sprouting underground stems of mature plants in the fall or winter. Choose a partly sunny area with rich, humusy soil that is moist but well drained, and away from strong winds. For planting in full sun, be prepared to water often. Do not plant close to walkways where bees can frighten visitors. Loosen roots of new plants at planting time, set plants 2 feet apart or more, mulch thickly to keep the soil cool and moist, and water deeply.

Growing Tips
Monarda, like most members of the mint family, can be invasive in moist soils. Pull excess plants, or cut them back and give the vigorous roots to another gardener. Plants may flop in wet weather but are too branchy to stake. Pinch new growth to encourage compact, bushy growth, or allow the plants to get large and rank.

Care
Fertilize lightly and frequently with a slow-acting or natural fertilizer, keep well mulched, and water deeply during hot dry spells. Insect pests are minor, though bees working the flowers can be a nuisance in small gardens. Mildew can cause most leaves to drop parts of the year; prune plants to rejuvenate with new growth.

Companion Planting and Design
Outstanding along woodland edges and moist areas of the garden, or in herb gardens where they have room to ramble. Interplant with large flowering mallows, native blazing star, Russian sage, and tiger lily.

Personal Favorites
The wild bee balm (*M. didyma*) or Oswego tea has scarlet flowers and bracts, with cultivars such as 'Croftway Pink', 'Snow White', and 'Cambridge Scarlet'. Bergamot (*M. fistulosa*) has lavender to light pink flowers and, along with spotted horsemint (*M. punctata*) with purple spotted yellow or pink blossoms, is best suited for naturalized or wildflower gardens.

Narrowleaf Sunflower

Helianthus angustifolius

When, Where, and How to Plant

Set out nursery-grown plants in the spring or fall, or dig, divide, and replant small plants from established colonies in the fall or winter. Space 2 feet apart or more in full or nearly full sun and average soil—even in areas that stay wet part of the year—and keep watered until established. Keep in mind the spreading nature of this vigorous native wildflower, and do not plant it too close to other perennials that may be crowded out.

Growing Tips

No need to water these plants other than an occasional deep soaking in very dry summers and early fall. Fertilize very lightly in the spring with an all-purpose fertilizer.

Care

Pinch the growing tips in June to make the plants branch out with many more flowering stems, which will be shorter and less likely to flop in the fall under the weight of flowers. Thin excess plants by simply pulling them up in the spring or summer. Leave plants intact after frost, for migrant birds to enjoy the rich seeds. This plant is pest free.

Companion Planting and Design

Plant sunflower at the back of a perennial border, or in a clump in the center of an island with blue or red flowers for a brilliant show. Plant in wildflower meadows or areas that are low and stay wet part of the year. It is naturally at home with goldenrod, asters, sumac, yucca, and other fall-performing natives, but contrasts well with evergreen shrubs such as nandina, hollies, and arborvitae.

Personal Favorites

The species in its wild form is perfect "as is," but 'Gold Lace' is less invasive, and flowers on naturally shorter plants (under 6 feet without pruning). 'Mellow Yellow' has pale yellow flowers. Jerusalem artichoke (*H. tuberosum*), whose edible tuberous roots are sold as "sunchokes," can be very invasive—but is beautiful as a screen.

This "tall boy" of the fall is one of the most spectacular native flowering perennials, and as easy to grow as it is beautiful. Each clump has several tall stems that radiate narrow, 6-inch-long leaves from spring to fall, making it a fine linear addition to the back of a flower border. When it comes into full bloom in October, its many dozens of inch-wide, yellow-orange flowers with chocolate-brown centers are very attractive to both people and wildlife, especially butterflies, and its seeds are very important sources of food for migrating birds. It tends to spread by underground runners, but is not a serious weed problem.

Other Common Name

Swamp Sunflower

Bloom Period and Seasonal Color

Yellow-orange blooms in fall

Mature Height × Spread

8 to 10 feet × 2 to 3 feet

Obedient Plant
Physostegia virginiana

Sometimes considered too invasive for polite gardens, this hardy native perennial definitely has a mind of its own, spreading in all directions into any type of soil. But its top quality, long-lasting, cut-flower spikes of white or lavender are beautiful, and irresistible to butterflies and hummingbirds—and its wayward stems are very easy to simply pull up and compost. Native to woodland edges and along sunny creek banks, the plant's deep green foliage and eye-catching spikes of flowers make it a wonderful "starter" plant for beginner gardeners or those who love excess or need lots of cut flowers. Its common name comes from the ability of individual trumpet-like flowers to be swiveled from side to side and remain in their new positions.

Other Common Name
False Dragonhead

Bloom Period and Seasonal Color
White or lavender flowers in spring and summer

Mature Height × Spread
2 to 4 feet × 2 to 3 feet

When, Where, and How to Plant
Set out container-grown plants any time of the year, preferably in the spring, or dig and separate plants from the edges of existing colonies in the fall or winter. It can be divided even when in full bloom as long as plants are cut back to prevent severe wilting—they sprout right back. For the best flowers, plant in sunny or bright areas in soil that is well drained but moist, with at least 2 to 3 feet between new plants (they will quickly fill in). Avoid planting where colonies can spread into poorly maintained moist areas, or it will take over. New plants may need staking to keep from flopping over.

Growing Tips
Obedient plant is somewhat aggressive in its spread, especially in moist soils, but not as horribly as some gardeners claim; extra plants can simply be pulled up and discarded, or given away (to grateful but unsuspecting new gardeners). During wet seasons, the plants may lean or flop over without staking, but the flowering ends of the stalks will turn upright toward the sky. Cut plants to the ground after the first fall frost.

Care
Water regularly during dry or exceptionally windy periods, and feed lightly, if at all, using slow-acting fertilizers or compost. There are no major insect or disease pests, but plants are susceptible to stem rots that cause them to die suddenly in midsummer—but this usually only thins out excess plants.

Companion Planting and Design
Obedient plant is very thick growing and can crowd out other plants quickly. Use with bold, sturdy plants such as palmetto or summer phlox, or interplant with equally vigorous artemisia, soapwort, or yarrow. Let it grow as a mass planting with a garden accessory as interest for when the plant is dormant.

Personal Favorites
'Summer Snow' is pure white, 'Vivid' is deep rose pink, and 'Variegata' is bluish pink with white-edged leaves. 'Miss Manners' doesn't spread.

Oxeye Daisy
Chrysanthemum leucanthemum

When, Where, and How to Plant

Set out container-grown plants or divisions any time of the year except when in full bloom, in full sun and well-drained soils of average fertility, or sow seeds in the late summer or fall and keep moist until seedlings appear. Water new transplants, but don't over-water—if young plants wilt, cut them back and they will quickly put out new growth that is better balanced with their roots. This is a very tough plant that tolerates a wide range of conditions. Leave 12 to 18 inches between them when planting in a border.

Growing Tips

In lieu of rain, water 1 inch per week until the plants are well established, and then during dry periods. It needs little fertilizer. Maintaining mulch helps control weeds, but these plants are pretty competitive by themselves.

Care

Regular deadheading can encourage longer blooming, but at least cut dead flowering stems back after plants have quit blooming to keep them looking neat; leave them long enough for seed to disperse or be eaten by songbirds. Divide clumps every few years in the fall or early spring. Insect pests on foliage are not serious enough to spray, considering the wildlife that visits the flowers.

Companion Planting and Design

It spreads easily, but is fortunately easy to transplant at any stage. In an area where it can naturalize, it multiplies happily to become a mainstay companion to spring-blooming black-eyed Susan, coreopsis, daylily, and iris, and is perfect to "interplant" with drought-tolerant daffodils. It also makes a striking solid-daisy border.

Personal Favorites

'May Queen' is perhaps the toughest spring daisy of all. Other good spring-flowering daisies include Shasta daisy (*C.* × *superbum* or *Leucanthemum* × *superbum*) and Nippon daisy (*C. nipponicum* or *Nipponanthemum nipponicum*), a good choice for coastal gardens.

This white daisy (sometimes listed as Leucanthemum vulgare), a European native that has spread and "naturalized" all over the South, begins to bloom in early April and lasts into June. Its crisp white flowers top strong, 18- to 24-inch stems and are a bright addition to a perennial border. Oxeye daisy can be the backbone of any wildflower meadow, since it's strong enough to compete with weeds and grasses. It also plays an important role for pollinators. Unlike other daisies (see Personal Favorites), oxeye is sturdy and never "flops" during wet springs. It is one of the few spring plants that will grow beside a mailbox a quarter mile from a garden hose—and not need water or get stolen.

Other Common Names
May Daisy, Daisy

Bloom Period and Seasonal Color
White blooms in late March to June

Mature Height × Spread
18 to 24 inches × 12 to 18 inches

Peony
Paeonia species

Nothing gets a Northern gardener's garden juices going better than peonies—their huge, lightly fragrant cut flowers, coarse foliage, and history make them almost irresistible. But the fact is, most varieties suffer terribly in the Deep South from mild winters, wet springs, and hot summers. Quite a few will grow but not flower except in higher altitudes in our northern counties, or where they are planted for maximum cold in the winter and minimum heat in the spring (north and east exposures). Gulf Coast gardeners can all but mark this plant off their wish list, or try some of the very early blooming ones listed in the Personal Favorites section.

Bloom Period and Seasonal Color
White, pink, red in early to mid-spring

Mature Height × Spread
2 to 3 feet × 3 feet

When, Where, and How to Plant
Plant peonies in the spring or fall, or divide mature plants in the fall so they can get established before the next summer. Peonies need lots of sun to flower, but an eastern exposure is best for Southern gardens to prevent sunburn and to keep them dormant until spring. They absolutely require very well-drained soil. Plant them shallow to prevent rotting in our mild wet winters, with no more than an inch of soil over the top of the rhizomes. Prepare the planting site right the first time, adding plenty of organic matter, bulb food (bone meal will do), and a cup of agricultural lime for each plant to reduce soil acidity. Mulch to protect against hot sun and fluctuating winter temperatures.

Growing Tips
Heavy peony flowers flop in our wet springs, so stake or cage them early. Remove old leaves in the fall to reduce problems with fungal leaf spot diseases, and reapply a thin mulch. Be sure to provide plenty of air circulation to reduce disease problems.

Care
Water only during extreme drought, or risk rotting the compact rhizomes. Fertilize lightly with a high-phosphorus bulb food in the spring. Leaf spots are a minor problem. Ants are frequently seen on peonies—which is a good thing since they eat the wax holding peony petals in the bud, allowing the flowers to open.

Companion Planting and Design
Plant peonies as specimens in raised beds or large tubs, in the light shade of crape myrtles or tall nandina, or in combination with early daffodils, bearded iris, and yarrow.

Personal Favorites
'Festiva Maxima', a white semi-double flower with red flecks in the center, has been popular even in Lower South gardens since it was introduced in the late 1800s, because it blooms early even after mild winters. Other early bloomers include fragrant dark red 'Big Ben', fragrant pink 'Edulis Superba', pale pink 'Shirley Temple', and the mid-season single pink 'Seashell'.

Purple Coneflower
Echinacea purpurea

When, Where, and How to Plant

Set out container-grown plants any time, being very careful to loosen potting soil or risk plants drying out too much. Or divide and transplant mature plants in the fall or late winter. Seeds need to be exposed to cold weather to sprout, so collect and sow in the fall, or give them two or three months of cold-damp treatment (called "stratification"). Purple coneflower does best in full or part sun, in well-drained soils of moderate fertility. Plant 1 to 2 feet apart in large groups or "drifts" and the plants will naturalize from there by seed.

Growing Tips

Water only during extreme dry spells, if at all. Plants need little fertilizer, but benefit from a spring feeding of compost. In light shade or during wet summers, tall flowering stems may flop over, but staking is rarely needed and can look out of place. Use flopped flowers for arrangements.

Care

Cut spent plants back after the first flush of blooms and they will rebloom. Leave a few seedheads intact for wild birds (especially finches), and the plants will spread by self-sown seeds. Carefully divide every three or four years to keep plants vigorous, making sure each division has roots. Coneflower petals are occasionally eaten by insects, but no real harm is done. A virus called aster yellows may distort flowers, but it seems to add to interest; seriously infected plants can be pulled up and discarded.

Companion Planting and Design

Purple coneflower makes an excellent back-of-the-border addition to a perennial flower bed, or with a picket fence backdrop. It is indispensable in wildflower and naturalistic plantings, especially when combined with orange daylily, salvias, black-eyed Susan, plains coreopsis, white yarrow, oxeye daisy, and grasses. Its medicinal use makes it appropriate for herb gardens.

Personal Favorites

Named selections include 'Kim's Knee High', 'Bright Star' with rosy pink flowers, 'Magnus' with 3-inch flowers that do not have drooping petals, and several white flowering forms.

This tough prairie native is usually rated as one of the top ten perennials for the South. A member of the aster family, it is very low maintenance. It grows into a leafy, green clump in the early spring, then pushes upward and blooms in May, June, and July, with repeat flowers throughout the rest of the season. Its magenta, flying saucer-like flowers have hot-pink petals surrounding a bristly orange cone—an energetic color and shape combination that is irresistible to people and butterflies alike. They also make excellent cut flowers for arrangements. There are many exciting new selections with more color combinations, but the native kind is just fine "as is."

Bloom Period and Seasonal Color
Pink-purple blooms in summer

Mature Height × Spread
2 to 4 feet × 1 to 2 feet

Rose Verbena

Verbena canadensis

Loving full sun, the old-fashioned, native perennial rose verbena grows wild along roadsides all across the South, where it thrives (its worst enemy is rich or poorly drained soils). Its thick spring and summer clusters of small, tubular flowers come in white, red, pink, and purple. In mild winters, rose verbena stays evergreen, but wherever it grows, it explodes in the spring with vigorous, densely leaved, spreading shoots. Verbena is fairly short-lived, but it is such an excellent plant for visual delight and butterflies and hummingbirds, that it is frequently replanted from cuttings taken in the summer.

Other Common Name
Verbena

Bloom Period and Seasonal Color
Rose, white, red, purple blooms in spring and summer

Mature Height × Spread
12 to 18 inches 2 to 6 feet

When, Where, and How to Plant

Set out rose verbena transplants in the spring and water until well established. Divide existing plants in the fall or spring, or root stem cuttings in late spring or summer. Plant rose verbena in full or nearly full sun in sandy or loose, well-drained soils, without which it can rot in the winter and spring, or at best come back scraggly and weak. Improve heavy soils by adding plenty of organic matter, but do not overdo it or verbena can dry out in the summer and need too much water, which can rot its crown. Place plants 2 feet apart of more.

Growing Tips

Except when grown in containers or high raised beds, verbena is extremely heat and drought tolerant; water only when absolutely necessary. Feed plants each spring with compost or a small amount of all-purpose fertilizer.

Care

In winter, remove leaves and mulch from around the crowns of the plants to decrease the chance of disease, but do not cut plants back, because foliage and stems protect them from winterkill. To increase plantings and keep plants healthy, regularly divide clumps. Clouds of tiny whiteflies are a problem some years, but sprays are rarely effective and can kill butterflies as well.

Companion Planting and Design

The bold colors of verbena work well in front of tall, bright yellows such as false sunflower, black-eyed Susan, or Klondike cosmos. A low, spreading plant, it makes a colorful walkway edging, ground-cover, or addition to a rock garden. It also thrives in raised beds or planters, attracting butterflies and admiring glances.

Personal Favorites

The best bets for starters are the widely available hybrids such as 'Homestead Purple' and 'Biloxi Blue'. However, anyone local with a good verbena in their garden will be more than glad to share a cutting or two. The brilliant purple roadside verbena (*V. rigida*) grows best in very poor soils and drought.

Ruellia
Ruellia brittoniana

When, Where, and How to Plant
Ruellia can be set out any time of the year, even when in full bloom, as long as adequate moisture is available to get plants established. Roots of container-grown plants are nearly always tightly wrapped and need loosening. Divide mature clumps in the late fall or winter, or root stem cuttings in water in the summer or fall. Plant in full sun or light shade, in nearly any type of soil, with moderate fertilizer, keeping in mind the plant's ability to spread into nearby areas. If new plants wilt, cut them back to relieve stress and they will quickly resprout with new flowering stems

Growing Tips
Keep plants in bounds by hand pulling or digging excess plants, or installing a sturdy edging at least 6 or 8 inches deep. Tip-prune new growth in the spring to create more compact mounds with more flowers. Mulch to keep roots cool and moist in the summer, and fertilize very lightly in the spring or early summer.

Care
Once plants are established, they are very tough and need little or no water or fertilizer. Keep free of tree seedlings that may sprout in the protected centers of old clumps. In the winter, cut plants all the way to the ground, and cover the area with mulch. Ruellia has no insect or disease problems, other than minor whitefly infestations.

Companion Planting and Design
The colonies are very thick and make excellent focal points in large gardens or under the light shade of small trees. Interplant with daylilies but be prepared to pull excess plants. Ruellia also grows well with elephant's ear, banana, canna, and other bold-textured plants.

Personal Favorites
The species is an all-time favorite, with its rich, dark purple-blue flowers. 'Chi Chi' has pale pink flowers. Compact, dwarf forms for edging beds include purple 'Katie', 'Colobe Pink', and 'Strawberries and Cream' with lavender blossoms and white-speckled leaves.

One of the hardiest perennials for the South, this summer- and fall-flowering beauty languished in cottage gardens for decades before being "discovered" by designers looking for really tough perennials. Those who grow it know how it can spread into good-size colonies—a potential problem in small spaces, but welcome in larger gardens where there is elbowroom. The large blue or pink petunia-like flowers, which appear in upper leaf joints of the bushy, many-stemmed, 3- or 4-foot plants, shimmer against the dark background of fingerlike foliage. This perennial is an easy, unkillable starter plant for beginner gardeners, and just as satisfying for seasoned gardeners who have plenty of room. Very compact dwarf forms are available for those who still have doubts.

Other Common Name
Mexican Petunia

Bloom Period and Seasonal Color
Blue or pink flowers from summer to fall

Mature Height × Spread
3 to 4 feet × 2 to 3 feet

Salvia

Salvia species

Ornamental salvias are shrubby plants, both native and non-native, with tall, slender spires of show-stopping blue or purple flowers that are perfect companions to nearly every other flower in the garden. These heat- and humidity-tolerant plants are heavily favored by hummingbirds, bees, and butterflies, and are good as cut flowers as well. Some flower all summer and fall, while others flower in a massive display only in the short days of fall (sometimes in the spring in coastal counties or after mild winters). Though perennial salvias are "hot" trendy plants, with many interesting hybrids coming onto the market all the time, several tried-and-true old garden favorites continue to dominate the summer garden.

Other Common Name
Perennial Salvia

Bloom Period and Seasonal Color
Blue, purple, red blooms in summer and fall

Mature Height × Spread
2 to 8 feet × 18 inches to 7 feet

When, Where, and How to Plant
Set out perennial salvias in the spring, in full or nearly full sun and in very well-drained soils high in organic matter. Spacing depends on growth habit: Some spread by rhizomes (underground stems) and take up lots of space, while others, such as autumn sage, grow into small shrubs. Leave enough space between transplants to allow for the full size of the plant.

Growing Tips
Salvias, though drought tolerant, benefit from regular watering when rapidly growing and blooming. Mulch plants in the winter to protect against winter cold. Fertilize each spring with a slow- or time-release fertilizer or compost.

Care
Prune salvias in late winter instead of fall, to avoid stem rot and late season new growth that can sprout during a midwinter warm spell. Deadheading through the summer prolongs blooming, and pinching new growth creates denser plants with more flower spikes. Whiteflies can be a major problem, to be treated with natural insecticidal soap, which does not burn plants or harm butterflies.

Companion Planting and Design
Perennial salvias are excellent by themselves, with a fence or birdbath for contrast. However, they are outstanding as flower border plants, with their spikes of flowers being perfect complements to daylily, ornamental grasses, lantana, sedum, and just about everything else.

Personal Favorites
Anise sage (*S. guaranitica* 'Argentine Skies' and 'Costa Rica Blue') is one of the best butterfly plants, and tolerates light shade. Autumn sage (*S. greggii*) is a short, almost woody plant with intense flower colors. *Salvia × sylvestris* comes in 'May Night', 'Blue Queen', and 'East Friesland' (violet). Bog sage (*S. uliginosa*) grows 4 to 5 feet tall, spreads vigorously especially in moist soils, and blooms a beautiful sky blue from spring to fall. Forsythia sage (*S. madrensis*) is a huge, yellow, shrubby perennial salvia that tolerates single-digit temperatures and can reach 7 or more feet tall and wide. There are others, including many hybrids.

Sedum

Sedum species

When, Where, and How to Plant

Set out sedum transplants any time, even in mid-winter, in full sun or light shade where they will get excellent drainage during rainy spells; do not add too much organic matter, as rich soil causes weak and floppy growth. Divide mature plants any time as well, or root stem cuttings in the spring and summer (keep cuttings on the dry side to avoid rot). Leave 1 to 2 feet between plants to give them room to grow.

Growing Tips

Sedum is drought tolerant to an extreme, and needs little or no water other than rainfall, even in severe droughts. Very little fertilizer is needed.

Care

Seedheads are attractive in the winter garden, so don't cut plants back in the fall. For bushier plants, pinch growing tips in spring or early summer. This also helps plants in partial shade, as they tend to get lanky. Sedum is long lived and pest free, with only a few problems with whiteflies or mealybugs.

Companion Planting and Design

Sedum is very popular as a border or edging plant, a companion to other perennials, or as a long-lived rock garden or outdoor container plant. It combines very well with iris and bulbs such as daffodils, because it both complements the flowers and tolerates the dry summer conditions the other plants require.

Personal Favorites

'Autumn Joy' (*Sedum spectabile* or *Hylotelephium spectabile*) is one of the most popular perennials sold. It forms a mass of large, flat, juicy leaves on 2- to 3-foot stems, topped with broccoli-like flower heads that open light pink then change to rose, then mature to a deep bronze or rust. Goldmoss sedum, sometimes called "moss" by country gardeners, is a creeping, cascading mass of small, light green succulent leaves topped with an impressive abundance of bright yellow flowers in the spring.

Sedums are drought-tolerant succulent plants with fleshy leaves. Also called stonecrop, sedum is carefree and is often found in dry or "xeriscape" landscapes that receive no extra watering. When planted in well-drained soils or containers, they can grow for years on rainfall alone. Sedums have showy foliage and clusters of small but interesting star-shaped flowers, and can be rooted quickly from stem cuttings or even leaf cuttings nearly all spring, summer, and fall. There are many species, cultivars, and hybrids, including landscape types and indoor "collector" plants, low-growing groundcovers to 2-foot tall plants with large heads of pollinator-attracting flowers. All are extremely low maintenance, with over-watering and over-fertilizing being their main problems.

Other Common Name
Stonecrop

Bloom Period and Seasonal Color
Yellow flowers in spring, or rose blooms in late summer to fall

Mature Height × Spread
6 inches to 3 feet × 1 to 2 feet

Soapwort
Saponaria officinalis

Once commonly seen growing along creek banks and even railroad tracks, this creeping, cascading evergreen perennial is nearly unkillable—even deer won't eat it. It has very attractive smooth foliage and clusters of pink and white flowers that are produced on short spikes from late spring to frost. The plant was introduced by European pioneer settlers for its use as soap—when crushed and mixed with water, its roots and leaves make a mild soapy lather used for washing clothes and hair (which is why it was planted along creeks). Another common name, "bouncing bet," comes from its use by English bar maids (generically called "Bet"), who used it to rinse used ale bottles.

Other Common Name
Bouncing Bet

Bloom Period and Seasonal Color
Pink and white flowers from spring to fall

Mature Height × Spread
12 to 18 inches × 2 to 3 feet

When, Where, and How to Plant
Set out container-grown plants any time you can get them, or divide existing plants in the winter or spring, cutting back new divisions to reduce stress and increase new branching. Plant in sun, in a well-drained soil that is not too rich or well prepared. Space plants 2 or more feet apart. Be aware that the plant can be invasive, so do not plant near smaller plants or desirable groundcovers. Cover the planting area with mulch to reduce weeds the first summer, and water deeply to get the plants established.

Growing Tips
No need to protect this incredibly hardy plant from cold—it can tolerate 40 degrees below zero! Cut scraggly foliage shoots and faded flower stems in the fall, and tip-prune new growth to keep plants compact and neat. Divide as needed to keep the plant in bounds.

Care
Soapwort is very drought tolerant and requires little or no fertilizer to thrive for decades. It has no major pests, but may become a little weedy itself, in need of keeping in bounds with a barrier or regular pruning. Because of its soapy taste, deer and slugs avoid it even when nothing else is available to browse.

Companion Planting and Design
Soapwort is either invasive or spreads, and cascades beautifully over rock walls and in rock gardens. It serves as a thick, durable underplanting to crape myrtle, althea, and shrub roses, and as a "skirt" for azaleas and other denser shrubs. It is also a good companion for sturdy perennials such as Louisiana iris, salvia, and artemisia. It grows very well with little care in large pots.

Personal Favorites
The single-flowered species is extremely invasive by underground runners, but the double-flowered forms 'Rosea Plena' (light pink) and 'Rubra Plena' (crimson, fades to pink), ramble over the soil surface without rooting as they go. A related species, rock soapwort (*S. ocymoides*), cascades with small pink flowers.

Spiderwort
Tradescantia virginiana

When, Where, and How to Plant
Most people want to know how to get rid of common spiderwort, which grows almost everywhere. Container-grown plants are available at some garden centers and mail-order nurseries from winter to spring, and can be set out any time you get them. Divisions of mature clumps are best done in the fall, winter, or early spring when plants are dormant. Seedlings can be transplanted any time if cut back before being dug. Plant spiderwort in full sun or shade, 2 feet or more apart in any type of soil—though it flowers best in slightly moist soils. Light fertilization and a good soaking at planting are about all this hardy native needs to get started.

Growing Tips
Spiderwort can get floppy in heavy shade or after lots of rain, so be prepared to cut plants back severely to force stouter new growth, or cage specimens so their flowering stems can remain upright. Divide every two or three years to keep plants vigorous, especially hybrids.

Care
Keep plants blooming and lush with an occasional soaking during hot, dry weather. No fertilizer is generally needed, other than an occasional light feeding in the spring. There are no major pests of spiderwort, but its own seedlings can become real weeds if you don't keep after them by pulling regularly.

Companion Planting and Design
Spiderwort is one of the most dependable natives for naturalizing, and grows well with wild blue phlox, ferns, columbine, and other woodland plants (it will come up through English ivy and Asiatic jasmine). Use as a "skirt" to shrubs. It can also take full sun with ornamental grasses, iris, daylily, and mallows.

Personal Favorites
'Sweet Kate' is compact with bright yellow foliage and deep blue flowers. 'Red Cloud' is reddish, 'Zwanenberg Blue' is a standard old deep blue, 'Purple Dome' is purple, 'Innocence' is pure white, and 'Bilberry Ice' is pale lavender with a deeper blush.

This sturdy native, which grows in moist woods and fields, is upright with juicy, grassy foliage topped with clusters of unusual three-petaled flowers that open only in the morning, and remain open only on cloudy days. In spite of the native wild species being somewhat hard to control, there are some choice, garden-quality cultivars (often sold as T. × andersoniana) with improved growth habit, sturdier foliage, and larger flowers in clear colors. This wild thing can be tamed for any style of garden.

Bloom Period and Seasonal Color
Blue, pink, or white flowers in spring and summer

Mature Height × Spread
2 to 3 feet × 2 to 3 feet

Stokes' Aster
Stokesia laevis

This chunky, clump-forming, ditch-bank native perennial with smooth, slick leaves erupts with short, many-branched stems loaded and bent over under the weight of masses of 3- to 4-inch-wide aster-like powder puffs of blue, purple, white, or even yellow. Each flower opens to reveal a central button of small disk flowers surrounded with many dozens of longer, thin ray flowers, almost like dandelion flowers on steroids. The evergreen plants tolerate difficult low, wet conditions and light shade, and can spread by seed into nearby areas but are easy to transplant and never weedy. It makes a good cut flower and is very attractive to butterflies and moths.

Other Common Name
Stokesia

Bloom Period and Seasonal Color
Blue, yellow, white, purple flowers in spring and summer

Mature Height × Spread
18 to 24 inches × 12 to 18 inches

When, Where, and How to Plant
Set out container-grown plants any time of the year, especially in the spring so you can enjoy their first season of flowers. Dig and divide mature plants in the fall, winter, or spring, cutting back some of the foliage to take stress off the plants. Plant in sun or moderate shade, in areas that stay damp part of the year (it is a native wetland plant). Set new clumps 12 to 18 or more inches apart so there is plenty of room to spread. Loosen roots of container-grown plants to encourage fast new root growth. Fertilize lightly, cover new plantings with mulch, and water frequently until plants are established.

Growing Tips
Cut old leaves off—never pull, or the resulting tears may lead to crown rot—and remove spent flower stems as they turn yellow. Sow mature seeds in moist potting soil for plenty of new plants later.

Care
Stokesia tolerates long periods of wet, but will need watering during prolonged summer or fall drought. No need to keep the plants wet, just moist. Fertilize very lightly in the spring with an all-purpose fertilizer or compost. There are no major insect or disease problems with this native perennial.

Companion Planting and Design
Stokes' aster is a fairly low clump-former, and can be used as a substitute for or interplanted with liriope in flower or shrub border edging. It grows very well in wet bog gardens, and in containers if watered regularly. Natural combinations would include phlox, verbena, garden lilies, Louisiana or Siberian iris, and blazing star.

Personal Favorites
All selections are a little taller than wide, with flower color being the most common variation. Easy ones include 'Blue Danube', deep purple 'Wyoming', pure white 'Silver Moon', 'Mary Gregory' with lemon yellow flowers, and 'Purple Parasols', whose powder blue flowers change to purple and magenta with age.

Summer Phlox
Phlox paniculata

When, Where, and How to Plant

Set out container-grown plants any time, even when in full bloom, but do not over-water if they wilt in the summer heat, or you will rot the roots. Divide mature clumps in the fall or spring, and pinch the growing tips from new plants to encourage more branching. Plant in full sun or part shade, with at least 3 feet or more between plants to reduce disease problems caused by overcrowding. Mulch newly planted phlox to reduce weed competition, and water only to get established. If plants wilt, resist the temptation to over-water; instead, thin out some stems.

Growing Tips

Summer phlox can get gangly and floppy under the weight of large flower clusters; stake as needed, or tip-prune new growth in the late spring to make plants compact and sturdier with even more flowers. When grown in full sun, flower colors may fade. Divide mature clumps every few years, replanting vigorous small plants from the outer edges.

Care

Phlox, being native, can withstand long periods of drought, but flower size will be greatly reduced. It requires little or no fertilizer, but compost will help make the plants sturdier and increase the color hue of flowers. Pests include aphids, whiteflies, and the fairly serious powdery mildew in the summer—thin crowded plants or plant mildew-resistant varieties.

Companion Planting and Design

A mature clump of summer phlox is statuesque by itself, especially against a picket or split rail fence, wagon wheel, or other "pioneer" artifact. Interplant in naturalistic meadows with other casual plants such as purple coneflower, orange daylily, tiger lily, black-eyed Susan, yarrow, artemisia, and naturalized daffodils. Mass at a woodland edge where the flowers can stand out against the backdrop of trees.

Personal Favorites

Mildew-resistant varieties include solid white 'David' and 'Mt. Fuji', 'Delta Snow' (white with purple eye), 'Nicky' (deep magenta), and 'Robert Poore' (violet pink). Seedlings of these cultivars tend toward the washed-out but natural pink.

The almost garish purplish pink of the tall native summer phlox is always sure to bring a smile to the face of an old-time gardener. It is reminiscent of old country cottage gardens, but fits well into modern landscapes that are beginning to include slices of perennial borders. It towers above other summer flowers, complementing the pink of purple coneflower and repeating the flower color of pink crape myrtle (in fact, phlox almost looks exactly like a dwarf crape myrtle from a distance). Other colors, with more mildew resistance, have become mainstream, but none are as beautiful—or natural—as a pink phlox covered with swallowtail butterflies.

Other Common Name
Garden Phlox

Bloom Period and Seasonal Color
Pink, white, purple, lavender, or red in late spring and summer

Mature Height × Spread
3 to 5 feet × 3 to 4 feet

Wild Blue Phlox
Phlox divaricata

This native phlox, which can be seen gracing shade gardens all over Europe, naturally lights up our own woodlands early in the dampness of spring just as ferns begin to unfurl. It is surprisingly easy to grow and as popular in a perennial flower border as it is in the shade garden. Wild blue phlox also has a sweet fragrance that adds a grace note to the landscape. This plant may go dormant in the summer from severe drought, but it happily returns on time every spring. There are white, bright blue, pale blue, and bright lavender selections. It is also an important early source of nectar for migrating hummingbirds.

Other Common Name
Wild Sweet William

Bloom Period and Seasonal Color
Blue, white, lavender blooms in spring

Mature Height × Spread
1 foot × 1 to 2 feet

When, Where, and How to Plant
Set out transplants or divide nearly any time except in midsummer when heat and drought are at their peak. Plant wild blue phlox in filtered light, such as the shade of deciduous trees, where soil is usually rich with natural leaf mould. Set plants 1 foot apart or more, mulch well, and water through the first summer to get them well established.

Growing Tips
Wild blue phlox likes moist soil, and will hold its foliage better when watered regularly in the summer. Maintain a natural leaf mulch to keep roots moist in summer. Plants require little fertilizer, but enjoy a spring feeding of compost.

Care
Phlox can look ratty up close in the late summer, so cut the foliage if necessary. However, leave it unpruned until seeds have dispersed in midsummer. There are no major pests.

Companion Planting and Design
This phlox is a natural companion for hardy ferns lining a woodland path, or naturalizing throughout a wooded slope. In a flower border, pair it with columbine or daffodils. This plant looks best when interspersed with plants with more attractive summer foliage such as iris, especially when the plant goes dormant in midsummer. It blooms about the same time as azaleas, making it a great "skirt" plant.

Personal Favorites
'Dirigo Ice' is pale blue, 'Blue Moon' is deep violet blue, and 'Louisiana' is intense purple blue. 'Chattahoochee' is a popular hybrid with dark green leaves and masses of fragrant, lavender-blue flowers, each with dark eye. A similar spring-blooming native, creeping phlox (*P. stolonifera*) grows 6 inches tall, blooms purple, and also thrives in the shade. Moss pink (*P. subulata*), often called "thrift," cascades down rock walls across the South with tiny, needle-like foliage and brilliant masses of pink, blue, lavender, or white flowers.

When, Where, and How to Plant

Set out container-grown plants any time, but be sure to loosen roots at planting time. Divide mature clumps in the fall or spring except when in flower. Plant in full sun or light shade. Yarrow is highly adaptable to soils and grows well in poor, exposed sites, but unless the soil is very well drained you will risk losing plants to root rot. Set plants 2 to 3 feet apart, fertilize lightly, and water just often enough to keep plants from wilting.

Growing Tips

Yarrow is heat and drought tolerant—it can be found growing along railroad tracks. It also needs little or no fertilizer, though a light application in the spring will increase its density and intensify its foliage color.

Care

Deadhead to increase blooms. Once plants have quit blooming, cut back dead flower heads. To increase plantings, divide clumps in the fall or spring. If common yarrow gets out of control, dig up unwanted plants and pass them along to friends. Do warn them, however, that this plant is aggressive, even invasive. Yarrow is pest free.

Companion Planting and Design

Yarrow is often used as a spreading groundcover between taller perennials in borders, or under the light shade of small flowering trees such as chaste tree or crape myrtle. It can be an excellent rock garden addition as well. Yellow selections are stunning with purple or blue salvias, oxeye daisy, coreopsis, and purple coneflower. It is one of the mainstay companion plants for daylily society show gardens, because it complements rather than competes with daylily flowers and foliage.

Personal Favorites

Varieties of common yarrow (*A. millefolium*) include deep pink 'Cerise Queen' and 'Fire King', a dark rose with yellow centers that spreads rapidly. Others include 'Lilac Beauty' and 'Fawcett Beauty'. Varieties of fernleaf yarrow (*A. filipendulina*) include 'Gold Plate' and 'Altgold'. The hybrids 'Coronation Gold' and 'Moonshine' have soft yellow blooms.

Easy to grow and long blooming, yarrow has pungently aromatic, ferny leaves which were often carried by soldiers and pioneers to use as a "wound wort" for wrapping bad cuts—a grow-your-own bandage, so to speak. Its spring and summer flowers, which are flat, round discs of white, yellow, gold, or rosy pink on sturdy long stems, can be cut and hung upside down in an airy place, where they will dry very well and retain their color in dried arrangements for months. Yarrow comes in many selections of different heights, with colors ranging from mustard yellow to brick red. Some types are invasive and may be difficult to contain.

Other Common Name
Milfoil

Bloom Period and Seasonal Color
White, yellow, rose, red, peach blooms in spring and summer

Mature Height × Spread
2 to 4 feet × 2 to 3 feet

Roses *for Alabama & Mississippi*

It's ironic that the beautiful, fragrant, historic rose—America's floral emblem—has such a bad garden reputation. Just ask around and you will find that nearly everyone who has tried to grow roses has run into difficulties ranging from how much sunshine is needed, what type of soil to grow them in, the right amounts of water and fertilizer, how to prune, and how to handle insect and disease problems. But you don't need to have a special rose garden to enjoy them. Forget the typical rose display gardens, cared for by meticulous rosarians and their trained helpers—there is no requirement that roses be grown in long rows with a sundial in the middle! Most roses can be worked quite easily into typical landscapes.

It is helpful to know that there are several completely different types of roses, and that each has many distinct varieties. Shrub roses can be large or small, and used as specimens or even hedges; climbing roses, which need a support, can be either once- or ever-blooming; miniature roses can be used as groundcovers, borders, or potted specimens. The most popular are the hybrid tea roses with long stems and cut-flower quality roses; many hybrid teas are prone to pest problems, but there are a few easy ones.

Antique roses are all the rage these days, but keep in mind that not all "old garden" roses (those grown before the first hybrid tea was introduced in the mid-1860s) are good roses—some were poor performers a hundred years ago, and still are. But while it is certainly true that some popular varieties, both modern and antique, are fussy, some great roses are easy! You've seen them around old home sites and country gardens, blooming their hearts out with no care at all. This chapter will highlight a few of the roses that are rewarding in our climate and busy lifestyles, without being troublesome. Choosing the right type of rose, and selecting its tried-and-true varieties, is a huge first step in your success and enjoyment, and will boost your confidence in growing roses until you, too, can call yourself a rose grower.

Hybrid Musk Rose 'Cornelia'

Container or Bare Root

Roses come either already potted and ready to go, or as "bare-root" plants, which saves growers on shipping costs. Roots of bare-root roses can dry out quickly and die, so most of the time their roots are kept in moist sawdust before being put into plastic bags for sale. If you choose to buy bare-root roses, have the soil already prepared so when you purchase them you can immediately soak their roots and plant as quickly as possible. Do not allow the roots to dry out—even for a few minutes! After planting, water deeply but do not keep plant roots wet or they can rot.

Most gardeners buy potted roses, which can be planted nearly any time of the year, as long as you can dig a nice hole amended with a little organic matter. In many cases, the roses were brought into the garden center in bundles of bare-root plants, and were potted up by garden center staff. Sometimes these roses will not be completely rooted in the containers, so when you pull them out of their pots the potting soil will just fall off. In any case, when planting container-grown roses, be sure to loosen some of the potting soil and spread roots out, which helps roses get off to a great start and get established to your own native soil more quickly.

Grafted or Rooted

Many commercially available roses have been created by grafting desirable roses onto sturdier roots, which helps them deal with heavy soils, root diseases, and nematodes (microscopic "root worms" found in sandy soils). Often the graft works for only a few years before the grafted (upper) part of the plant dies, in which case the rootstock—usually a rambling sort of red rose—sprouts and takes over.

"Own-root" roses are grown from cuttings and can live for many years. To help plants with weaker roots have their best chance at survival, take extra time and effort with soil preparation, making sure the soil is dug wide (2 or more feet across) and partly amended with organic matter. You can root your own roses by taking pencil-size or larger cuttings from recent growth in the late fall and sticking them into a sunny, well-drained flower bed, even without "rooting hormones," and they will root over the winter. Some roses root better than others, but this is how it has been done for many centuries. Transplant in the spring. For the best success with roses, adhere to the following good gardening practices.

Planting and Growing Roses Well

Roses like rich, fluffy soil with excellent drainage. Do whatever you have to do to achieve that. Dig your native soil—no matter what the quality—a solid shovel's depth and extra wide, then add a fair amount of organic matter such as bark, peat, compost, or manure (better yet, a blend of several types). Mix one part

Shrub Roses with Bearded Iris

organic matter to two parts native soil. If a soil test has indicated you have overly acidic soil, now is the time to work lime into the bed. Choose a site that has as much sun as possible. Give the roses plenty of room for air to circulate to reduce diseases. When planting, set plants slightly above the soil around them and mound soil up to them, to ensure proper drainage. Cover the soil surface with enough pine straw, shredded bark, or other mulch to keep the sun from shining directly on the soil, and add enough extra mulch to allow for settling.

Water deeply, not frequently. Roses need a deep soaking only when they get really dry; established plants in well-prepared soil can go for weeks without water. Mulches will help conserve moisture. Fertilize sparingly. Some roses bloom for years without being fed. However, yours will do much better if you broadcast an all-purpose fertilizer under the shrubs at least once a year in late March or April, and perhaps a light second feeding in late August.

Pest Control

The best thing to do for pests and diseases is either to not look at your roses too closely, or to start an all-consuming pesticide spray program—there's no in-between approach. Two common rose diseases are blackspot and powdery mildew, and the best defense is a good offense: planting disease-resistant roses. Tiny spider mites suck sap from the undersides of leaves, and thrips (very small cigar-shaped insects) get into and distort flower buds; there are no great controls for either. Tidiness helps, however. Remove fallen leaves and petals from beneath the plant (insect pests and fungal diseases use these as a breeding ground), and remove discolored or damaged leaves from the shrub.

Prune for a Reason

Don't make this difficult. Most roses bloom on new growth, so prune them by a third or half in late winter to keep them compact and bushy, and again after blooming or in late summer for sturdy new fall growth. Those that bloom only once in the spring can be pruned after they finish. Climbers need only a few errant canes removed. But never prune a grafted rose below the knotty-looking graft, or you will end up with only a wild rootstock rose.

Use hand pruners that work with a scissors-like motion to cut cleanly through stems. Loppers may be easier to use on thick stems. To promote strong new growth and to open up the plant for better air circulation, most rose growers recommend pruning right above a "five-leaflet leaf" that points outward from the center of the plant; however, most folks just cut off faded flowers and let it go at that. When cutting long-stemmed roses for flower arrangements, have a deep bucket of fresh water handy. Immediately put the cut roses into it, covering as much of the stem as possible, or the cut ends will seal off and your flowers won't last as long. Cut the ends again when placing in the arrangement.

Rose Companions

A surprising number of combinations of roses and other plants grow well together and complement one another in shape, form, texture, and color. So-called "companion" plants can also be used to help one another blend and fill the garden through all the seasons, as long as they tolerate the same basic growing conditions (sun, soil, water, and, especially if you choose to spray, pesticides). A few good companions for roses are:

- Bulbs such as daffodils, rain lily, chives, blazing star, garlic, and painted arum
- Annuals including pansies, violas, pentas, marigolds, and narrow-leaf zinnia
- Perennials such as salvia, iris, soapwort, yarrow, daylily, rosemary, and artemisia

- Groundcovers such as ivy, liriope, and mondo grass
- Evergreen accent plants, especially boxwood, juniper, arborvitae, and nandina
- Airy large shrubs or small trees such as yaupon or possumhaw holly, or chaste tree

And all roses look good when grown near some sort of "hard feature" such as a large urn, bench, birdbath, formal sculpture, arbor, or contemporary art. Choose something that suits the style and scale of your house and garden.

Floribunda Rose 'Playboy'

Different Types of Roses

There are many different types of roses you can grow well, even without owning a pesticide sprayer. Below are the most popular ones and just a few favorites of each, based on beauty, fragrance, and low maintenance. Try a few of these and some companions in appropriate settings, and see if they don't either satisfy your romantic landscape desires, or whet your appetite for more roses than you ever dreamed possible.

Hybrid Tea

'Peace'

This popular rose type outsells all other kinds of roses combined, but is the one that gives roses their fussy reputation. Hybrid tea roses were bred for long stems and shapely flowers (both in bud and fully open). Their plants, which reach 6 feet or taller, have several sometimes-spindly stems with foliage that is prone to diseases, and require frequent feeding, pruning, and watering for best growth. Some gardeners treat them as short-lived plants and replace them as needed. They are best used as specimens or in rows to make care and cutting for bouquets easier.

Personal Favorites: 'Mr. Lincoln' (red), 'Tropicana' (orange), 'Lafter' (orange-pink and yellow), 'First Prize' (pink), 'Oregold' (yellow), 'Peace' (pink and yellow), 'Summer Sunshine' (yellow), and 'Garden Party' (white)

Floribunda

'Iceberg'

Floribundas are usually medium-sized shrubs that constantly produce very large sprays of small, sometimes hybrid-tea-like roses. They are generally low-maintenance bushes that make outstanding informal hedges, low borders, barriers, or container plants, or can be planted to peek through fences. They tolerate shearing better than other larger roses, which will make them produce abundant flowers over a long period of time.

Personal Favorites: 'Europeana' (red), 'Showbiz' (red), 'Eutin' (the old red rose seen in most small towns), 'Betty Prior' (pink), 'Gene Boerner' (pink), 'First Edition' (orange and pink), 'Sun Flare' (yellow), 'Sunsprite' (yellow), 'Iceberg' (white), 'Trumpeter' (orange-red)

Grandiflora

These vigorous shrubs sometimes grow to 10 feet tall and nearly as wide, with cut-flower-quality, hybrid-tea-like flowers sometimes in long-stemmed clusters. Many are crosses between hybrid teas and floribundas, combining the flower form of the former and the sturdiness of the latter. They are easily used in masses for stunning color effect (and more cut flowers—or lots of petals for special occasions), or as background and barrier hedges.

Personal Favorites: 'Queen Elizabeth' (pink), 'Pink Parfait' (pink), 'Tournament of Roses' (pink), 'Gold Medal' (yellow), 'White Lightnin' (white)

'Gold Medal'

Polyantha

Similar to floribundas but older, polyanthas have multiple, small flowers on compact shrubs. They bloom continuously throughout spring, summer, and fall. Many are disease resistant and some are fragrant. Because they are smaller plants than many roses, they are well suited for use as borders, groundcovers, or low hedges, and are well-behaved additions to perennial and shrub beds. 'The Fairy', which dates back to 1932, remains one of the most popular polyanthas.

Personal Favorites: 'The Fairy' (pink), 'Caldwell Pink' (pink), 'Cécile Brünner' (light pink, the famous old "sweetheart" rose), 'Clotilde Soupert' (white double with pinkish centers), 'La Marne' (pink blend), 'Marie Pavie' (very fragrant pinkish white), 'Perle d'Or' (peachy yellow)

'La Marne'

Shrub Roses

'Carefree Beauty'

Shrub roses have been bred for general landscape use, and combine cold-hardy, disease-resistant, many-branched plants with showy, usually ever-blooming flowers. Modern shrub roses produce open, single or double flowers in a soft pastel range, with aging flowers usually fading into muted shades. They are commonly used in parks and public gardens because of their low maintenance. The several types of shrub roses include hybrid musk roses (large shrubs or small climbers), English or David Austin roses, groundcover roses, and miscellaneous others.

Personal Favorites: 'Knock Out' (pinkish red), 'Belinda's Dream' (hybrid-tea-like pink), 'Will Scarlet' (red hybrid musk), 'Cornelia' (pink hybrid musk), 'Heritage' (pink David Austin), 'Flower Carpet Pink' (deep pink groundcover), 'Graham Thomas' (golden yellow David Austin), 'Bonica' (pink), 'Carefree Beauty' (rose pink), 'Simplicity' (pink), and the Meidiland series

Tea and China Roses

'Mutabilis'

Until the "discovery" of ever-blooming and yellow roses from China, most European roses were once-bloomers in hues of red and pink. Hybridizers quickly crossed these different types of ancient plants to change rose history by creating the hybrid tea rose. China roses are large shrubs that love the South and are used as specimens, as hedges, and in borders. Tea roses are tall, upright shrubs with bronzy-red new foliage and a strong, distinct green-tea-like fragrance.

Personal Favorites: 'Old Blush' (pink China), 'Martha Gonzalez' (little red China), 'Mutabilis' ("butterfly" rose, multi-color large China), 'Sombreuil' (climbing white tea), 'Duchess de Brabant' (very fragrant pink tea), 'Cramoisi Superieur' (red China climber), and 'Louis Philippe' (crimson China)

Miniature

"Minis" are small ever-blooming replicas of hybrid tea and floribunda roses, most under 18 to 24 inches tall and in varied flower colors. They are accepted in competition as "show" roses. Very hardy outdoors, they are ideal for small gardens, borders, window boxes, and containers—even indoors in cool, sunny windows. They require more frequent watering than larger roses with more wide-ranging roots. Though most are "own-root" plants, they require attention to pruning, and especially pest control.

'Rise 'n' Shine'

Personal Favorites: 'Rise 'n' Shine' (yellow), 'Snow Bride' (white), 'Green Ice' (white), 'Giggles' (medium pink), and 'Fairhope' (pale yellow)

Climbing

Climbers have graceful, arching canes that grow from 10 to 30 feet long. They come in a variety of types, including old-fashioned ramblers (which need a lot of space and bloom fabulously once a year), and large-flowered climbers (many are repeat bloomers). Not true vines, climbing roses require sturdy supports to which their arching canes must be tied; prune by thinning old or wayward stems right after they flower in the spring. For more information on climbing roses see the Vines chapter.

'New Dawn'

Personal Favorites: 'New Dawn' (creamy pink), *Rosa banksiae* (the Lady Banks' rose, soft yellow and fragrant white forms, blooms only in the spring, thornless), 'Altissimo' (blood red), 'Dortmund' (fragrant, dark red), 'Climbing American Beauty' (deep pink, fragrant, once-blooming), 'American Pillar' (reddish pink rambler), 'Zephirine Drouhin' (dark pink, nearly thornless), 'Climbing Old Blush' (pink ever-bloomer), and 'Red Cascades' (small intensely red rambler)

Shrubs *for Alabama & Mississippi*

Shrubs—often called "bushes"—ask little and give a lot. Provide them with the right amount of light, fairly good soil, a little fertilizer, and a blanket of mulch over their roots and they are good to go, often for many decades with little or no problems. And no job is too big or too small for shrubs. They can be used to tone down or hide a home's foundation, "anchor" the corners visually, and balance a structure's features. They can "tie" bigger plants together or be used to divide large landscapes into smaller, more manageable "rooms." They can attract and focus attention as strong accents, or lead the eye around a space through repetition. They carry a garden through all the seasons, as other plants come in and out of flower.

Large shrubs can protect smaller shrubs and shade-loving perennials, or line a walk as small trees do. They can screen views, and provide important food and shelter for birds and other wildlife. Small shrubs can fill space that otherwise would be high-maintenance lawn. They can provide seasonal flowers, foliage texture and color, and fruit. They provide greenery for holidays, and can conjure memories of people and places past. Given the right conditions, most shrubs are easy to grow, and will work for you for many years, through thick and thin. These characteristics can help decide placement of new shrubs, in general order of importance:

- Mature size and shape (tall-, medium-, or low-growing; upright or spreading; round or pointed)
- Evergreen or deciduous
- Light requirements (sun or shade)
- Foliage texture (bold or fine) and flowers (season and color)

Oakleaf Hydrangea—Alabama's Official State Wildflower

Azaleas

- Special features (berries, fragrance, being attractive to wildlife)
- Tolerance of native soil (who wants to keep amending the soil?)
- Ease of care (pruning needs, potential serious pest problems)
- How many you really need considering the holes you will have to dig)

Basics of Digging a Good Shrub Hole

The first big mistake often made is choosing the wrong plant for the wrong space, and the second most important mistake, made even by professional landscapers, is doing a poor job of preparing soil, which can make or break a shrub's chances of survival. The old adage is, "It is better to dig a five-dollar hole for a fifty-cent plant than a fifty-cent hole for a five dollar plant." The better job you do preparing the soil, the better the shrub will grow and the less trouble it will be later.

When digging a hole for an individual shrub, dig it just deep enough to set the plant's rootball flush with the ground around it, but dig it really wide—two or three times wider than the rootball. Then loosen the soil a little in the bottom of the hole, and chop up and roughen the sides. Then always— always—loosen the potting soil and roots of the plant. Never deviate from this. Stir the potting soil with maybe a little extra bark or compost (a shovelful or two per plant) into the native soil, and use that to fill in around the new plant. Water the plant really well to settle the soil mix around roots, and cover the area with bark, pine straw, or even grass clippings to shade the soil and keep it from compacting in the sun and rain. Sometimes you can mix in a little all-purpose fertilizer with the backfill soil, but usually store-bought plants come with enough to feed them for a few weeks or months. And that's it: Dig wide, add a little stuff, loosen roots, water, and mulch. For entire shrub beds, do the same thing, only wider or longer.

Some garden centers, especially those that sell to professional landscapers, carry "balled and burlapped" shrubs and trees, which are field-grown in regular soil, dug in the winter, and their cut roots wrapped in burlap, sometime secured within a wire cage. They are often excellent plants because their roots are already accustomed to growing in "real dirt." When planting them, be sure to loosen the burlap at the top of the root ball, and tuck it back into the soil out of direct sunshine to keep it from acting like a wick and drying the plants out. If you can remove the wire cage and most of the burlap without the

Beautyberry

root ball falling apart that is even better; unlike natural materials used in the past, most burlap today is synthetic and does not decay well underground. Twine, burlap, and wire cages left strapped to shrubs and trees can actually strangle roots and prevent them from growing out into the surrounding soil, leading to the eventual decline of the plant. When planting, remember to watch your back—"B-and-B" plants are usually much heavier than container-grown ones.

Now, if after you have dug such a perfect hole and carefully planted the shrub, you decide to move it, don't despair. "When can I move a shrub?" is a frequently asked question. Sometimes gardeners have made honest mistakes. Sometimes they are living with the shrubby mistakes of homeowners who preceded them. Wait until the shrub goes dormant, say December or January, and move it to the desired spot. This gives it time to get re-established before the summer heat and minimizes "transplant shock."

Watering Shrubs

Most shrubs can live for years on just rainfall— if you don't believe it, just look around your neighborhood. But a slow, deep soaking every few weeks helps them tremendously. Frequent shallow watering will encourage the shrubs to grow roots near the soil surface, which are more likely to be damaged by a subsequent lack of water, or even severe cold. Over-watering—including the weekly use of an irrigation system—can also cause roots to rot, so don't do it. Newly planted shrubs are more likely to need extra watering, especially their first summer. And plants enduring a severe drought—even plants that have been in the garden for years—can need relief. Mulch helps to keep moisture in the ground around the roots and this simple step can lessen the drought stress on the shrubs and the work you will have to do to keep the plants thriving.

Pruning Shrubs

Well-chosen and placed shrubs may never need pruning except to remove dead or wayward growth. Shearing new growth creates a tight, neat appearance, but usually requires even more shearing later.

Holly

Thinning only tall growth may not look as neat, but can be accomplished with pruners or loppers. "Pick-pruning" and "cloud pruning" are methods that give a more natural shape to shrubs; simply clip back any growth that has extended past the general shrub shape, cutting it a little deeper into the shrub to allow for later growth and let in some light. "Limbing up" large shrubs into small trees saves much work in the long run, because you only need to worry about sprouts forming along the trunk and can basically let the top grow.

To rejuvenate a completely overgrown shrub, such as a forsythia, you can whack the entire thing back (depending on the type of shrub) to a foot or so, or cut back some portion (maybe one-third) of it to 8 to 12 inches from the ground each year for two or three years. Which method you choose—drastic and short-term or careful and long-term—depends on the type of plant and how valuable it is to you. Some shrubs respond to pruning better than others, and you should never cut conifer branches back to where there is no green growth or you will likely lose the entire branch. Most deciduous shrubs will branch better if you cut back to a "node," or point where there are leaves or branches; if you cut a stem between nodes you might have to look at stubs for a while. Flowering shrubs should be pruned after they finish blooming. For more information on pruning, see the general introduction in the front of this book.

Since shrubs and trees form the "backbone" of the landscape, it is important to choose them wisely and site them well—they will be with you a long time. Assess your current landscape and your needs, and research your options before installing any significant plantings. These days there are numerous shrub options available, for every garden situation. While it is good to have an overall plan for your yard, you can minimize the amount of labor (and the expense) incurred at any one time by spreading out the planting of the larger elements across several seasons.

The goal is to make gardening simpler, not more complicated. If you are planning a new landscape or major overhaul, you should perhaps consult a designer about shrubs and trees. They will be your biggest investment of time and money. But don't get locked into someone else's vision for your garden—remember, some people think poison ivy is pretty in the fall!

Abelia

Abelia × grandiflora

One of the hardiest evergreen shrubs for low-maintenance gardens is abelia, a medium-to-large bush with long, arching, brown-barked branches and small, glossy, pointed leaves. Abelia grows well in sun or shade, and is tough enough to grow for decades with little care, and can be pruned into a tight form or allowed to spread into a large, airy mass. Clusters of white flowers, each with a pink bract that remains after the flower sheds, are produced from spring to late summer (later if you tip-prune), and are rich in nectar and pollen. Abelia will be covered not only with butterflies, hummingbirds, and clear-wing moths, but also honeybees—so many bees, in fact, that you should not plant it too close to a busy sidewalk or patio.

Other Common Name
Glossy Abelia

Bloom Period and Seasonal Color
White flowers and pink bracts in spring and summer

Mature Height × Spread
3 to 6 feet × 4 to 6 feet

When, Where, and How to Plant

Container-grown abelia is readily available all year, and can be planted any time. It flowers well in sun or shade, but foliage is denser in full sun. Abelia tolerates a wide range of soils, but is susceptible to root rot in heavy, wet soils. Dig a wide hole, amend very lightly if at all with organic matter, and loosen roots when planting. Keep a layer of mulch over roots to reduce water needs and to protect trunks from string trimmer damage. Most container-grown plants have been heavily fertilized during production and do not need a lot of fertilizer the first year in the ground.

Growing Tips

Water only the first summer to get plants established, and feed very lightly every two or three springs by broadcasting an all-purpose fertilizer under the spread of the branches.

Care

Prune long shoots to make the shrubs more compact and produce more flowering stems—this is easily done with tip-pruning in spring and summer—or simply thin a few long stems to maintain a loose informal shape. Heavy pruning, to a foot or so tall, can be done in winter or spring to get overgrown plants back to a manageable size. There are no major insect or disease problems.

Companion Planting and Design

Formal designs require abelia to be pruned quite often, so use it as a very good informal hedge, or mass planting in large areas. Work it into the back of a shrub or flower border, or in front of trees such as pine or Southern magnolia. It is a good complement to camellias. Dwarf forms can be interplanted with perennials, bulbs, and roses.

Personal Favorites

'Francis Mason' is compact and low growing with yellow variegated leaves. 'Prostrata' makes a good groundcover. 'Sherwoodii' is a densely compact form. Chinese abelia (*A. chinensis*) is a loose shrub with extra-large, thick clusters of flowers. 'Edward Goucher' is a very popular dwarf, pink-flowering hybrid.

Althea
Hibiscus syriacus

When, Where, and How to Plant
Plant container-grown shrubs any time of the year, or plant young seedlings or bare-root plants in the winter when they are available. Althea roots readily from pencil-size stem cuttings taken in fall or winter. Rose of Sharon blooms well in sun or light shade, but requires a very well-drained soil. For a thick hedge, set plants 4 or 5 feet apart. Dig or till an area at least twice as wide as the rootball and mix a little compost or soil conditioner and all-purpose fertilizer with your native soil. Water deeply and add a layer of mulch.

Growing Tips
Established plants need little water if any, even in severe summer droughts (they are native to the arid Plains of Sharon of the Old Testament). Fertilize lightly in the spring, but do not overdo it or expect leggy growth and few flowers.

Care
Althea blooms on new growth, so prune in late winter or spring. Leave unpruned to enjoy the papery husky seedpods, but expect to pull the few seedlings that will result from letting the plant form seeds. Althea is susceptible to aphids and whiteflies, but neither is usually serious enough to spray. Old leaves turn bright yellow before shedding, a process which may start early and look like a problem.

Companion Planting and Design
Plant where you will enjoy its summer blooms, near a patio or deck, for instance. In a large garden, it is useful as a summer-blooming hedge or barrier between garden areas, and can be trained to grow and flower over an arbor almost like a climbing rose. Plant smaller shrubs and medium-sized perennials such as yarrow, daylily, or salvia in front to hide the leggy lower trunks of althea, and underplant with spring bulbs like grape hyacinth and small daffodils.

Personal Favorites
Though there are many great old-fashioned varieties to root from plants in other gardens, three of the best althea varieties are the large-flowered, ever-blooming, non-seeding white 'Diana', dark pink 'Aphrodite', sky blue 'Blue Bird', and lavender-violet 'Minerva' with its dark red eye.

A hardy, old-fashioned shrub, althea dresses up the garden for summer with large, hollyhock-like blooms and pretty yellow fall color; it blooms fairly well even in moderate shade. Althea was common in gardens around the turn of the twentieth century and is one of several old-fashioned shrubs coming back into vogue. It needs plenty of space unless you prune it back every spring. Left to form a natural shape, it makes a pretty summer-blooming hedge in a large or country garden. Old-fashioned selections of althea reseed, and are easy to come by if you know someone who has them in their garden. There are many selections in the nursery trade, including new hybrids that bloom up to three or four months and have large flowers that do not form viable seeds.

Other Common Name
Rose of Sharon

Bloom Period and Seasonal Color
Purple, red, pink, blue, white, and striped blooms in summer

Mature Height × Spread
6 to 12 feet × 6 to 12 feet

Arborvitae
Thuja occidentalis

Arborvitae means "tree of life"—and the shrub, or at least its modern forms, continues to bring gardens to life. The traditional arborvitae is a large, teardrop-shaped shrub with dense, flattened fans of bright green foliage (that can harbor wasp nests). Once ridiculed as hopelessly old-fashioned and overbearing, with its new dwarf cultivars in more manageable shapes and variety of foliage hues it has become one of the hottest trends in European and cottage gardens. Arborvitae also offers versatility and hardiness through thick and thin and all seasons. Tough enough to grow without special care, modern enough to fit beside a contemporary glass house, rustic enough to blend with wood cottages, this plant has something to offer every gardener, regardless of what snooty designers say.

Bloom Period and Seasonal Color
Evergreen with bluish summer and fall fruits

Mature Height × Spread
2 to 10 feet × 2 to 6 feet

When, Where, and How to Plant
Plant arborvitae any time of the year, in full sun or light shade where water does not stand for more than two or three hours after a heavy rain. Dig a moderately wide hole, lightly amend with organic matter, and loosen potbound roots. Plant a little on the high side with soil sloped up to the plant's original soil line, and mulch lightly with pine straw. Space 2 to 6 feet apart, depending on the cultivar.

Growing Tips
Water deeply but only occasionally the first summer, and feed very lightly in the late winter or spring to encourage a good flush of new growth.

Care
No need to ever prune these compact growers, whose shape is predetermined by what variety you buy. Shearing new foliage lightly in the early summer will help make the plants bushier, but is not recommended. When working close to an arborvitae in the summer, always prod the plant to check for wasp nests. The worst pest is bagworm, a caterpillar that crawls around with a silk-and-twig bag. Handpick or spray with biological worm spray.

Companion Planting and Design
Arborvitae is so easy to use in any setting—historic hedge, Oriental garden, suburban foundation corner planting, strong accent for contemporary style buildings, large containers, or as "bones" in a perennial border for summer contrast and winter interest. Its odd shapes and bright colors help it complement nearly anything: Leyland cypress, nandina, azalea, daylily, iris, soft tip yucca, crape myrtle, bulbs, anything at all. Combining several cultivars with different colors and forms looks good also.

Personal Favorites
'Emerald' is a dense, narrow cone to about 15 feet tall and 4 feet wide; 'Globosa' remains a tight ball about 4 feet high; 'Rheingold' is cone shaped, bright golden, and slow growing to about 5 feet tall; 'Woodwardii' is an old-fashioned globular type that grows slowly to about 8 feet tall. There are many others.

Beautyberry
Callicarpa americana

When, Where, and How to Plant
Plant container-grown shrubs almost any time of the year, even in the summer, if watered regularly. Transplant small wild shrubs (with permission from the landowner) in the fall or winter; prune transplants to help compensate for root loss. Plant in sun or light shade, in rich, well-drained soil. Allow at least 5 feet between beautyberry and a structure or between shrubs in a border. Dig an area at least twice as wide as the rootball (three to five times as wide is better, but no deeper than its height). Mulch to protect new plant roots until they become shaded by foliage.

Growing Tips
Water this very hardy native shrub only during extreme dry spells, just to preserve the fruit for fall, and to keep the large leaves from shedding too early; too much water can cause leaf diseases. Feed lightly in the spring, perhaps not even every year.

Care
Beautyberry blooms on new growth, so can be cut back in late winter to control size and create lots of branches for more flowers and berries. Beautyberry is free of major pests, though whiteflies may be a nuisance; no control is recommended. In the hot summer, beautyberry's large leaves naturally wilt during the day, but revive at dusk.

Companion Planting and Design
Beautyberry makes a good specimen plant in front of an evergreen background, and does well in shrub borders, especially in natural areas under high shade. Plant where you will walk by or can easily enjoy its berries and the birds attracted by the berries. This large species can overtake nearby shrubs; underplant with spring bulbs that will flower when beautyberry is dormant. For a spectacular fall display plant asters, goldenrods, sunflowers, and ornamental grasses nearby.

Personal Favorites
The native species is big and bold, and has a white-berried form (*C. americana* var. *lactea*). Asian beautyberries, especially *C. dichotoma*, smaller with cascading foliage and smaller berries, are more refined and suitable for small garden areas.

Beautyberry is so exotic looking that most people who see it in landscapes are amazed that it could be a common woodland native. The mounding, medium-sized shrub does grow naturally—almost prolifically—in the dry woods of the Southeast, but it really isn't invasive or hard to control. Every leaf joint on its long branches produces a loose bunch of small, pale pink blooms in spring and summer, which turn into golf-ball-shaped clusters of hot purple-pink berries that birds can easily spot. The berries, which birds love, are edible to humans, but are very mealy and bland tasting. The berries persist until after the large leaves shed in late summer and early fall.

Other Common Names
French Mulberry, Spanish Mulberry

Bloom Period and Seasonal Color
Pink blooms in spring and summer, purple berries in late summer and fall

Mature Height × Spread
3 to 8 feet × 4 to 8 feet

Blueberry

Vaccinium species

Talk about a four-season shrub—pretty, pinkish-white, bell-shaped flowers in early spring; fantastic sweet blue fruit in the summer; eye-popping red fall colors; and an architectural form with pretty, peely bark in the winter. That's what native blueberry shrubs offer. Even if birds get a lot of the fruit, the plants are outstanding landscape plants. They produce the largest, sweetest berries when two or more different varieties are interplanted, which also extends the harvest season by up to two months. Commercial growers have come up with extra-sweet, extra-large, extra-early varieties that home gardeners can get for their own landscapes. Make room for several types if you can.

Other Common Names
Rabbit-eye Blueberry, Southern High-bush Blueberry

Bloom Period and Seasonal Color
Pinkish-white spring blooms, blue summer fruit, red fall colors

Mature Height × Spread
5 to 8 feet × 3 to 6 feet

When, Where, and How to Plant

Blueberries bought as container plants can be set out any time but require watering. Bare-root plants or suckers cut from mature plants must be planted in the fall or winter. Plant in full sun or light shade, spaced 3 to 6 feet apart, depending on whether you want a hedge or individual plants. Blueberries require rich, acidic soils high in organic matter, so mix lots of peat moss and bark with native soil. Mulch deeply with pine straw.

Growing Tips

Water shallow-rooted blueberries generously in the summer, to help fruit firm up and to encourage new flower bud formation for the next year. Weekly soakings are ideal, but a good soaking at least every two or three weeks is acceptable; soaker hoses make this much easier. Fertilize extremely lightly in mid-spring with an all-purpose fertilizer or an acid-forming azalea-camellia fertilizer. A scant handful per plant is plenty.

Care

Pruning is not tricky, but should be precise: Tip-prune new growth as it appears in spring and early summer to make it branch out for more berries next year; stop pruning by early summer. After harvest, completely cut down the tallest stems and any wayward branches to rejuvenate the plants, regardless of how well they produced or how much new growth they have. Blueberries suffer sometimes from twig dieback that should be pruned out immediately, and from stinkbugs and birds. Netting helps deter the latter.

Companion Planting and Design

Blueberries grow well in hedges or small mixed groups for easy picking. Use them as understory shrubs under high pines. They show up well against a backdrop of dense evergreen magnolias or a fence or wall. Underplant with liriope or mondo grass, which tolerates intense growing conditions.

Personal Favorites

Good rabbit-eye (*V. ashei*) varieties include 'Climax' (early), 'Tifblue' (midseason), 'Powderblue' (midseason), and 'Centurion' (late). Good southern high-bush varieties (hybrids between rabbit-eye and northern high-bush blueberries) include 'O'Neal' (early), 'Georgiagem' (early), 'Magnolia' (mid), and 'Summit' (mid to late).

Bottlebrush Buckeye
Aesculus parviflora

When, Where, and How to Plant

Plant container-grown shrubs almost any time of the year, even in the summer, but water deeply and fairly often the first summer to get plants established, especially when grown near other mature plants. If new plants wilt, don't over-water—instead, snip off some older foliage to reduce demand on struggling roots. Plant in light shade, in rich, moist, "woodsy" soil, and mulch heavily. Space plants at least 6 or 8 feet apart and they will quickly grow together with suckers; for one large specimen plant allow 10 or 12 feet from other shrubs, trees, or structures.

Growing Tips

Water deeply as needed during dry spells, especially when the shrubs are grown under thirsty trees, but don't over-water if leaves appear to droop during the day; wait to see if they perk up in the evening. Feed very lightly in the spring with an all-purpose fertilizer, and keep a thick natural leaf mulch under plants to encourage sucker growth.

Care

Rejuvenate older, overgrown bottlebrush buckeye plantings only when they extend far out of bounds, by sawing large plants close to the ground and pruning suckers back to about a third of their height. Thin growth that gets too close to walkways. No real pests bother this native beauty, but root rot can occur in heavy or wet soils.

Companion Planting and Design

In nature, it grows in colonies in wooded areas, along creeks and rivers. It is a good choice for planting in drifts and naturalizing or lining a shady path, but put it far back from the walk and allow it to spread forward. Bottlebrush buckeye also works well in a shady hedge or as a specimen shrub in front of an evergreen background. Interplant with the contrasting foliage of evergreen Florida leucothoe, holly, and abelia.

Personal Favorites

The species is stunning enough, but the somewhat hard-to-find *A. parviflora* var. *serotina* 'Rogers' has much longer flowers, up to 2 feet long or more, blooming later than the species or variety.

This stunning plant should be considered one of the top ten native shrubs for the landscape—you can see a lot of it in the woods, growing in thin colonies; but in the garden and at the edge of woodlands it gets thicker and fuller, spreading by underground "suckers" to make sometimes large colonies. Its leaves, which are divided into several long leaflets in a palmate pattern, create a large, graceful mound of handsome green. This shrub is topped from May to July or later with showy, upright white plumes 10 to 15 inches long, that attract butterflies. The fall color is golden yellow. Planting it behind a low rock wall, backed by equally stunning Southern magnolia, creates a wonderful "sense of place" landscape.

Bloom Period and Seasonal Color

White blooms in summer with golden yellow fall foliage

Mature Height × Spread

8 to 15 feet × 8 to 12 feet

Boxwood
Buxus sempervirens

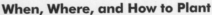

Nothing says "green shrub" better than boxwood. Slow-growing and dense, boxwoods are aristocrats of the Southern garden, used for many centuries in Europe and around the Mediterranean, then in colonial America. Large, older specimens around antebellum homes and old home places are architectural treasures. Today, boxwood remains popular among herb gardeners, restorers of historic gardens, people who enjoy the clipped garden effect, and those who just have a fondness for the shrub. Stem cuttings are used in flower arrangements. Common boxwood can get over 10 feet tall and wide, but can be pruned easily to keep it within bounds, or smaller types can be used. Its tiny flowers and small, oval leaves are lightly fragrant; some people enjoy the scent while others do not.

Other Common Name
Box

Bloom Period and Seasonal Color
Evergreen foliage

Mature Height × Spread
3 to 20 feet × 3 to 15 feet

When, Where, and How to Plant
Plant any time of the year, even in the summer. Boxwoods can grow in full sun, but do even better (with less foliage burn and spider mite damage) when planted in light shade. Plant boxwood in rich, moist, well-drained soil. Boxwood grows slowly, but remember to allow plenty of space for its mature size. Set foundation plants 3 to 4 feet or more from the house, allowing 3 feet between shrubs in a hedge (closer for smaller varieties).

Growing Tips
Water boxwood deeply during summer drought, especially in the fall, or risk losing parts of the shrub to sudden hard freezes; do not keep wet. Mature plants require little fertilizer, so apply an all-purpose fertilizer only in the spring.

Care
Shearing old growth in the late winter and new growth in the summer promotes denser growth. Avoid shearing in the fall or risk winter damage to new growth. Old leggy plants may require heavy pruning; however, because boxwoods are slow to return from heavy pruning, this is best done in late winter or early spring. Clean out dead leaves under plants. Leaf miners and spider mites can discolor leaves, but sprays are difficult and have to be repeated regularly.

Companion Planting and Design
In addition to its use as a foundation planting, for lining walks, or creating boxed parterre gardens, boxwood is charming planted in containers. Dwarf boxwood is good for edging, as a small entrance plant, or a very low hedge. Best companions are smaller edging groundcovers such as mondo grass, or hardy bulbs, including daffodils, spider lily, painted arum, and grape hyacinth.

Personal Favorites
'Graham Blandy' is narrow and columnar; English or "edging" boxwood (*B. sempervirens* 'Suffruticosa') grows slowly to about 3 feet tall. Coastal gardeners should consider the more heat-tolerant littleleaf boxwood (*B. microphylla*), which generally only gets 4 or 5 feet tall, and its Japanese subspecies that gets 6 or so feet tall.

Butterfly Bush
Buddleia davidii

When, Where, and How to Plant
Plant container-grown buddleias any time, in full or part sun and away from other shrubs that hold humidity close (the fuzzy leaves can get mildewed with poor air circulation). Good drainage is essential, so do an especially good job of soil preparation, as you would for a rose, with plenty of organic matter added to your native soil. Apply a 3-inch layer of mulch. Allow at 6 or 8 feet between plants.

Growing Tips
Occasional deep soakings and two or three light feedings from spring to midsummer promote heavier flower production. However, don't irrigate regularly, or expect mildewed foliage and root damage.

Care
Butterfly bush blooms on new spring growth. In late winter cut shrubs back to about 2 feet to control size and stimulate strong new growth. It is very important to cut or break off spent flower heads as soon as they fade, to promote faster new flower production. Whiteflies and aphids may be problems some summers, but no control is usually needed. Sudden hard freezes may damage plants, but they usually come back from the roots.

Companion Planting and Design
Used as a specimen plant, in a shrub border, or as a hedge, butterfly bush is at its best when mixed with perennials—especially bold-flowered hibiscus, coarse-textured canna, black-eyed Susan, and ornamental grasses—and winter bulbs and pansies to bloom when the shrub is bare. It also looks good with bright annuals such as ornamental sweet potato and verbena.

Personal Favorites
"Weeping Mary" (*B. lindleyana*) is an unusual old "pass-along plant" that grows best in the southern half of our states. It spreads, and has cinnamon-colored peely bark and 2-foot cascading spikes of purple flowers. Of the "regular" butterfly bushes, 'Black Knight' has dark, almost purple flowers; 'Empire Blue' produces lovely, long-lasting periwinkle blue flowers; 'Ellen's Blue' is very fragrant. The Nanho series are dwarf and good for smaller gardens. 'Harlequin' has variegated leaves and reddish-purple flower spikes.

Old-fashioned and exotic, butterfly bush is a spring- and summer-blooming delight. When not in bloom, the irregular branches of the deciduous shrub, which can reach 8 feet tall or more, are easy to overlook, in spite of long, thin, green leaves that are white and fuzzy underneath. But the shrub is stunning in flower, with fat, mostly upright or cascading spikes of flowers covered with butterflies. Flowers are purple, blue, pink, or white. Sometimes damaged by sudden severe freezes, buddleja can be cut nearly to the ground each year to resprout with vigor. It has become weedy in some areas of the country, but generally stays put for us. Many selections are available, all of which require good drainage, an occasional soaking, and light pruning to keep flowers coming in abundance.

Other Common Name
Buddleia

Bloom Period and Seasonal Color
Purple, pink, white blooms in summer

Mature Height × Spread
6 to 8 feet × 6 to 8 feet

Camellia

Camellia japonica

The "rose of winter"—Alabama's official state flower—is produced on a stately, evergreen shrub that can easily get well over 10 or 12 feet tall with glossy, dark green foliage, in sun or shade. There are many hundred-year-old camellias in small towns across our states. The sometimes fist-size, rose-like blooms of pink, white, red, or streaked, produced from midwinter to mid-spring, can be single, double, or semi-double, and often produce enough buds to survive a few flowers being caught by a deep freeze. Most are not fragrant at all, but depend on beauty alone to attract admiring glances and pollinating bees. Plant early, mid-, and late-season varieties to have landscape color for many weeks when little else is in flower.

Bloom Period and Seasonal Color
Pink, white, red, striped blooms in winter

Mature Height × Spread
10 to 20 feet × 5 to 10 feet

When, Where, and How to Plant
Container-grown camellias can be set out any time, but in the winter when they are flowering you can see exactly what you are buying. It is often difficult to prepare the soil properly in midwinter or midsummer. Camellias have been grown for decades in full sun and moderately dense shade, but foliage and flowers usually look best when grown in light shade or with protection from hot afternoon sun. They will not tolerate heavy wet soils or very alkaline soils. Dig an extra-wide hole, and amend up to one-third with peat moss, bark, or other acid-forming amendment. Loosen roots when planting, and mulch heavily. Allow 5 to 10 feet between plants

Growing Tips
Water camellias deeply but not frequently, especially in mid- and late summer when winter flower buds begin to form. Fertilize lightly in the late winter or spring, if possible with a specialty acid-forming camellia-azalea fertilizer, or just an all-purpose fertilizer. Keep a thick layer of mulch over the entire planting area to keep roots cool and moist in the summer and protected from sudden winter changes.

Care
Prune camellias only to remove wayward branches, or lightly tip-prune new growth in the spring to thicken up summer growth and increase the number of flower buds. Scale insects on undersides of leaves can be treated with dormant oil in the late winter, and leaf gall can be picked off and removed from the area. Yellow leaves may be a sign of scale insects, root problems (usually too much water), or alkaline soil.

Companion Planting and Design
Camellias make excellent specimen trees, hedges, or understory fillers between pines. They contrast well with Japanese maples, crape myrtles, oakleaf hydrangeas, and azaleas, and help shade ferns, cast-iron plant, and caladium.

Personal Favorites
There are many good ones—and no two gardeners agree on which are the best; the best survivors from gardens of long ago include 'Pink Perfection', 'Elegans', 'Debutante', 'R.L. Wheeler', and 'Alba Plena'. There are many, many others.

158

Chinese Fringe
Loropetalum chinense

When, Where, and How to Plant
Set out container-grown plants any time of the year. They have good color in both sun and light shade, and will tolerate reflected heat from pavement when planted around pools or patios, and when espaliered against walls. Space plants 3 to 5 feet and expect them to quickly grow together. Dig wide holes and add plenty of peat and compost to create well-drained, slightly acidic conditions. Mulch after planting.

Growing Tips
Plants are very drought and heat tolerant, so water only to get young plants established or to help mature plants through very hot seasons. Fertilize lightly in the spring with an acid-forming azalea-camellia fertilizer or slow-acting soil-feeding cottonseed meal.

Care
No need to prune except to shape lopsided or overgrown shrubs by thinning unwanted limbs and branches; leave no stubs when pruning this way. Larger forms can be espaliered against a wall, or limbed up into small trees. Do not shear or you will ruin the naturally loose form of the plant. Minor whitefly infestations are the only concern, and they are usually not serious enough to warrant treatment.

Companion Planting and Design
The almost gaudy foliage of burgundy varieties is difficult to use judiciously except as companions in perennial and mixed shrub borders. Out in the open, plant in masses for a stunning effect. Complement with ornamental grasses, including miscanthus cultivars and burgundy fountain grass, with purple coneflowers and cannas, 'Autumn Joy' sedum, and blue-green groundcover junipers. Or go for a big splash with contrasting golden euonymus and 'New Gold' lantana. Underplant with winter bulbs.

Personal Favorites
The newer burgundy foliage varieties are becoming over-planted in some areas, but are still attractive. Examples include 'Burgundy' (red foliage fades to purple green, deep pink flowers), 'Razzleberri' (bronze red leaves fade to olive green, fuchsia pink flowers), and 'Fire Dance' (ruby red leaves fade to reddish purple, with deep pink flowers), and others.

Years ago, the witch-hazel flowers of Chinese fringe were less than impressive because they didn't bloom for very long, though the shrubs did offer tiers of arching branches and snappy green leaves. Now there are dazzling new burgundy, red, and purple foliage types available with pink flowers, bordering on gaudy, and they have grown dramatically in popularity. The clusters of flowers in spring, summer, and maybe a few in the fall are interesting with narrow, twisting petals, and the foliage is a real traffic stopper. The tough, pest-free plants will also hold up in heat and drought, which makes them all the more endearing.

Other Common Name
Chinese Witch Hazel

Bloom Period and Seasonal Color
Winter and spring flowers, all season color

Mature Height × Spread
4 to 15 feet × 3 to 12 feet

Cleyera

Ternstroemia gymnanthera

Evergreen and elegant, fast growing, and easy to prune, or allowed to grow into a small tree, cleyera is a darling of landscape designers. The polished, oval leaves resemble those of a rhododendron, but are smaller and arranged in attractive whorls. New growth is bronzy, and winter foliage takes on a mauve cast. Normally thought of as a medium-sized shrub, it can also reach 15 feet or more in height. Disease-resistant cleyera has attractive and highly fragrant late spring flowers that can be somewhat messy around a walk or deck, but are easy to sweep or blow away. Still, it is an ideal shrub anywhere you need a handsome, relatively carefree evergreen shrub, hedge, or small tree.

Bloom Period and Seasonal Color
Yellow blooms in May, red berries in fall

Mature Height × Spread
8 to 15 feet × 6 to 8 feet

When, Where, and How to Plant

Plant container-grown cleyera any time you can dig a wide hole. For a hedge effect, plant no closer than 6 or 8 feet. It is very thick when grown in full sun or light shade, but gets leggier in moderate shade and needs more pruning to stay compact. Avoid heavy clay soils, or amend them for better drainage. Spread roots wide during planting, cover the soil with mulch, and water during the first summer.

Growing Tips

Once established, cleyera thrives on little or no care at all—it is very drought tolerant, pest free, and in need of only occasional feeding every few years.

Care

Young cleyeras are fairly fast growing, but settle down with time and as new growth is pruned or "pinched" to make it fuller. Keeping cleyera pruned into small or medium shrubs is a never-ending task, but larger shrubs are easy to maintain with only occasional thinning of tall stems. Hard winters in northern counties may kill some branches, which are easily pruned off. The slick leaves, both upper and undersides, are not easy for diseases or insect pests—even whiteflies and scale—to get started on, which makes this one of the lowest-maintenance shrubs you can plant. Mulches protect roots from sudden freezes in northern counties.

Companion Planting and Design

Cleyera is almost too easy as a foundation planting, but works better at corners where it can be allowed to get full size than under windows where it will need constant pruning. It makes a great hedge, but is attractive enough to use as an evergreen specimen, even in a large container. Plant with contrasting nandina, palmetto, leucothoe, painted arum, and ferns.

Personal Favorites

'Variegata' has dark green leaves with creamy white edges that turn pink in the winter; the new growth of 'Burnished Gold' is bright golden and fades to bronzy green; 'Bigfoot' has large, glossy, light leaves and a notably upright habit.

Deciduous Azalea
Rhododendron species

When, Where, and How to Plant

These plants are difficult to transplant, but can be moved in fall and winter. Plant container-grown shrubs any time of the year, especially in the late winter and spring, when you can select the right flower color with assurance. Plant in light shade, or full sun with plenty of mulch and water during dry spells. Prepare soil by working in plenty of peat moss, bark, and compost—and some native woodland soil if you can get it. Handle the delicate roots gently, separating only the most tightly rootbound ones. Water deeply and mulch heavily, but do not add a lot of fertilizer at planting time; let plants get established before "pushing" them. Allow 4 to 6 feet between plants.

Growing Tips

Water deeply and frequently during long dry spells, especially young plants. Feed with a very light application of azalea-camellia fertilizer, or a light dusting of cottonseed meal in the spring.

Care

If necessary to remove tall or wayward stems and dead growth, prune immediately after azaleas bloom. Native azaleas are pest free but attract an occasional caterpillar.

Companion Planting and Design

Use tall deciduous azaleas in small or formal gardens as single specimen accents, against fences or walls where flowers and forms create lovely silhouettes, or in groups scattered throughout naturalistic gardens. Place toward the back of shrub borders where their legginess won't be too noticeable, but close enough to walkways for their fragrance to be enjoyed. Interplant with Virginia sweetspire, between and behind oakleaf hydrangeas, camellias, and other small to medium shrubs. Native woodland ferns, blue phlox, and dwarf crested iris are great underplantings.

Personal Favorites

Piedmont azalea (*R. canescens*) is pink; flame azalea (*R. calendulaceum*) is orange, red, pale yellow, cream, pink, or red; plumleaf azalea (*R. prunifolium*) is bright red and blooms in early and midsummer; there are many others, and stunning hybrids such as 'Colonel Mosby' with frilly salmon pink blooms with a yellow flare.

Around the first of April, creek banks and moist shaded hillsides come alive with the airy flowers of leggy native azaleas. The common, deciduous shrubs are naturally hardy, grow from the coast and up into our hills, and make splendid specimen shrubs or small trees. Colorful native azalea species and astonishing hybrids are finally becoming more widely available and popular in the nursery trade. Though the soft hues and delicate form of these so-called "wild honeysuckles" are often calm and soothing, the plants can usually hold their own when grown beside flashier imported "regular" evergreen azaleas. Native azaleas make lovely accent shrubs and wave a flag of welcome to newly arriving hummingbirds.

Other Common Name
Wild Honeysuckle

Bloom Period and Seasonal Color
Pink, white, orange, red, gold blooms in spring

Mature Height × Spread
6 to 10 feet × 4 to 6 feet

Doublefile Viburnum

Viburnum plicatum var. *tomentosum*

There are almost too many great viburnums to select a favorite—who doesn't admire the big, showy "snowball bush" (V. macrocephalum *and others), arrowwood (V.* dentatum), *coarse-textured leatherleaf (V. rhytido-phyllum), and other diverse and very useful species? But if there were just one to choose, it would have to be doublefile, for its haunting, lace-like white spring flowers held above the stems in mid-spring, and its red berries in the fall, which are a feast for the eye and for birds. Throw in its purple fall colors, and you have one fine but (sadly) underplanted shrub. One reason more people don't plant this viburnum is that it doesn't look great while young and in a nursery pot. But it really performs in the garden!*

Bloom Period and Seasonal Color
White blooms in spring with red fall berries

Mature Height × Spread
8 to 12 feet × 8 to 15 feet

When, Where, and How to Plant
Set out container-grown shrubs any time, but fall and winter are the best times so roots can get established over the winter. Plant in sun or part sun, in a well-drained soil, and provide deep soakings every two or three weeks through the first summer. Provide plenty of space for these plants, no closer than 10 feet apart.

Growing Tips
Keep doublefile viburnum moist, not wet, with heavy mulch and occasional deep soakings during prolonged dry spells. Fertilize in the spring, but only lightly, especially in full sun, or you may stimulate too much growth that can cause fruits to shed later in the season.

Care
Prune only to limb up into a small tree-like effect, and to thin wayward branches and cluttered limbs; do not shear or you will lose the plant's natural horizontal branching habit. Light thinning is best done in midwinter when you can better see what you are doing, but you will of course lose some of your spring flower show this way. Don't leave stubs that can rot. Toward the end of a hot, dry summer, you may see a little leaf scorch, which could also be caused by spider mites if the shrub is grown in full sun. No control is recommended.

Companion Planting and Design
Because of its spreading growth habit, it looks good against a dark backdrop of evergreens such as Southern magnolia, between camellias or tall pines, or partially espaliered to grow nearly flat against a wall or solid fence. Underplant with dark green dwarf hollies, English ivy, mondo grass, or winter-red compact nandina. Bulbs and native ferns grow well in its light shade.

Personal Favorites
'Shasta' is perhaps the most popular selection for its horizontal habit (to 15 feet wide, on a shrub only 10 feet tall) and large flowers. 'Summer Snowflake' blooms from spring through fall. 'Pink Beauty' has pink flowers.

Dwarf Palmetto
Sabal minor

When, Where, and How to Plant
Available only as container-grown plants, which can be set out any time of the year. Plant 3 or 4 feet apart in partial shade in areas that stay moist most of the year. Palmetto will tolerate very heavy soils and even drought if protected from hot sun and away from harsh winds that tear up the leaves. Dig or till an area at least twice as wide as the root-ball, and loosen it deeply to make room for the long taproot. Water well as often as needed to keep moist, but not wet, the first summer.

Growing Tips
Mature palmetto will survive intense drought for many months, but will not put on a lot of new leaves without regular moisture, especially the first summer or two; keep moist, not wet. Fertilize very lightly every spring with an all-purpose or slow-release fertilizer high in nitrogen, and keep a thick layer of natural leaves or compost around the base.

Care
No need to prune except to saw off unsightly old leaves as they die and turn brown. Leave tall "flower" stalks until all the black seeds have matured and fallen (collect and plant seeds in pots of potting soil left outside; they will sprout the next spring). No major pests, but strong winds can tatter the leaves.

Companion Planting and Design
Use dwarf palmetto as an accent plant near an entryway or at the corners of a house for a strangely exotic or contemporary effect. Plant in high shade under limbed-up bald cypress, along with horsetail, Louisiana iris, ferns, and aucuba for a prehistoric tropical look.

Personal Favorites
There are no cultivars of this ancient plant. The closest palm relative that is hardy outside is windmill palm (*Trachycarpus fortunei*) with its hairy trunk, but it is dependably hardy only in the southern counties of our states.

This native of our moist woodlands and fields is prehistoric—fossils have been uncovered throughout southeastern lowlands as far north as Oklahoma. The large, exotic-looking leaves unfold from accordion-like pleats into fans 4 feet or more across on 3-foot stalks, which arise from a central trunk that rarely gets taller than 2 or 3 feet. The entire plant may only reach 5 or 6 feet tall and wide. Landscape designers like dwarf palmetto's dramatic flair. Its biggest drawback is being very difficult to transplant from the wild because of its deep taproot, and though it is easy to grow from seed, it is very slow. It is available commercially from native plant growers who supply the garden center trade.

Bloom Period and Seasonal Color
Evergreen foliage

Mature Height × Spread
5 to 7 feet × 4 to 8 feet

Evergreen Azalea
Azalea hybrids

Evergreen azaleas are so commonly planted and so stunning, they are almost "color thugs" that steal the spring scene from other plants. Still, hundreds of thousands are grown every year at nurseries to satisfy a never-ending demand. They are the showiest of all spring shrubs, with eye-popping masses of flowers from late March to April, and there are a few fall-blooming ones. Some selections are hardy from the Tennessee state line to the Gulf Coast, while others do well only in southern counties. These evergreen shrubs come in large, medium, and small types; each has many different varieties from which to choose—based on flower size and color, and leaf size and color—to fit every desire.

Bloom Period and Seasonal Color
Pink, white, red, purple spring blooms, some fall colors

Mature Height × Spread
3 to 10 feet × 3 to 10 feet

When, Where, and How to Plant
Plant nursery-grown azaleas almost any time, but those planted in spring or summer will need watering every two or three weeks the first summer. Azaleas have fewer problems when grown in light shade, but will tolerate full sun if they have good roots. Dig extra-wide holes and amend up to one-third with peat moss and bark. Loosen tightly wound roots, and mulch heavily at planting time. Allow 5 or 6 feet between large-growing azaleas, and 3 or 4 feet between smaller types.

Growing Tips
If possible, water azaleas deeply every month in the summer and fall when they are forming flower buds, but do not keep them wet! Water deeply before a predicted hard freeze to protect roots. Fertilize in early spring, and give those growing in sandy soils another light feeding in midsummer. Keep mulch under them at all times.

Care
Prune azaleas after flowering to keep them more compact; tip-prune new shoots by late June to allow time for new growth to mature and set flower buds before fall. Azaleas, especially those in full sun, are susceptible to sudden freeze damage, scale insects, lacebugs, spider mites, and whiteflies. Fertilizing and watering help them outgrow most pests with few or no sprays.

Companion Planting and Design
Azaleas are common foundation shrubs, but an even better use is in masses under tall pines and other high shade. Combine them with shrubs that bloom before, during, and after azalea season, including spirea, kerria, viburnum, oakleaf hydrangea, and althea. "Skirt" azalea plantings with iris, liriope, ferns, dianthus, peonies, and lamb's ears.

Personal Favorites
Southern Indica azaleas ('Pride of Mobile', 'George L. Taber') are large shrubs with large flowers best suited for southern counties; Glenn Dale hybrids ('Geisha', 'Fashion') are very cold hardy. Kurume ('Coral Bells', 'Hino-Crimson') and Satsuki azaleas (Gumpo hybrids) are compact with smaller leaves and flowers and more cold tolerance. Encore hybrids are touted as fall bloomers, but have yet to prove themselves in popularity.

Evergreen Holly
Ilex species

When, Where, and How to Plant

Plant any time of year, in sun or shade, clay soil or sandy. Japanese hollies (*I. crenata* 'Helleri' and 'Compacta') in particular are susceptible to root rot in wet soils, especially when planted as foundation shrubs where rain water runs off a roof—do an extra good job of creating a raised bed for those. Spacing, from 3 to 12 feet apart, depends on the mature size of individual cultivars. Add a fair amount of organic matter to the native soil, and spread tangled or tight roots at planting. Mulch to keep soil loose and cool.

Growing Tips

Once established, hollies are perhaps the most durable landscape plants of all and need little or no water or fertilizer; a deep soaking during extreme drought is much better than regular irrigation. Broadcast a light amount of all-purpose fertilizer in the spring to help keep them growing steadily.

Care

Shear non-berried hollies from spring to late summer, but not in the fall. Berry-producing hollies flower in the spring, so wait until you see where the berries will be before thinning wayward branches or tip-pruning new growth. Treat scale insects, if necessary, by spraying the undersides of leaves with dormant oil spray. If Japanese hollies die suddenly in the summer from long-term root problems, rework the soil with more amendments and replant.

Companion Planting and Design

Use hollies for everything, from foundation plantings to edging, hedges, screens, accents, and large containers. They complement or contrast with nearly all other plants, especially loose-growing nandina, soft-tip yucca, ornamental grasses, and bulbs.

Personal Favorites

Popular hollies include spiny-leaved Chinese holly (*I. cornuta*), including large-growing 'Burfordii', 'Dwarf Burford', 'Needlepoint', compact 'Rotunda' and 'Carissa'; small-leaved Japanese holly (*I. crenata* 'Compacta' and 'Helleri'). Native yaupon holly selections (*I. vomitoria*) include tall, weeping 'Pendula'; small, round 'Stoke's Dwarf'; and tall, needle-like 'Will Fleming'.

Hollies are fast growing, economical, and tough. Exotic or native, large or small, evergreen holly shrubs are perhaps the most versatile and useful group of plants for our landscapes. There are dozens of different types of hollies, each with excellent cultivars prized for their year-round garden structure as creative accents, dense hedges, and tight "gumdrop" or "green worm" foundation plantings around almost all of our homes and businesses. Many have red, black, or even yellow berries on which birds feast as they nest in the shrubs. Their flowers, which are thick clusters of creamy white hidden in the new growth of spring, are excellent sources of nectar for bees, which pollinate between the male and female holly plants (necessary for berry formation).

Bloom Period and Seasonal Color
Red berries in fall, evergreen foliage

Mature Height × Spread
3 to 20 feet × 3 to 12 feet

Fatsia

Fatsia japonica

Fatsia is reminiscent of the type of plants seen in tropical rain forests—a clump-forming thicket of strong stems topped with emerald green leaves, each a big shiny umbrella almost a foot wide, all reaching for rays of sun that filter through the forest canopy. A native of Japan, fatsia is evergreen and shade loving, a favorite of landscape designers for gardens with natural, exotic, contemporary, or oriental themes. Fatsia usually produces tall clusters of golf-ball-like white flowers in the late fall, which freeze in central counties. In the northern counties and higher elevations, fatsia sometimes gets burned to the ground by freezes, but returns from the roots in the spring.

Bloom Period and Seasonal Color
White blooms in fall, evergreen leaves

Mature Height × Spread
4 to 6 feet × 4 to 8 feet

When, Where, and How to Plant

Plant container-grown plants in the spring or early summer, to give them time to get root-established before fall. Fatsia requires shade even in the winter, so do not plant on the south side of a building where deciduous trees can let the plants scorch or stay too warm and become susceptible to winter injury. Add plenty of organic matter to the soil, in a wide hole or bed, to encourage fast root development. Water well, and keep slightly moist until plants are established. Cover with a natural leaf mulch to "feed" the soil as it decomposes. Give fatsia plenty of room to grow up and spread out, at least 4 or 6 feet between plants.

Growing Tips

Fatsia is moisture loving, so water slowly and deeply during extreme dry spells, but do not keep it wet, or root diseases and leaf spots may show up. Fertilize lightly with a nitrogen fertilizer in the spring.

Care

Thin crowded clumps as needed, and cut winter-damaged growth close to the ground in midwinter so new growth can come up clean in the spring. The thick foliage of fatsia is resistant to diseases and insect attack, though it will scorch in the sun, even in the winter. It grows so thick and dense it may provide a cool place for slugs—and the little garden snakes that eat slugs.

Companion Planting and Design

With its wide leaves, fatsia is a good accent beside a shady water feature or reflecting pool. It combines well with gold-spot aucuba, holly fern, and cast-iron plant, provides a good contrast to mahonia, and makes a terrific container plant even indoors.

Personal Favorites

'Variegata' has leaves edged with gold or creamy white. Fatshedera (×*Fatshedera lizei*), a perfect cross between fatsia and a type of ivy (*Hedera hibernica* or *Hedera helix* 'Hibernica'), has 5-inch-wide, ivy-like leaves on sturdy semi-upright vines, and comes in variegated and 'Media-Picta', which has a golden spot in the middle of each leaf.

Florida Anise
Illicium floridanum

When, Where, and How to Plant
Plant container-grown shrubs any time of the year, in light shade and well-drained soil high in organic matter. In groups, allow plants at least 6 or 8 feet for good growth. Prepare a very wide hole or bed, and thoroughly blend in a generous layer of several different types of organic matter, including bark, compost, and partially decomposed leaves, which blend together with your native soil to create a rich "woodsy" mix to which anise is naturally adapted. Loosen potting soil and mix in with your garden soil, spread anise roots out as best you can, and water deeply to get plants started. Use a natural leaf mulch.

Growing Tips
Keep this plant moist, not wet, through the summer, and it will flower prolifically the next spring. Natural leaf mulch decomposes to feed the soil, further helping the woodland roots grow far and wide. Feed with compost or manure rather than harsh chemical fertilizers.

Care
If it has enough space to grow to full size, anise usually does not need pruning. To reduce its size, thin tall or crowded stems rather than cutting the plant back severely; this preserves the naturalistic shape. Anise is pest free.

Companion Planting and Design
Use in small groups for a natural-looking evergreen hedge in a moist, shaded, heavily mulched landscape. Its big, bold foliage works well in shaded tropical gardens, to provide an evergreen accent when other bold plants are dormant. Interplant with nandina, azaleas, fatsia, leucothoe, caladiums, surprise lily, and evergreen groundcovers, or just mulch for a naturalistic touch.

Personal Favorites
'Halley's Comet' is compact, making it more suitable for smaller shade gardens, with larger, redder flowers than the wild species; it often reblooms a little in the fall. 'Alba' has white flowers, 'Variegata' has subtle variegation but burgundy flowers, 'Woodland Ruby' has starfish-shaped ruby-pink flowers over a long period. Native yellow anise (*I. parviflorum*), with yellow flowers, is larger and more tolerant of sun than Florida anise.

One of our best shade-loving native evergreen shrubs, anise has large, pointy-oval, shiny leaves up to 6 inches long, each with a prominent midrib, like that of small bay trees or even rhododendrons. Its thick foliage has a very spicy, pungent aroma when brushed or crushed. Two-inch, waxy, red flowers, like spidery pinwheels on 2-inch stalks, are almost hidden in the big leaves in the early spring, but are easily recognized from their musky fragrance that some people find a little unpleasant. This large shrub, found growing naturally in our moist wooded bottomlands and along creeks, provides an outstanding choice for those of us with low areas in shaded landscapes.

Other Common Name
Anise

Bloom Period and Seasonal Color
Maroon blooms in late March, April, early May

Mature Height × Spread
8 to 12 feet × 6 to 10 feet

Florida Leucothoe
Leucothoe populifolia

Too bad such a great plant has such a weird name, because every garden that has a leucothoe (pronounced loo-CO-thow-ee) is a special place. The Leucothoe genus also includes woodland groundcovers with arching stems and drooping spring flowers. Stick with Florida leucothoe, a bigger plant that some botanists have renamed Agarista populifolia. The large, spreading, multiple-stem evergreen shrub has long branches with glossy, rich green leaves, and fragrant but not very showy early summer flowers. Florida leucothoe looks almost like glossy, arching bamboo; its open, airy form makes a manageable evergreen woodland screen. The stems are long lasting when cut and make excellent greenery for floral arrangements or decorating.

Other Common Name
Fetterbush

Bloom Period and Seasonal Color
Evergreen with cream-colored flowers in early summer

Mature Height × Spread
8 to 12 feet × 6 to 10 feet

When, Where, and How to Plant
Plant container-grown shrubs almost any time of the year, or divide mature clumps in the fall or early winter. Cut plants back when dividing, and they will recover more quickly the next summer. Plant leucothoe in light shade and away from the hot reflected heat of pavement or a south-facing wall. Prepare the soil ahead of time by working in generous amounts of compost, old leaves, and bark to create a deep, well-drained "woodsy" soil condition. Place plants 6 to 8 feet apart and they will fill in rather quickly.

Growing Tips
Leucothoe grows best in rich, moist soil, so keep a thick layer of natural leaf mulch around its stems, and water deeply during prolonged drought. Instead of using chemical fertilizers, apply compost around the plants in the spring to enrich the soil and feed earthworms, which aerate the soil and help water penetrate more deeply.

Care
Prune lightly in late winter to remove old canes and open up the plant to show off its interesting arching stems. Feed very lightly in the spring, or spread compost in the fall to feed roots over the winter. Leucothoe is subject to a leaf spot fungus that causes minor cosmetic damage, but does not kill the shrub.

Companion Planting and Design
Leucothoe makes an excellent woodland or shade garden screen or naturalistic hedge. Use it as a broad accent plant behind a water feature. Good companions include azaleas, ferns, hosta, impatiens, and any type of hard feature such as rustic fence, large rock, or old log.

Personal Favorites
Only the large species is available. Drooping leucothoe (*L. fontanesiana*) is a native semi-evergreen groundcover that reaches only 4 or 5 feet tall; interesting cultivars include 'Rainbow' with yellow, green, and pink markings on its foliage, and 'Scarletta' with brilliant red spring leaves that turn green by summer, then deep red in fall and winter.

Flowering Quince
Chaenomeles species

When, Where, and How to Plant
Dig and divide suckers from older plants in the fall or winter, or plant bare-root shrubs in the winter when they become available. Stem cuttings taken in late winter and stuck in well-drained garden soil will root quickly and can be transplanted the following fall. Container plants can be set out any time of the year. Quince shrubs flower best when they get at least eight hours of direct sunshine a day in the summer, but often flower in old gardens that are overgrown and more densely shaded. The plants, which are sometimes found growing and blooming perfectly well in old cemeteries and around abandoned houses, are not fussy about soil, and will tolerate many weeks of drought. But they must have well-drained soil or their roots may rot. No real need to mulch these plants.

Growing Tips
Water only occasionally, if at all, in the late summer when flower buds are forming. Fertilize lightly every two or three springs.

Care
Prune overgrown flowering quince soon after blooming, by cutting back old canes close to the ground to encourage flowering stems for the following spring. A few stems can be cut to the base, to control size or promote flowering. Whiteflies and aphids can be troublesome, but are not serious pests to the plants. There are no major diseases.

Companion Planting and Design
Flowering quince makes stunning accents when you least expect color in February. Best as groups or scattered through informal shrub borders or toward the rear of large perennial beds where they jump-start the season. Plant with yellow forsythia, white spirea, camellias, and lots of spring bulbs. Place the shrub so it is not "front and center" after the spring show since it does not have an attractive form when not in bloom; vining clematis in it can also help "dress it up."

Personal Favorites
Some good cultivars of *C. speciosa* are 'Apple Blossom' (white with pink tinge), 'Contorta' (very interesting twisted branches with white or pink flowers), 'Orange Delight' (low, spreading shrub with orange-red flowers, great with daffodils). There are many others, all equally tough.

This old-fashioned pass-along plant never fails to flower in February and early March—often the only plant in bloom other than camellias and early daffodils, even before forsythia—and continues for several weeks. The plant itself is scraggly, with thin, thorny branches and sparse leaves, but when it pops into flower, every stem becomes a blaze of flowers, usually candy-apple red or cotton-candy pink. Bring budded branches indoors in January to flower in a vase of water. Easy to grow, common flowering quince has a spreading habit and small knobby, yellow-green, apple-like fruits (which, though sometimes used for jelly, are not the same as the big pear-like quince used to make preserves, which grow on a small tree named Cydonia oblonga).

Other Common Name
Japonica

Bloom Period and Seasonal Color
Red, coral, white, pink flowers in mid- to late winter

Mature Height × Spread
4 to 6 feet × 5 to 8 feet

Forsythia

Forsythia × intermedia

This leggy, deciduous shrub, with its spirited, yellow February and March flowers, is a spring tonic. The old-fashioned shrub, which can be found growing around old home sites and even escaped into nearby woods, is fast growing and nearly indestructible—it is winter hardy well into Canada and Alaska! Like flowering quince, its stems can be cut and brought in during the midwinter to sprout in vases of water as an early touch of spring. Though it can be pruned into very tight shrubs, even sheared, this naturalistic shrub should be left alone to grow into a large, spreading mass of long, arching branches with narrow, toothed leaves that turn maroon in the fall. Forsythia is tolerant of heat, drought, and pollution.

Other Common Names
Yellow Bells, Golden Bells

Bloom Period and Seasonal Color
Yellow blooms in February with maroon fall foliage

Mature Height × Spread
6 to 8 feet × 8 to 10 feet

When, Where, and How to Plant
Plant bare-root forsythia or dig and divide suckers from beneath old shrubs in the winter, and water through the first summer. Plant container-grown shrubs any time in full sun or light shade. No special soil preparation is generally needed, just a wide hole and mulch after planting. Allow 8 to 10 feet or more between plants.

Growing Tips
Once it is established, there is no need to water forsythia, ever. Light feedings will help the plants retain better foliage, but too much actually cuts down on flowering the next spring by promoting lush growth instead of flower bud formation. Root stem cuttings of forsythia right after the shrubs stop flowering.

Care
To maintain forsythia's vigor and graceful natural form, prune older canes to the base immediately after flowering, to encourage strong new arching branches. Do not prune after midsummer—including fall and winter—or you will lose the next spring's flowers. Shearing into square boxes and round meatballs is often done and can be interesting, but seems a shame when there are so many shrubs that actually enjoy being treated that way! Pests are generally not a problem with forsythia.

Companion Planting and Design
Frequently used as a specimen, hedge, border planting, or naturalized in a large, colorful mass on a hillside, a single forsythia will draw attention to itself. Underplant with grape hyacinth or white daffodils (yellow daffodils simply disappear when yellow forsythia comes into bloom). Plant with summer blooming (butterfly bush, chaste tree) and fall-color shrubs (burning bush, Virginia sweetspire) for a full season shrub border.

Personal Favorites
Getting beyond the common 'Lynwood' found in garden centers, look for the variegated-leaf 'Fiesta' and the delicate pale yellow 'Spring Glory'. The popular old 'Beatrix Farrand' reaches up to 10 feet tall with 2 1/2-inch flowers in deep yellow marked with orange. 'Gold Tide' is a dwarf selection that grows only a couple of feet tall but spreads by suckers to twice that wide, yet still bears a heavy load of blooms.

French Hydrangea

Hydrangea macrophylla

When, Where, and How to Plant

Hydrangea cuttings root easily in spring or summer, and can be transplanted in the fall. Container-grown shrubs can be set out any time, but watering enough without rotting them can be tricky the first summer. Plant in bright light, preferably where the plants get morning sun and afternoon shade, or light shade all day. When preparing the soil, add generous amounts of organic matter to fluff up and increase drainage. Dig a wide hole, not deep, so roots can quickly grow outward. Allow 3 to 5 feet between plants.

Growing Tips

Water deeply and frequently, if possible, without overdoing it and rotting roots. Keep a thick layer of organic mulch under plants to continuously feed the soil. Fertilize lightly in the spring, not in the fall, or risk winter damage to tender twigs. To make flowers pink, add lime to your soil; to make them blue, acidify the soil by adding sulfur or aluminum sulfate (available at garden centers).

Care

Prune French hydrangea immediately after it blooms, thinning tall stems back nearly to the ground. Tip-prune new growth early in the spring for thicker plants the next year. Whiteflies may be troublesome some years, as is root rot if planted in poorly drained soil.

Companion Planting and Design

Use French hydrangeas in shrub borders, toward the back of perennial borders, as stunning lawn specimens or accent plants, or as low seasonal hedges. The plants are bold by themselves, but also work well with crape myrtles, evergreen conifers, and early-blooming spring bulbs and pansies that flower underneath before hydrangeas leaf out.

Personal Favorites

The old standbys 'Nikko Blue' and 'Domotoi' are still great, but the hot hydrangeas now are the rebloomers that flower on new growth, including 'Dooley', 'Penny Mac', 'Endless Summer', and the "lacecap" types with flat clusters of small flowers surrounded with a ring of larger flowers, including 'Blue Wave' and the variegated-leaved 'Variegata' (which looks good just as a foliage plant).

Trying to predict how to make a hydrangea bloom is nearly impossible. Do everything just right, and you have a fifty-fifty chance; then you see an old country garden with nothing done right, and the plants are glorious. But the gamble is worth it to have medium-sized shrubs with large, almost tropical leaves and huge nodding flower heads of usually gaudy pink or electric blue. What they need is morning sun, afternoon shade, rich soil with plenty of organic matter, lots of mulch, and an occasional deep soaking. And hope the weather cooperates and a cold snap doesn't kill all the buds. Luckily, there are selections that bloom on new growth, so you can still have flowers even after a hard late freeze.

Other Common Name
Big-leaf Hydrangea

Bloom Period and Seasonal Color
Pink, blue, red, or white blooms in late spring and summer

Mature Height × Spread
3 to 6 feet × 3 to 5 feet

Gardenia

Gardenia augusta

Gardenia fragrance—the stuff of bride's bouquets—is unforgettable, especially when it hangs in the air on a summer evening. Silky white, highly perfumed flowers glow against a backdrop of lustrous, dark green foliage before fading to dull yellow. Gardenias can be frozen when winter temperatures dip into the single digits and lower teens in the winter, but usually return from the roots. They can also be grown in pots and cut back to keep over the winter in the garage. If you can't find one at a garden center, find a hardy shrub in an old garden near you and root a tip cutting, while in flower, in a glass of water.

Other Common Name
Cape Jasmine

Bloom Period and Seasonal Color
White blooms in late spring and summer

Mature Height × Spread
5 to 6 feet × 4 to 5 feet

When, Where, and How to Plant

Root gardenia cuttings in early or midsummer, and transplant in the fall. Or set out container-grown plants any time. Gardenias flower well in full sun or light shade, but require an acidic, highly amended soil that drains very well. Add plenty of peat, bark, and compost to your native soil over a wide area (three or four times the diameter of the rootball), plant the shrub on the high side with soil mix mounded up to it, and mulch heavily.

Growing Tips

Water gardenias regularly during the summer with slow, deep soakings every two or three weeks. Fertilize lightly and frequently, from early spring through midsummer, using an acidic azalea-camellia fertilizer or cottonseed meal. Keep well mulched.

Care

Gardenias naturally shed old leaves as the temperatures heat up; some gardeners become alarmed when the leaves turn bright yellow, but this does not indicate a problem. Rather than shearing, prune by thinning tall stems from deep within the shrub in the late winter and spring. Gardenias suffer from whiteflies whose sugary excrement drips down and causes black "sooty mold" to grow on leaves—rinse it off with soapy water followed by clear water, and treat with insecticidal soap.

Companion Planting and Design

Gardenias make good specimen plants, especially in out-of-the way places where you can see the flowers and smell the fragrance without the whiteflies and sooty mold bothering you. Skirt leggy plants with pachysandra, and interplant with nandina or tall crape myrtles.

Personal Favorites

For variety, grow both the larger, old-fashioned "cape jasmine" gardenia, which reaches 5 to 6 feet in height, and the smaller-leaved, knee-high 'Radicans' cultivar, which is a more tender groundcover. 'August Beauty' is one of the more popular regular-sized gardenias with large double flowers blooming over a long time, and is less rangy than the standard old 'Mystery'. 'Kleim's Hardy' is noted for its cold hardiness, down to zero degrees Fahrenheit.

Japanese Kerria
Kerria japonica

When, Where, and How to Plant
Plant container-grown shrubs any time of the year, or dig and immediately replant suckers from the edge of a colony in fall or winter, using a sharp spade to cut through woody underground stems. Cut transplants back to keep them from overpowering the reduced root system. Plant in light shade in areas that do not stay wet in the winter. Light soil preparation includes adding a fair amount of organic matter to a wide bed, spacing new plants 4 to 5 feet apart, and mulching heavily.

Growing Tips
This drought-tolerant plant needs little or no irrigation, but an occasional deep soaking in dry summers will increase its flower bud production and help leaves remain longer on the shrub in the fall. Fertilize lightly in the spring, and replenish mulch as needed.

Care
Kerria is a naturally loose shrub, and shearing or tip-pruning causes odd new growth to form high in the plant. Better to prune kerria only to thin wayward, cluttered, and old stems, cutting close to the ground right after flowering; this renews the plant with new growth. Kerria is relatively pest free, but whiteflies may be troublesome some years.

Companion Planting and Design
Kerria is an eye-catching accent along shady informal paths and between mature evergreens such as ligustrum, camellia, evergreen azaleas, and pieris. It complements spireas and contrasts well with flowering quince, but is too golden to hold up against brilliant forsythia. Its arching branches provide a good framework for smaller flowering shrubs, perennials such as peonies and iris, and flowering bulbs. Kerria is perfectly at home in cottage or old-fashioned gardens, and also makes a good show in mass plantings in large informal garden borders.

Personal Favorites
The species is single-flowered and includes early-blooming 'Shannon' and low-growing (to 4 feet) variegated 'Picta' ('Variegata'). The most common form found around small towns and country gardens is the double-flowered 'Plenifora' ('Flora Pleno') with golden yellow pompoms at every leaf joint; it spreads steadily by underground stems.

In late March and April, the "yellow rose of Texas" bursts into a wild, ranging spray of school-bus-yellow flowers that loudly announce its presence. The shrub grows into a fountain of long, slender stems from 5 to 10 feet tall, forming an open spray of long, slender stems, which are zigzag and remain green. Flowers are fuzzy buttons of golden-orange in showy clusters at every leaf joint, with the best show in the spring, though a few flowers will spritz into summer. Coupled with the small, toothed, yellow-green leaves, the flowers create a green-and-gold show. Tolerant of a wide variety of conditions, including moderate shade around old home places, the easy-to-grow heirloom plant spreads easily from short suckers that are simple to dig and share.

Other Common Names
Yellow Rose of Texas, Jerusalem Rose

Bloom Period and Seasonal Color
Yellow blooms in spring and summer

Mature Height × Spread
4 to 10 feet × 4 to 6 feet

Japanese Pieris
Pieris japonica

The slender, bent, sculptural form of Japanese pieris adds an elegance and touch of mystery to the shade garden. This distant cousin of the azalea is evergreen, covered with narrow, lustrous leaves in whorls. New growth emerges rosy red and on some selections is very showy, especially when contrasted with the flowers, which begin in late winter. The tips of every stem of the small shrub drip with multiple cascading chains of white, pink, or red bell-like flowers that look like lily-of-the-valley. Best of all, it is tough, growing perfectly well into Canada. Along the coast, pieris needs regular deep watering, and protection from all-night heat, especially that absorbed during the day and radiated at night from nearby walls or paved areas.

Other Common Names
Japanese Andromeda, Lily-of-the-Valley Shrub

Bloom Period and Seasonal Color
White blooms in spring

Mature Height × Spread
4 to 8 feet × 3 to 5 feet

When, Where, and How to Plant
Plant pieris as you would a camellia, in the fall or winter, or be prepared to water carefully during the first summer. Plant the small shrubs in partial shade or morning sun only, and out of hot summer breezes, in rich, light, moist, acid soil. Allow 3 to 4 feet between shrubs in a border, foundation, or mass planting. Dig an area at least twice as wide as the rootball, and mix one-third to one-half compost or soil conditioner with topsoil. The first summer, water deeply and frequently so roots can get well established, but avoid overwatering. Mulch heavily with natural leaf mulch.

Growing Tips
Treat pieris like a treasured azalea or camellia, with occasional deep soakings in the summer and dry fall, and light feedings of acid-forming azalea or camellia fertilizer in the spring. Keep a thick layer of mulch around the roots.

Care
When needed, thin out tall stems but leave the overall shrub in its naturally loose form. Sun and drought, like overfeeding and over-watering, can weaken the plant and make it more susceptible to leaf spots; otherwise, it is both trouble and pest free.

Companion Planting and Design
Pieris is an ideal small specimen plant along a turn in a wooded walk, oriental garden, or in a large container left outside all winter. It contrasts well with deciduous native azaleas, or evergreen fatsia and aucuba. Planted in groups of three to five, it does a lovely job of naturalizing an area in the shade because of its loose, informal habit. Interplant with evergreen holly fern and cast-iron plant.

Personal Favorites
There are many good selections, but the most common ones found in the trade include 'Mountain Fire', which has attractive, red new growth, and 'Variegata', which looks almost like a miniature poinsettia when it's covered with new leaves of green, cream, and pink.

Mahonia

Mahonia bealei

When, Where, and How to Plant

Plant container-grown plants any time, but fall or winter is less stressful to new plants, which need to be watered through their first summer. Plant in light shade, or prepare an extra wide and rich bed for their roots to grow deep and stay cool and moist. Avoid wet soils, which can cause root rot. Plant 5 or 6 feet apart. Prepare wide holes or beds and amend with sand and organic matter to help drainage. Loosen and spread out roots of pot-bound plants, water them well, and mulch to keep roots cool and moist the first summer.

Growing Tips

Keep soil moist during prolonged dry spells, but not wet, which can rot mahonia roots. Fertilize in the spring with a light application of all-purpose or natural fertilizer.

Care

Prune tall or excess stems down close to the ground where they will resprout. Prune in the spring after enjoying the flowers and some of the fruit display. Mahonia has no major pests.

Companion Planting and Design

Mahonia is best as a striking architectural specimen against a brick, stone, or gray wood wall where its winter flowers and berries will be noticed. Don't plant too close to walks or the spiny leaves will snag people who pass by. Also good naturalized along woodland trails with azaleas and hollies. Great shade-loving companions include variegated aucuba, crape myrtle (for its trunks), camellia, hellebore, cast-iron plant, and holly fern. A skirt of grape hyacinths makes the blue berries really stand out.

Personal Favorites

The species is a favorite. A close relative, Oregon grape holly (*M. aquifolium*), is only 5 or 6 feet tall and spreads by underground runners into small colonies, with bronze new growth that turns purplish in the fall or when grown in the sun. Its fruit makes a decent jelly; 'Orange Flame' is only 2 feet tall and has bronzy orange new growth that turns wine red in the winter.

Mahonia is a popular plant in shaded gardens. Looking like a hybrid between a holly and nandina, its multiple trunks are topped with whorls of foot-long leaves made up of many spiny, holly-like leaflets. Chains of golden yellow fragrant flowers cascade from the tops of the stems in January and February, and are followed by clusters of blue-black grape-like berries coated in sky-blue wax. Some designers claim that this woodland understory plant can tolerate sun, but the resulting bronzy golden fall color is really sunburn. It is best to give the plants plenty of room to spread out and make a strong architectural statement against a wall or near a window, and enjoy its show in an otherwise dreary time of year.

Other Common Name

Leatherleaf Mahonia

Bloom Period and Seasonal Color

Late winter yellow flowers, spring and summer blue fruit

Mature Height × Spread

6 to 10 feet × 5 to 8 feet

Mountain Laurel
Kalmia latifolia

There are few sights as inspiring as mountain laurel in the spring and early summer, blooming atop hill-country ridges and along steep banks of creeks and streams. Mountain laurel falls into a category of shrubs that frequently lays claim to being "America's best loved native shrub." A slow-growing, sculptural evergreen, mountain laurel has angular, woody branches and elliptical, waxy, dark green leaves, which provide a striking backdrop for its 5-inch clusters of flattened star-like bells of rose to pale pink flowers with contrasting centers. Many named selections in varying sizes and flower colors do much better in landscapes than "rescued" wild mountain laurel, which is extremely difficult to transplant.

Bloom Period and Seasonal Color
Pale pink blooms in spring, evergreen foliage

Mature Height × Spread
6 to 10 feet × 4 to 8 feet

When, Where, and How to Plant
Treat exactly as you would a camellia, planting carefully any time you can find a good potted plant to set out. Plant in full or light shade, in perfectly well-drained soils or on a slope, or raised a bit above the surrounding soil. Dig a wide hole and amend with long-lasting, acid-forming peat moss and bark. Mulch deeply and water through the first summer. Space 4 feet apart or more.

Growing Tips
Though wild plants seem to grow with no water at all, when you look closely you'll see that many of them are half dead. Every two or three weeks without rain, give mountain laurel a good, deep soaking—just like azaleas and camellias—and they will hold up for many years. Fertilize lightly in the spring with an acidic azalea or camellia fertilizer, or a good dusting of cottonseed meal, which feeds earthworms that eat and carry mulch deep around roots. Maintain a thick layer of natural leaf mulch under shrubs.

Care
Prune only dead or broken branches, thinning each plant into a unique, small, evergreen tree form. In humid areas, mountain laurel's foliage is bothered by leaf spot, which causes cosmetic damage, but does not kill the shrub. It also occasionally suffers insect damage. Apply a winter spraying of dormant oil to suppress problems.

Companion Planting and Design
Shade-loving mountain laurel is a good candidate for naturalizing in woods or along stream banks. It works well in a formal shade garden with camellias, rhododendrons, azaleas, pieris, and oakleaf hydrangea, and fits into the back of a small shrub border or shady rock garden, or as a specimen shrub. It can be grown in a large tub if kept watered. Plant ferns and wildflowers underneath.

Personal Favorites
'Elf' is a lovely dwarf form with blooms in natural pale pink. 'Bullseye' has a dark cinnamon-purple and white coloring. 'Sarah' has bright, reddish-pink blooms.

Nandina
Nandina domestica

When, Where, and How to Plant

In the fall or winter, use a sharp spade to dig into and divide old clumps of nandina, replanting immediately. This can be done even in the summer if you water enough afterwards, or pot up divisions to plant later. Set out container-grown shrubs in sun or shade any time of the year, but be sure to loosen tightly potbound roots. Do not plant in standing water. Fertilize very lightly, and cover the area around young plants with thick mulch. Space 3 to 4 feet apart, depending on the cultivar.

Growing Tips

Water and fertilize nandina only when you have little or nothing else to do—the tough shrub needs nothing at all from humans to grow and thrive for decades; however, a little fertilizer every few years will increase its berry production.

Care

Control height by cutting out taller canes in the spring or summer, after berries have started to form so you don't cut too many of them off. Cut a few inches from the ground to encourage strong new stems that will flower and berry the next year. Keep clumps from spreading by burying a metal barrier from ground level down a foot or so. Nandina is bulletproof when it comes to pests.

Companion Planting and Design

Use nandina anywhere you need a small to medium-sized evergreen or a spot of red—as an accent, group planting, foundation plant, or container specimen (even left outside all winter). Companions include lamb's ears, purple coneflower, daylilies, daffodils, grasses, yucca, 'Autumn Joy' sedum, spider lily, hardy mums—anything and everything.

Personal Favorites

'Moyer's Red' is a favorite standard size nandina with good winter color and early berries. 'Compacta' reaches only 4 or 5 feet tall; 'Gulf Stream' is more compact. 'Plum Passion' has deep purplish-red spring and winter foliage. Dwarf varieties include 'Harbour Dwarf' and 'Nana', the latter with twisted foliage.

It's difficult to imagine life without the ubiquitous nandina. In the face of complaints that it is overused, and potentially invasive, gardeners generally find neither to be true—in fact, it is one of the most companionable shrubs available! Heavenly bamboo is an attractive foliage plant with upright, cane-like stems topped with whorls of ferny foliage that complements nearly everything around it, both in its summer greenery and fiery wine-red winter colors. Lacy late spring panicles of white flowers are followed in the fall by loose upright clusters of stunning red berries that persist through the following spring. On top of its aesthetic attributes, nandina is hardy, pest free, and economical, and thrives on utter neglect.

Other Common Name
Heavenly Bamboo

Bloom Period and Seasonal Color
White spring flowers, red fall berries, red and purple winter foliage

Mature Height × Spread
3 to 8 feet × 3 to 4 feet

Oakleaf Hydrangea

Hydrangea quercifolia

One of the most stunning of our native shrubs, and an exceptional addition to shade gardens, this woodland hillside beauty is acclaimed the world over for its bold foliage and huge clusters of flowers and flower bracts. Blooming in May and June, oakleaf hydrangea grows from 6 to 8 feet tall, has attractive gray-green foliage through summer, then puts on a dramatic fall show as its leaves turn bronze before they drop, revealing upright, spreading stems with scaling, cinnamon bark that is very attractive in winter. Oakleaf hydrangea has another claim to fame—several years ago, after intensive lobbying, it was voted Alabama's "official state wildflower."

Bloom Period and Seasonal Color
White to creamy pink blooms in summer with bronze fall foliage

Mature Height × Spread
6 to 8 feet × 6 to 8 feet

When, Where, and How to Plant
Plant container-grown shrubs in the fall or winter, or any time if watered regularly without rotting roots. Oakleaf hydrangea will tolerate full sun, but does much better with protection from hot afternoon sun and reflected heat from brick walls or pavement (it grows naturally on wooded slopes). Plant in richly amended, "woodsy" soils, in near perfect drainage, allowing 4 to 6 feet or more between shrubs, depending on the cultivar. If your garden is flat, create a small raised area, like a baseball pitcher's mound, for better drainage. Mulch heavily to simulate natural growing conditions, and water deeply until established.

Growing Tips
Water deeply as needed in prolonged drought, but do not keep wet, or roots will rot. Note that the big leaves wilt naturally during the day, but perk up at night—don't try to revive a wilted plant by watering without first checking it the next morning.

Care
Prune oakleaf hydrangea by thinning too-tall or wayward trunks and branches, cutting dead stems to the base of the shrub so new growth can occur. Prune other stems back to new wood. There are no major pests.

Companion Planting and Design
Use oakleaf hydrangea in front of an evergreen border or screen, such as bayberry or holly. It also looks attractive against a wall or fence (though avoid west-facing structures), in a mass planting, or lining a driveway. It is a good choice for naturalizing under high shade with native ferns. Underplant with erosion-controlling mondo grass and spring bulbs when planted in southern exposures.

Personal Favorites
The wild oakleaf hydrangea is beautiful, and tough enough to transplant during winter native plant "rescues" (coordinated by local forestry commissions and beautification boards, usually around planned new construction sites). Named selections, such as 'Snowflake', 'Harmony', and 'Snow Queen', have impressive flower clusters on plants ranging from a few feet tall to over 10 feet tall and wide. There are also dwarf varieties.

Pittosporum

Pittosporum tobira

When, Where, and How to Plant

Plant container-grown plants any time you need to, in sun or shade in well-drained soils that do not stay wet in the winter. In northern counties provide protection from sudden deep freezes or cold or drying winds—plant on the east side to keep plants from staying too tender in the warm winter sun, which can cause more freeze damage. Prepare soil with organic matter so it does not hold water during the wet season, especially when using pittosporum as a foundation plant, in locations where rainfall runs off the roof. Space 4 to 6 feet apart.

Growing Tips

This plant is drought hardy and slow growing, with no need to water or fertilize it more than normal—deep soakings during very dry spells, and a light feeding in the spring.

Care

This shrub needs no pruning, other than limbing up into small trees in southern counties. Pittosporum is vulnerable to scale, which spraying with horticultural oil helps to control. It is also extremely sensitive to temperatures below 15 degrees Fahrenheit.

Companion Planting and Design

Pittosporum is often used as a foundation plant, evergreen hedge, or border, providing a deep green backdrop for flowers. In southern counties it is often pruned into a small tree. Dwarf selections work well in containers near entryways or steps; they are also ideal for spaces under windows. The plants are very dense, making growing anything under them difficult. Use as a foil or contrast under taller crape myrtles or wax myrtle; between pines; between roses; or behind drought-tolerant perennials such as daylily, iris, sedum, and bluestar.

Personal Favorites

'Wheeler's Dwarf', which gets about 4 feet tall and wide, is very common in the trade, though not as cold hardy as the species. 'Variegatum' is reliable and up to about 8 or 10 feet tall with gray-green leaves edged in white. 'Cream de Mint' is a low, compact mound to 2 1/2 feet tall and wide, with mint-green leaves edged in white.

This once popular Japanese shrub is coming back into favor as a foundation plant, after a devastating loss from a long, deep freeze that killed many old plants in our northern counties. Slightly irregular, round headed, and spreading, it is a smooth contrast to other shrubs, especially the variegated type. In the spring it boasts orange-scented creamy white flowers. The rest of the year it is "only" a lustrous mass of green—just what the landscape designer ordered. A choice foliage plant even as a potted specimen in northern areas, pittosporum is easy to grow and a good shrub for natural, contemporary, oriental, tropical, or low-maintenance gardens. A friend to coastal gardeners, pittosporum is tough enough for even "primary dune" seaside plantings.

Other Common Name
Mock Orange

Bloom Period and Seasonal Color
White blooms in spring with evergreen foliage

Mature Height × Spread
4 to 12 feet × 4 to 8 feet

Rhododendron

Rhododendron catawbiense

The native rhododendron heralds springtime in the hills. In moist ravines and along river and creek banks where few tourists venture, the huge flower trusses glow in the woods. An irregular, straggling shrub, the heat-tolerant Catawba rhododendron varieties grow wild in central and northern counties (except in the Mississippi Delta), where it can reach heights of 20 feet. It is a parent of many modern hybrids (crossed with exotic Asian rhododendrons); now there are countless different sizes and flower colors, most reaching from 3 to 10 feet in height. "Rhodies" make outstanding specimens, and are good for naturalizing under high shade, especially on the lower sides of wooded slopes. Choose native selections or hybrids adapted to warmer areas.

Other Common Name
Rhodie

Bloom Period and Seasonal Color
Pink, lavender, white blooms in spring

Mature Height × Spread
3 to 10 feet × 3 to 8 feet

When, Where, and How to Plant
Plant almost any time of the year, but summer planting can cause watering woes. Plant in full or light shade, with no more than early morning sunlight, in high beds amended extremely well with peat moss and a little bark for drainage. Raised beds or mounds are required in flat gardens; most gardeners plant "rhodies" with the top of the rootball out of the soil, covered with lots of mulch. Space 3 to 8 feet apart, depending on the variety.

Growing Tips
Rhododendrons need regular, even moisture, which means watering somewhat frequently in the over-prepared soil they require. Overhead sprinkling done in the morning will not cause diseases as badly as that done late in the day. Drip irrigation rarely does the job well enough for the large, fibrous root masses. Note that the large leaves typically wilt during the day as a natural water conservation mechanism—don't think the plants are dying and then kill them with over-watering! Fertilize lightly in late spring—after flowering—to avoid forcing new growth early that can interfere with blooming; use an azalea-camellia fertilizer. Keep well mulched.

Care
Rhododendron does not need much pruning, other than pinching new growth in the spring to encourage branching and more flowers the following spring, thinning tall growth, and removing spent flowers. There are no major pests other than stem dieback caused by root rot in plants grown in flat gardens, heavy clay, or wet, poorly-drained soils.

Companion Planting and Design
Plant in masses on moist slopes or in raised beds in light shade (under pines is ideal) or early morning sun, with deciduous azaleas, pieris, camellia, mountain laurel, Virginia sweetspire, and woodland ferns.

Personal Favorites
Good heat-tolerant choices include: 'Piedmont' (a rosy pink, dwarf cultivar of the native species), 'Anna Rose Whitney' (bright pink), 'English Roseum' and 'Roseum Elegans' (both lavender), 'Album' (white), and 'Lee's Dark Purple'. There are many others.

Sasanqua Camellia
Camellia sasanqua

When, Where, and How to Plant
Plant sasanquas any time, but the best time for selection is in the fall when they are in bloom. They grow and flower best in light shade, in well-drained soils high in organic matter. Shield from north winds. Allow 10 to 12 feet for specimen plants, 6 to 8 feet for borders and foundation plants, 3 feet for an uncut hedge. Mulch well.

Growing Tips
Water deeply every two or three weeks in the summer to promote flower bud formation, but do not over-water. Feed lightly in the spring with an azalea-camellia fertilizer. If leaves turn yellow with darker green veins, apply chelated iron according to directions.

Care
In late winter, thin or limb up sasanquas for size and shape. In spring (but be sure it's well before summer starts) lightly tip-prune new growth for more flowers in the fall. Sasanquas are susceptible to petal blight. Clean up and remove the spent blooms to ward off fungus. Spray horticultural oil for tea scale on the undersides of leaves.

Companion Planting and Design
Sasanqua camellia is frequently pruned into a low-growing foundation plant or espaliered to climb a wall or fence. Most commonly it is used as a tree-form specimen or accent by entryways or patios, or as an understory tree in high shade. Companions include evergreen azaleas, pieris, ferns, hydrangea, and hard features such as an antique urn or bench.

Personal Favorites
Cold-tolerant selections include 'Apple Blossom' (single white flowers), 'Sparkling Burgundy', and 'Cleopatra' (rose pink, semi-double). 'Shishi-Gashira' is an outstanding "groundcover" hybrid, with semi-double rose red flowers from October to March (some years) on shrubs that are only 3 feet tall but 5 feet wide. 'Yuletide' is a small hybrid that starts blooming bright red in December. For gardeners in very high elevations and northernmost counties, ask a garden center to order some of the other new cold hardy camellia hybrids, with names such as 'Polar Ice', 'Winter's Star', 'Pink Icicle', and 'Snow Flurry'.

The camellia commonly called "sasanqua" blooms out of context—in the fall, often right before our first frost of the season. But that's okay, because the plant (or some of its newer forms) is totally winter hardy. In late October or early November, when the rest of the garden is in its last blaze of fall color, this serene shrub—which during the spring and summer is just a nice, neat evergreen with shiny leaves—breaks out in pink, white, or lipstick-red flowers. Small blooming branches can be brought indoors for the holidays where their glamour will be appreciated up close. Because the shrub has smaller leaves and flowers, it is considered more versatile than Camellia japonica.

Other Common Name
Sasanqua

Bloom Period and Seasonal Color
Rose, pink, white, red blooms in late fall

Mature Height × Spread
6 to 15 feet × 4 to 8 feet

Spirea

Spiraea species

Heirloom spireas are among the toughest shrubs you can plant—and they will be there decades later. Mostly spring blooming, every branch of the round-headed or upright, arching shrubs will be covered with clusters of small, white, dusty-smelling posies. Long stems can be cut in the winter and brought indoors to "force" into flower in a vase of water. Compact shrubby varieties, most with pink or rosy flowers in flat heads held above the plants, bloom from late spring and well into summer, or even in the fall. The ones that bloom with azaleas make perfect fine-textured complements without stealing the show, and if the azaleas die, the spirea will remain as a "garden friendly" plant on its own.

Bloom Period and Seasonal Color
White, pink blooms in spring and summer

Mature Height × Spread
3 to 8 feet × 3 to 8 feet

When, Where, and How to Plant

Dig and divide multiple-stem shrubs in the fall or winter, root cuttings in the fall or winter to transplant the following fall, or set out container-grown plants any time. Spireas grow equally well in sun or shade, and tolerate all but the most waterlogged soils. When planting, loosen and spread roots to get them started growing out into your native soil. Space 3 to 6 feet apart, depending on the mature size of your selection.

Growing Tips

Once established, spireas are boring to maintain—there is nothing you need to do, except spread a little all-purpose fertilizer under the shrubs every four or five years.

Care

Thin tall growth as needed to maintain its natural shape, or cut close to the ground immediately after flowering to control size. Spireas are pest free and tolerant of city conditions.

Companion Planting and Design

Spireas are ideal for historic, cottage, country, or informal gardens. They look lovely against an evergreen backdrop, and make excellent hedges and mass plantings, especially in shaded older gardens. Interplant with azaleas and camellias, cedars, magnolia, arborvitae, and large crape myrtles, or "skirt" with large-flowering bulbs, pansies, iris, and dianthus.

Personal Favorites

Baby's breath (*S. thunbergii*) is very early with single white blossoms in February and decent yellow fall color on narrow leaves. True bridalwreath spirea (*S. prunifolia*) blooms next with clusters of tiny double button-like white flowers in March, and can be 6 to 8 feet tall. Reeves (*S. cantoniensis*) blooms white in April in clusters surrounding thin arching stems. Of the white flowering spireas, the large Vanhoutte (*S. × vanhouttei*) blooms latest with large (2-inch) showy, flat clusters of white held atop arching stems and angular, fingernail-like green leaves. Small, 3-foot, shrubby, "pink" spireas such as 'Anthony Waterer' (*S. japonica*) bloom from May to July or August. 'Gold Mound' and 'Limemound' have gold and lime green foliage.

Strawberry Bush
Euonymus americanus

When, Where, and How to Plant
Plant container-grown shrubs almost any time of the year—really, any time you can find them for sale. Or dig and transplant native plants (with permission, of course) in the fall or winter—be sure to wear hunter orange, because you will be walking the woods during deer season! Find a suitable area in woodland shade for planting this naturalizing shrub. Dig a wide, shallow bed and amend with native or natural leaf mould and compost, spread the roots out during planting, water deeply, and mulch heavily.

Growing Tips
Water this durable native plant only during extreme drought. Spreading or just raking a thick layer of natural leaf mulch (which you probably have already) around the base will generally feed the plant, but you can feed very lightly in the spring with cottonseed meal, compost, or a light application of all-purpose fertilizer.

Care
Prune to thicken the plant, or it will remain leggy and thin. Remove tall branches that cause the plant to lean over, and tip-prune what is left to encourage dense branching. There are no major pests, though whiteflies can be a nuisance if you brush the plant as you walk by.

Companion Planting and Design
Strawberry bush is at home in informal or native gardens, but also works well in tropical collections for its green winter stems, and in contemporary or oriental gardens as a unique specimen planted against a backdrop. It creates a naturalistic effect when planted under small groups of trees, but shows up best with a backdrop. Companion plantss include hellebores, daffodils, ferns, and creeping phlox.

Personal Favorite
There are no cultivars for this underused native shrub.

This curiously beautiful ornamental is native throughout our woodlands, both high and dry and in bottomlands. In the wild it can seem thin and scraggly, growing in extreme drought and shady thickets with airy stems that remain green even in the winter. In spring, the strawberry bush sprouts small, oval, green leaves and pale greenish-white blooms in the leaf axils. By late summer it wakes up with leaves burning bright red, orange, and yellow (it's in the same family as the incendiary winged euonymus). And if colorful foliage wasn't enough, the shrub's unusual strawberry-red fruit capsules crack open to reveal purple insides as they shove out dangling orange seeds like gaudy clip earrings—or heart's-a-bustin', as some gardener's call it.

Other Common Names
Hearts Bursting, Heart's-a-Bustin'

Bloom Period and Seasonal Color
Greenish spring flowers, yellow-red fall color, red and orange winter fruit

Mature Height × Spread
4 to 6 feet × 3 to 4 feet

Sweet Olive

Osmanthus fragrans

Sweet olive has the type of sweetly delicate but persistent fragrance that wafts through the night in romance novels (or should); though not overpowering. One shrub can scent an entire neighborhood. This big, broad-leaved evergreen is named for its fruity scent that comes from clusters of tiny white flowers hidden in the foliage at leaf joints. Blooming mostly in the fall and spring, many flowers will open even on warm winter days. It is often planted as a surrogate fragrance for showier camellias, which often bloom at the same time but have no scent. Sweet olive has an irregular, upright form with glossy leaves and grows 10 to 15 feet tall, even taller in ideal conditions.

Other Common Name
Fragrant Tea Olive

Bloom Period and Seasonal Color
Pale yellow, orange, or white blooms fall and spring

Mature Height × Spread
10 to 15 feet × 6 to 10 feet

When, Where, and How to Plant
Plant container-grown shrubs almost any time of the year, if watered regularly. Sweet olive grows best in light shade but can tolerate sun if it has a good root system. Dig a wide hole and amend with plenty of organic matter, then water deeply but not frequently to encourage wide-ranging roots. In northern counties plant it in a sheltered location to protect it from winter cold and winds. Space plants 4 to 6 feet apart.

Growing Tips
Water deeply every few weeks in hot, dry summers to ensure plentiful flowers in the fall. Fertilize lightly in the spring, but not too heavily or you will have all leaves and fewer, less scented flowers. Feeding in the late summer can lead to over-tender growth that is more likely to freeze.

Care
Sweet olive needs little pruning. Pinch tips from new growth in spring for a thicker shrub. If damaged by severe cold, cut out the dead wood and let the shrub grow back from the roots. It is pest free and fairly easy to grow, if given the right conditions.

Companion Planting and Design
Use it as a specimen plant near a walkway, patio, or window where you can better savor its fragrance. Sweet olive is also used in large shrub borders, hedges, foundation plantings (if pruned), and seaside gardens. It's an excellent companion for camellias, even in containers in cool greenhouses.

Personal Favorites
'Butter Yellow' and 'Orange Supreme' have yellow and orange flowers. The form *aurantiacus* has narrow leaves and orange flowers that are heavily scented in the early fall. Relatives include hybrid fortune osmanthus (*O. × fortunei*), or fortune tea olive, which is smaller, more compact, and more cold hardy with fragrant white flowers in fall. False holly (*O. heterophyllus*) has spiny, holly-like leaves and fall blooms that are fragrant. Devilwood (*O. americanus*) is a native of our coastal swamps that flowers in March and April.

Virginia Sweetspire
Itea virginica

When, Where, and How to Plant
Divide and move small plants from colonies in the fall or winter, and cut them back to reduce stress on new roots. Plant container-grown shrubs any time of the year. Plant in light shade, or full sun with lots of mulch and water, giving plants plenty of room to spread naturally—set out new plants 3 or 4 feet apart for a fuller initial effect. Prepare beds by tilling in organic matter. Loosen roots of container-grown plants during planting. Water deeply to settle soil around roots, then cover the area with mulch.

Growing Tips
Water occasionally, especially if plants have spread into dry woodland areas where other plants may soak up available moisture. Feed lightly in the spring, but no more than once a year to encourage better fall color. Use a natural fertilizer rather than fast-acting chemicals.

Care
It is not necessary to prune sweetspire, except to cut out dead wood any time, or to rejuvenate overgrown plants by cutting old stems close to the ground in late winter or spring, while the shrub is still dormant. Virginia sweetspire is pest free and attracts butterflies and hummingbirds, so treating with chemical pest controls does more harm than good.

Companion Planting and Design
Use it for mass plantings in wooded or lightly shaded areas underneath Japanese maples, native azaleas, wax myrtle, oakleaf hydrangea, and 'Little Gem' magnolia. Sweetspire's fall color has more impact in large masses, especially in front of a green background, such as an anise hedge. Spring bulbs and native woodland perennials such as blue phlox and alumroot blend in well with the arching foliage of sweetspire.

Personal Favorites
'Henry's Garnet', the most popular commercially available selection, is named for its fall color. It gets about 4 feet tall by 6 feet wide. 'Little Henry' is more compact and a mere 3 feet tall. 'Long Spire' has 7-inch flower clusters, 'Sarah Eve' has pink-tinged flowers, and 'Saturnalia' features orange, purple, and wine-red fall colors.

A graceful shrub native to our woodlands, Virginia sweetspire would probably replace other shrub choices for fall color if only more people outside the native plant and landscaping industry knew about it. The problem is, Virginia sweetspire simply doesn't look like much in a small garden center pot in the spring. Mounding and colony-forming in wooded areas, this deciduous shrub has arching, reddish-green branches and narrow, oval leaves that are 4 inches long and dark green. The foliage ignites into ruby red, purple, and orange in the fall and hangs onto the plants well into winter—sometimes until new spring growth forces them off the plant. Its creamy white flowers, held aloft in midsummer, are tightly packed clusters up to 6 inches long, small but fragrant.

Bloom Period and Seasonal Color
White blooms in summer with red fall foliage

Mature Height × Spread
3 to 10 feet × 3 to 8 feet

Wax Myrtle
Myrica cerifera

Southern wax myrtle almost always surprises gardeners by its fast, vigorous growth—a small shrub can become a small tree in two years. A native of the Coastal Plains in the southern counties, it is sometimes seen growing wild along roadsides everywhere except in our highest elevations. It can survive hard freezes to come back from sturdy roots and make small trees by midsummer. Wax myrtle quickly develops into an airy multiple- trunk shrub with a wide canopy, covered with narrow, toothed, oddly olive-colored leaves. Its twigs are densely crusted with bluish gray berries whose waxy covering is used in making candles. In most gardens, the plants need annual pruning to stay in bounds.

Other Common Name
Bayberry

Bloom Period and Seasonal Color
Evergreen foliage

Mature Height × Spread
4 to 20 feet × 4 to 15 feet

When, Where, and How to Plant
Set out container-grown plants any time of the year, in full sun or light shade, in nearly any type of soil except pure clay. Dig a wide hole or bed and amend your native soil (especially heavy clay) with organic matter and loosen tightly potbound roots at planting time. If your soil is clay, raise the bed by adding more sand and organic matter for better drainage. Water deeply, and cover the planting area with pine straw or other loose mulch. Space 4 to 10 feet apart, depending on the type.

Growing Tips
Water only during extreme dry spells; this hardy native grows well in both dry soils and wet. Fertilize lightly in the late winter or spring, but avoid excess fertilizer that can lead to growth even more rampant than already occurs. Maintain a layer of mulch underneath.

Care
Wax myrtle needs annual pruning, either to thin tall branches or to clean small sucker growth off lower trunks, or shearing to increase foliage density. Wax myrtle hedges do need shearing. Prune any time of the year except late summer or fall, which can stimulate tender new growth too late in the season. Other than occasional leaf spot, there are no major pests.

Companion Planting and Design
Plant wax myrtles behind oakleaf hydrangeas, line a sidewalk with a row, or plant as a filler in high shade between tall pines. Use as a specimen in large planters, limbed up into small evergreen specimen trees. Companions include pines, Southern magnolia, ornamental grasses, and small Kurume azaleas.

Personal Favorites
The species is fine for large areas. 'Luray' is very compact, only 4 or 5 feet tall and wide, and the form *pumila* reaches only 3 feet tall but spreads into a groundcover mass. *M. pensylvanica* is more cold hardy and denser, with green leaves and fruit coated in the fragrant white wax that is used in bayberry candles.

Weigela
Weigela florida

When, Where, and How to Plant

Weigela, though widely produced, is often difficult to find commercially, but can easily be ordered through customer-service-oriented garden centers, mail-order, or Internet nursery sites. They are also extremely easy to root from cuttings taken in the fall or winter, to be planted the following fall. Plant bare-root shrubs in the winter before they leaf out, or container-grown plants any time of the year. Weigela grows and flowers best in full sun or light shade, with no protection from winter cold (it is hardy into Canada). Avoid low, wet sites, digging a wide hole and lightly amending with organic matter. Mulch to protect roots. Space 3 to 6 feet apart, depending on the mature size of the variety.

Growing Tips

There is generally no need to water weigela—ever. It is about as tough a shrub as you could find, with old neglected specimens flowering around country homes. Feed very lightly every few years with an all-purpose fertilizer spread under the shrub in the spring.

Care

To promote new growth, more flowers, and attractive foliage, cut back one-third of the older canes nearly to the ground every year and then leave them alone. There are no major pests to contend with, other than whiteflies.

Companion Planting and Design

Use it as a foundation plant in rustic settings, as a distant hedge, low screen, or mass along a hillside. This shrub is a hummingbird magnet. It is coarse textured, and sets well against a backdrop of ornamental grasses, evergreen cedar or holly, and precedes the flowers of althea. Underplant with daffodils.

Personal Favorites

Our great-grandmothers grew the common red, pink, and white weigelas and they are still good plants. 'Variegata' has deep rosy red flowers and green-and-white foliage. 'Lucifer' has extra-large deep red flowers, and 'Wine and Roses' has bright pink flowers set against leaves that start out deep purple and by fall are nearly black.

Growing as wide as it does tall, the gangly old-fashioned weigela shrub is not very attractive in summer, winter, or fall, making it seem like a difficult shrub to work into a landscape. But when it comes into flower in late spring—long after the glory of azaleas has subsided—this heirloom shrub's long, arching branches nod to the ground under the weight of many dozens of inch-long, funnel-shaped, red, pink, or white flowers. Look again at the Latin name—"florida" means lots of flowers, not the state. Not surprisingly, it is popular with butterfly and hummingbird enthusiasts.

Bloom Period and Seasonal Color

White, pink, red blooms in mid- to late spring

Mature Height × Spread

3 to 10 feet × 3 to 12 feet

187

Winged Euonymus
Euonymus alatus

This exotic Asian shrub, with its dense, mounding, green form, is a sleeper in the summer, and we wonder why it is so commonly planted around interstate exits and shopping mall parking lots. But as soon as the days shorten in the fall and night temperatures begin to drop, the dull green foliage becomes perhaps the most astonishing blaze of red of any plant on Earth. It's no wonder that one of its common names is "burning bush." Unfortunately, this eye-popping show is only seen in the northern counties and higher elevations; in mild winter areas it remains plain green in the fall. Even after the leaves shed, the densely twiggy shrub is interesting with unusual corky "wings" along its stems, hence its most common name.

Other Common Name
Burning Bush

Bloom Period and Seasonal Color
Scarlet fall foliage

Mature Height × Spread
3 to 15 feet × 3 to 15 feet

When, Where, and How to Plant
Plant container-grown plants any time of the year, although for areas where watering is not going to be practical, plant in the fall so plants will be root-established before hot summer comes around. Plant in full sun (in the shade fall color is pink at best), in a wide bed only lightly amended with organic matter, just enough to get plant roots started out right. Mulch heavily. Space the species winged euonymus no closer than 6 feet apart.

Growing Tips
This is another tough plant that needs little or no supplemental watering and can go for years without fertilizers. Water big plants grown in small areas during extreme drought—if possible—and feed lightly in the spring if you must.

Care
Prune only if absolutely necessary, either by cutting severely to "rejuvenate" or by selectively thinning cluttered or taller stems. If plants get scale, spray with horticultural oil.

Companion Planting and Design
Winged euonymus is used by landscape designers to call attention to a special feature, make a bold color statement (forming a bright red hedge), or create a symphony of different colors—greens, reds, and yellows—in the fall garden. Its cold hardiness and drought tolerance make it ideally suited for difficult-to-water and tricky-to-mow slopes, parking lot dividers, schoolyards, and other full-sun, exposed sites. The best companions would be backdrop evergreens such as magnolia, pines, and cedar, or pampas grass. It's stunning also near the yellow foliage of ginkgo and the reds and oranges of red maples in the fall. Underplant with hardy evergreen groundcovers such as wintercreeper euonymus, creeping juniper, or Asiatic jasmine, or just mulch and add lots of naturalizing types of daffodils.

Personal Favorites
The species is way too big for anyone with a normal-size garden. At a mere 6 or 8 feet tall and wide, 'Compactus' is smaller and denser than the species, hides its lower limbs better, but is just as showy in the fall. 'Rudy Haag' is very compact and only 3 to 5 feet tall and wide.

When, Where, and How to Plant

Small yucca "pups" can be twisted or cut off the base of existing clumps any time of the year, and either potted up for later planting or stuck directly into freshly prepared planting sites. Plant container-grown plants any time. Plant in full sun or light shade, in well-drained soil or on a slope. Space clump-forming yuccas 2 or 3 feet apart and they will quickly grow together. Loosen the roots and spread out any runners or suckers you find growing from the rootball. Water one time and be done with it.

Growing Tips

No need to water this native plant—ever. Feed with a slow-release or natural fertilizer in the spring.

Care

There is no pruning at all, other than snipping off the faded flower stalks and perhaps trimming away dead lower foliage once a year. The worst pests are spider mites and lacebugs, which seriously discolor older leaves. Use insecticidal soap in the late spring and summer.

Companion Planting and Design

Clump-forming yuccas make perfect single accents either in the ground or in containers left out all year. They help naturalize a small meadow or woodland garden, provide winter texture to perennial borders, and are perfect contrasts to small or medium evergreen shrubs such as nandina, holly, and boxwood. They work well with grasses, sedum, salvia, herbs, purple coneflower, and perennial bulbs as well.

Personal Favorites

Though the parentage is somewhat confused, good cultivars to look for are 'Bright Edge' with yellow edges; 'Variegata' with creamy white edges that turn pink in the winter; and 'Garland's Gold' with a yellow stripe down the center of each leaf. Spanish dagger (*Y. gloriosa*) has a sharp name, but is a very gentle clump-forming yucca that gets up to 3 feet tall, with soft leaves that bend downward toward their tips under their own weight, and huge flower stalks.

Yucca causes most people to think "No! Too pointy and dangerous!" But that's only the tall, stiff Spanish bayonet (Yucca aloifolia). The most commonly grown yucca, Adam's needle (Y. filamentosa var. flaccida or Y. filifera), a hardy native throughout the eastern United States and into Canada, is actually a safe, clump-forming evergreen plant. It makes a perfect all-season accent and companion to flower beds and shrubs alike—in sun or shade. It stays put, and doesn't try to poke you in the eye or skewer your beach ball. And its tall spike of white flowers adds to the interest. It and other "soft tip" yuccas can grow in tight, hot, dry spots that little else can survive, and are well worth adding to any garden.

Other Common Names
Adam's Needle, Bear Grass

Bloom Period and Seasonal Color
Evergreen with tall spikes of white summer flowers

Mature Height × Spread
2 to 3 feet × 2 to 3 feet

Trees *for Alabama & Mississippi*

Trees are more than oxygen machines and home to wildlife—they are the low-maintenance framing "walls" and "ceiling" of our landscapes, they block unsightly views, and help conserve energy. Plus, they generally lift human spirits weary of pavement and wall-to-wall grass. Many popular trees are fast growing but relatively short-lived (thirty years is a long life for some), and some like Bradford pears and dogwoods are fussy. Other trees can be slow growing but long-lived and stately workhorses, more valuable to future generations. They range from magnificent evergreens such as live oak, longleaf pine (Alabama's state tree), magnolia (Mississippi's state tree), red cedar, and American holly, to deciduous oaks and cypress.

A clear trend in landscaping is planting naturalistic groups of trees, like "woodland islands" in the lawn. Connecting them with mulch and underplanting with smaller shade-tolerant trees, shrubs, and perennials helps trees grow better and reduces their maintenance—and that of the lawn—dramatically. Keep in mind when selecting and siting a tree in your landscape that it is not something you can move easily. Know the tree's mature shape and ultimate size, and give it enough room to grow. When buying trees to plant, keep in mind that small ones will outgrow larger ones of the same species nearly every time—at a much lower cost and higher chance of survival. And you don't need to dig as large a hole!

Prune Trees the Right Way

Remove limbs and branches from trees without changing the natural shape. Simply cut them off at their points of origin—to the outside of the swollen area near the trunk, called the "collar." For faster

Kousa Dogwood

healing, do not leave stubs, which will decay and possibly cause internal tree rot. There is no need to use so-called "pruning paints," which are simply cosmetic and have no long-term benefit.

Topping trees is *not* good for them! If a tree is in the way of a power line, carefully prune so the tree grows around the line (better yet, have a professional tree trimmer do it). Tree topping creates a lot of succulent (and brittle) growth, which is more likely to be broken off in high winds, and ruins the natural (and more stable) branching pattern of the tree. Topping also causes a great deal of stress to the tree, which can encourage pests and diseases.

Slash Pines

Cutting a few surface roots generally will not harm a mature tree, but covering or compacting or digging all the way around can cut off major roots and cause slow decline or death. Keep in mind that the most active roots of a tree are at the perimeter of the drip line (the outer spread of branches). Protecting roots from compaction and other damage only near the trunk is not enough to keep the tree from possible irreparable harm, which might not show up for years. If you are undergoing construction on your property, place protective fencing around your trees, as far out as the widest spreading branches.

Planting Under Trees

Planting under mature trees can be tricky, if not downright impossible. First of all, the soil under large trees is often compacted and hard, in which case it may take two or three digging sessions to get the soil loose enough, deep enough. When possible, do this a day or two after a good rain, or after the area has been soaked deeply, which softens the soil dramatically; avoid digging when the soil is sticky wet, or it can ball up and be worse than ever. Each time you dig, loosen the soil as deeply as you can and let water soak further down to soften it even more.

Red Maples

Avoid cutting or burying large roots! They are the main pipelines between the tree trunk and many hundreds of smaller "feeder" roots, and cutting them off essentially cuts off the tree's ability to absorb water and nutrients. Covering the area with several inches of topsoil is not a wise idea either since it can suffocate a tree's shallow roots (roots need oxygen as well as water). Also, over-watering or overfeeding to compensate for root damage can actually rot the roots that remain! Use a shovel, not a tiller, to dig around and between large roots as best you can, poking organic matter into pockets here and there. Since it is generally dry under large trees, be sure to use drought-tolerant plants.

After planting under large trees, mulch heavily to replicate natural leaf mulch, which will slowly decompose and work its way into the soil to "feed" the soil and further improve the growing conditions. Before you know it, earthworms will return to the once-hard soil and continue the digging job that your shovel began. One last thing about planting under large mature trees: Any deep digging—especially while installing or replacing sewer, water, or irritation pipes, cuts off all the roots outside the dug area. Doing this to more than a third or so of the area under a tree severely damages its roots.

Trees for Energy Conservation

At the height of summer solstice, the sun actually rises in the northeast and sets in the northwest, but by midwinter it makes a low arc across the southern sky. Cool summer breezes typically come from the south in the summer, and harsh winds from the north-northwest. For protection from hot summer sun, plant shade trees so they will cast a shadow on east and west walls and by northeast and northwest corners, where they will block morning and afternoon summer sunshine. Plant smaller deciduous trees on the south side so they will not block cooling summer breezes that will carry heat off your roof, and when they drop their leaves in the winter they will let warm sunshine help heat the house. For protection from cold winter winds, plant evergreen screens—both trees and large shrubs—on the north and northwest corners of the house where they will block and lift winds up over your house.

Tree Guidelines

Here are few things to consider for success with trees:

- Pick the right tree for the right spot, especially for soil drainage. Always look up before planting, to make sure the tree won't grow into utility or power lines, and check with utility companies before digging so roots won't interfere with water, sewer, or buried utility lines, or sidewalks.
- When possible, plant trees in the fall or winter so their roots can take advantage of seasonal rains and they can get established before enduring their first hot, dry summer.
- When planting new trees, dig a wide hole, not a deep one, and loosen the soil an extra shovel's width or so around the hole to help new roots grow into your native soil. Loosen potting soil and tightly wrapped roots on container-grown trees to get them growing outward.
- Do not over-water new trees (most grow poorly in wet, swampy soil conditions, which irrigation systems often create). Give trees a slow, deep soaking every two weeks their first summer, and they will quickly develop strong, deep roots like their country cousins. If your soil is very poorly drained, plant trees a little high and slope soil up to them—like a baseball pitcher's mound.

- Mulch newly planted trees with a ring or "doughnut" of pine straw or shredded bark, which mimic's natural woodland conditions, conserves moisture, keeps grass away from the roots, and keeps the lawn mower and string trimmer from nicking tender young trunks (the single leading cause of new tree death).
- Feed trees by broadcasting all-purpose fertilizer under the outer spread of the branches (the drip line) and beyond; if you feed the lawn, you will also feed nearby trees.
- As trees grow, cut off lower limbs or spreading branches that interfere with people walking nearby or otherwise get in the way.

Chaste Tree

American Holly

Ilex opaca

Native holly trees, which stand out in the winter woods across the South, are slow growing and tolerant of poor soils. The American holly forms a sculptural green pyramid atop a pale gray trunk. Its spiny leaves can be glossy or dull, and a fairly heavy crop of red winter berries attracts a host of birds. There are hundreds of named selections of American holly and many hybrids, with different leaf shapes and tree forms; in many cases the hybrids have a more abundant berry crop than the wild species. The trees are long-lived enough to make good living memorials, and can be found in many older landscapes. While wild American holly plants are either male or female, with both needed for berry production, some hybrids are self-fertile.

Bloom Period and Seasonal Color
Evergreen foliage, red berries in winter

Mature Height × Spread
40 to 50 feet × 15 to 40 feet

When, Where, and How to Plant
When possible, to prevent leaf drop, plant American hollies in the fall or in winter if the ground is not frozen. In nature, holly occurs in the woods under high shade, but it thrives in full sun; avoid dry, windy sites. American holly likes loose, moist, acid soils that are well drained, but will tolerate a little standing water in the winter. Allow 10 to 15 feet between plants (or a building), depending upon the selection. Prepare a planting area three to five times the diameter of the rootball. Add a controlled-release, nitrogen-rich, tree-and-shrub fertilizer to the soil, according to directions. Loosen the roots of container-grown trees. Mulch after planting.

Growing Tips
In lieu of rain, water newly planted trees deeply every two or three weeks the first summer, than only as needed. Fertilize every year or two. Leave lower branches and limbs on trees to help hide leaf litter on the ground below.

Care
American hollies suffer from leaf scorch, especially on young plants or those suddenly exposed to the sun, or after a hot, dry summer. Though these hollies are rarely bothered by deer, their appearance can be marred by "tar spot" fungus and leaf miners, for which there are no practical controls.

Companion Planting and Design
Find a special place in your landscape for this stately specimen tree, or use it as a thick screen. Unless you choose a self-fertile cultivar, make sure you have at least one male for every two or three females for berry production. Underplant with liriope or other groundcovers to hide the slow-to-decompose fallen leaves. Though often used this way, American holly does not make a good foundation plant close to a house.

Personal Favorites
'Croonenburg' has both male and female flowers on the same plant and saves you the trouble of buying two hollies; 'Canary' has yellow berries. Another great group of hollies are hybrids between American and other hollies, notably *Ilex × attenuata*; favorites include the self-fruitful 'Foster's #2', 'Savannah', and 'East Palatka'.

Bald Cypress
Taxodium distichum

When, Where, and How to Plant
Set out container-grown trees any time you can dig a wide hole, but plant bare-root saplings in the winter when they are still dormant. Plant in full sun or very light shade, but remember to look up for power lines—cypress grows straight and tall! It tolerates a wide range of soil conditions, from damp (creek or pond banks) to dry. Dig a wide hole and very lightly amend it to help roots grow outward quickly. Allow 20 feet between trees or between cypress and any structures.

Growing Tips
Small cypress trees planted any time of the year generally lose their leaves early the first fall. Water young cypress trees during long dry spells the first year or so, but don't think you have to keep them wet. Feed sparingly if at all, especially if a fertilized lawn is nearby where tree roots can forage for nutrients.

Care
Bald cypress usually needs a little thinning of lower limbs and branches, to make the tree look more "tree-like" and expose its attractive spreading trunk. Simply snip off branches and limbs that are not growing in the direction you want. Spider mites and occasionally bagworms can affect the leaves, as can a bluish ball-like fungus, but no controls are needed.

Companion Planting and Design
Though bald cypress tolerates dry settings, it is ideal for wet areas, especially where its knobby root protrusions ("knees") will not interfere with mowing. Its narrow, conical form works well as a specimen tree or in a natural grouping. Underplant with Louisiana iris, which flowers even in the shade and also loves moist soil; in drier settings use vinca, liriope, or ferns. Where space permits a long view, combine with Southern magnolia, pines, and Japanese maple for a stunning contrast.

Personal Favorites
There really are not any selections of bald cypress, but the species is great as it is. Pond cypress (*T. ascendens*) grows faster than bald cypress, is more narrow, and has leaves that stand upward rather than in whorls around the stem.

The bayous of the Deep South are filled with cypress trees, with turtles sunning on the eerie cypress "knees" sticking up out of the dark water. But they can also be seen high and dry in botanic gardens, and as street trees in holes cut into concrete sidewalks. Truth is, they are very versatile trees whose only real water requirements are for seed sprouting. Their light green, feathery leaves turn rusty brown before shedding in autumn, but they are small and do not pose a leaf litter problem. The beautiful peely bark and dense, finely branching twigs are striking in winter. Bald cypress was heavily logged a century ago, but in protected areas of the South there are awesome, gnarly-kneed trees 400 to 800 years old.

Other Common Name
Cypress

Bloom Period and Seasonal Color
Deciduous with bronze fall foliage

Mature Height × Spread
50 to 70 feet × 20 to 30 feet

Chaste Tree

Vitex agnus-castus

This small, round-topped tree (sometimes multi-trunk) dresses itself in long, showy spikes of blue flowers from late May to autumn. The old-fashioned plant, loved by gardeners and honey producers alike, has come back into popularity as a fast-growing specimen that stops traffic when in bloom. Plus it is a butterfly and hummingbird magnet. When not in flower, chaste tree's deeply divided leaves, each with several long leaflets spread out like a hand, is appealing—though it looks suspiciously like marijuana—and has a strong, pungent, musty aroma when bruised. The common name "chaste tree," and the less common "monk's pepper," comes from the myth that the seeds encourage chastity.

Other Common Names
Vitex, Monk's Pepper

Bloom Period and Seasonal Color
Blue, lilac, pink, white blooms May through September

Mature Height × Spread
15 to 25 feet × 10 to 20 feet

When, Where, and How to Plant

Plant chaste tree any time you can get it and can dig a wide hole. Flowering best in full sun, the tree tolerates intense drought, and must have well-drained soil or its roots will rot. Usually used as a wide-growing specimen tree, you can plant other trees 20 feet or more away without crowding. Mulch the tree to keep roots moist the first year, or plant a groundcover beneath it.

Growing Tips

Water new plants until established, but do not keep wet. Cut young plants back to get them to branch out closer to the ground. Do not overfertilize or trees will grow weak branches that can snap in ice storms, or even during hard summer rains if they have a heavy flower load.

Care

Thin out excess trunks and limbs in the winter when you can better see what you are doing. Tip-pruning after the first big flush of flowers will result in a uniform display of many more flowers later. It can also be cut back hard in late winter to resprout from the base, to control size. Vitex can get a fungal leaf spot during muggy summers, and a little leaf-tip burn when roots are kept too wet. And the bees that it attracts can be bothersome to visitors, or to people passing underneath.

Companion Planting and Design

Because of its width and unusual color, it works best as a specimen in a lawn, or the back of a flower border where it has plenty of room. Chaste tree is fun to plant within view of a window to enjoy the summer show from inside. For a more formal garden, "limb it up" to take on a tree form and plant in groups or rows for impact. Underplant with daylily or purple coneflower, which contrasts well with the flowers.

Personal Favorites

There are several named selections, including 'Fletcher Pink', 'Montrose Purple' (rich violet), 'Shoal Creek' (blue-violet on flower stems over a foot long), 'Rosea' (pink), and the form *alba* (white).

Cherry Laurel
Prunus caroliniana

When, Where, and How to Plant
Container-grown plants can be set out any time of the year, and though it is always best to transplant seedlings in the fall or winter, small plants under 3 feet tall can be moved any time, with supplemental summer watering. Plant in sun or shade, in a well-drained, moderately amended soil, and mulch to recreate natural woodland conditions. Place those grown as trees at least 10 feet from structures to give them room to spread; for a hedge, plant no closer than 4 or 5 feet apart. Avoid planting over a formal patio where fruit litter will be a problem.

Growing Tips
Once established, hardy native cherry laurel requires little or no water, but responds readily to a light spring application of an all-purpose fertilizer, especially if sheared as a hedge.

Care
Where there is room to grow, leave it natural or remove selected lower limbs for a more graceful tree. For a more formal effect, shear in the late spring after flowering, but be aware that shearing often causes temporary leaf mutilation. To create an interesting multiple trunk specimen, cut a small plant close to the ground when young. It occasionally suffers from leaf spot (the same disease that devastates red tip photinia), but this only results in a little leaf shedding.

Companion Planting and Design
Use as a woodland specimen to stand out in the winter garden, as a large sheared formal hedge, or in a naturalistic group. It is an excellent evergreen backdrop for large flowering shrubs and is a good replacement in northern counties for less hardy privet. Underplant with mondo grass or liriope, which tolerate the shade and from which seedlings are easily pulled.

Personal Favorites
Dense, more compact 'Bright 'n Tight' ('Compacta') is an outstanding landscape selection for hedges or foundation plantings. The similar *P. laurocerasus* 'Otto Luyken' is more of a shrub at 3 to 4 feet tall and 6 to 8 feet wide and is widely available in nurseries.

One of the sturdiest small evergreen trees for the Southern landscape, this glossy-leaf native is a woodland understory tree that thrives in shade or sun—one of the few very good hedge plants for shade. Though grown for its foliage, the short, dense spikes of creamy white spring flowers give a white-cloud effect and are very attractive to bees, and glossy black fruits are favorites of birds. It takes very well to pruning as a dense evergreen shrub, either specimen or hedge, and it remains dense longer than other shrubs, requiring less frequent follow-up pruning. The fruit litter may be messy around a patio, and seedlings sprout readily in nearby flower beds—all the better for sharing with gardening friends.

Other Common Name
Carolina Cherry Laurel

Bloom Period and Seasonal Color
Spring white flowers, evergreen

Mature Height × Spread
25 to 35 feet × 15 to 25 feet

Chinese Pistache

Pistacia chinensis

A hardy import, Chinese pistache is a favorite of landscape architects and designers. The medium-sized street tree grows quickly into a rounded, shady canopy in summer. Though its flowers are rather insignificant, the many-leaflet foliage rivals maples for red, orange, or yellow fall color, even along the coast. The tree shows off interesting, exfoliating bark in winter. Pistache trees can be male or female, but only when one of each is nearby will a gardener ever see the small clusters of tiny fruit in the fall (the ornamental types are not the same as the pistachio nut trees).

Other Common Name
Chinese Pistachio

Bloom Period and Seasonal Color
Deciduous with yellow, orange, red fall foliage

Mature Height × Spread
35 to 60 feet × 30 to 50 feet

When, Where, and How to Plant
Plant pistache trees in the fall or winter so their roots will be better established before it gets hot and dry in summer. Plant in full sun at least 20 feet from other plants, or risk losing the characteristic rounded shape. Avoid planting where dripping sap from minor insect pests could fall on parked cars or patio furniture below. Chinese pistache likes average, well-drained soil. Its root system is not invasive, so it can be used close to a patio or house, even between a walkway and the house. Mulch the entire area with a 2- to 4-inch layer of pine straw or bark.

Growing Tips
Water pistache trees only during extreme drought; keeping them wet can cause root rot. Feed in the late winter or early spring very lightly if at all (especially if tree roots can get to a fertilized lawn where more nutrients might be available), or risk having a poor show of fall color.

Care
This tree has poor branch structure when young, making it gawky and floppy. Stake young trees to help form a straight trunk, and prune off lower limbs to get the trees above head-high. Autumn leaves drop over a short span of time, making for a low maintenance, one-time cleanup. The dripping of sticky "honeydew" from aphids is a minor problem.

Companion Planting and Design
Outstanding at a distance for its round shape, feathery foliage, and fall colors, or in the middle of a large terrace where its heat tolerance helps it provide welcome summer shade. Underplant with nandina (especially 'Compacta') whose winter foliage and berries complement the pistache bark.

Personal Favorites
Chinese pistache doesn't have selections available, so plant the species. Texas pistachio (*P. texana*) is not as large as the Chinese pistache, and is semi-evergreen where temperatures don't get below the mid-teens. It makes a nice feathery screen and grows well in limestone soils.

When, Where, and How to Plant

Plant this tough tree any time you can dig a decent hole, except for small bare-root plants that need planting while dormant in the fall or winter. Plant in full sun with excellent air circulation to help prevent powdery mildew disease; crape myrtles grown in partial shade bloom less and are more susceptible to mildew. They like rich, well-drained, slightly acid soil. Prepare a planting area three to five times the diameter of the rootball, and work in a little all-purpose fertilizer. Mulch the entire planting area.

Growing Tips

Water young crape myrtles only when they get dry, and fertilize lightly to stimulate growth—but not enough to cause rank leaf production at the expense of flowering.

Care

Crape myrtles rarely "need" pruning, unless for shaping or to limb them up so the attractive bark is more visible. Regularly remove inward-growing branches and "crossing" limbs where one begins to grow over the top of another. Light pruning in the late winter (to growth about the diameter of a pencil) will encourage more uniform flowering; a second light pruning in midsummer, after the first flush of flowers, will cause uniform new growth that produces a stunning show later in the summer or early fall. Call your county Extension agent for recommended controls for mildew and aphids.

Companion Planting and Design

Use as specimen trees, in pairs or groups to create a screen or wall of color, or as an allée down a walk or drive. In winter, their handsome bark and form are beautiful displayed against a contrasting wall or fence. Underplant with dwarf nandina, silvery-white artemisia, or Asiatic jasmine, and add some tall daffodils for a late winter show.

Personal Favorites

Old favorites include 'Near East' and 'Watermelon Red', but they are susceptible to problems. New "Native American" varieties with names like 'Natchez', 'Comanche', and 'Sioux' have superior flowers, bark, cold hardiness, and disease resistance. 'Dynamite' has stunning dark red flowers and reddish new growth.

Crape myrtle, the "lilac of the South," is an all-season tree, with gorgeous bark; upright, graceful form; small leaves with good autumn color (that don't require raking); and brilliant clusters of crepe-papery flowers of pink, white, red, or lavender from June through September. It works hard enough to be considered the South's favorite summer-flowering tree. It's also tolerant of the urban environment—both air pollution and reflected heat from pavement—and is often seen in cemeteries and around old abandoned houses. Standard sizes range from dwarf (about 3 feet tall) to 30 feet or more tall, in upright or mounding forms, so be sure you select the right size for your site.

Other Common Name
Southern Lilac

Bloom Period and Seasonal Color
Red, white, pink, purple blooms in July to September with red, orange fall foliage

Mature Height × Spread
3 to 30 feet × 4 to 30 feet

Deciduous Holly
Ilex decidua

Possum haw makes a handsome winter specimen tree in any garden. Female trees radiate with winter color, displaying bright orange-red or scarlet berries on completely naked, pale gray stems—a great attraction for migratory birds. The berries are also vividly contrasted against pale chartreuse fall foliage just as they are beginning to "red up." The small, rounded, multi-stemmed tree has a spreading dark green canopy in an overall form similar to crape myrtle. It is a tough and adaptable tree, as evidenced by how it grows naturally along highway fencerows. There are separate male and female plants, so at least one pollinator male is needed for good berry set.

Other Common Names
Possum Haw, Winterberry

Bloom Period and Seasonal Color
Orange-red berries in fall and winter

Mature Height × Spread
10 to 20 feet × 8 to 20 feet

When, Where, and How to Plant
Plant in the fall when plants first start showing up in garden centers. If transplanting from the wild, be aware that only some are berry-producing females, and a male pollinator is needed as well (young plants may take years to mature to flowering size). It is better to buy rooted, mature plants that you know will do well. Plant in full or mostly full sun, with a male pollinator holly nearby so bees can go back and forth between plants (so berries are produced later). Deciduous holly grows best in well-drained soils, with mulch to keep roots from overheating in the sun. Plant 8 to 10 feet apart.

Growing Tips
Water with a slow, deep soaking when absolutely necessary, such as after two months of drought, which can cause fruit drop. Fertilize lightly every two or three springs with an all-purpose fertilizer.

Care
Do not prune heavily, or risk losing spring flowers and therefore the next winter's berries. Thin out tall or wayward branches only, or tip-prune new growth in late spring to encourage more branching in summer for flower set by fall. No serious pests, other than cedar waxwing birds that can devour all the berries in one quick swoop.

Companion Planting and Design
Possum haw flourishes beneath the high shade of tall pines and hardwoods, and also grows amazingly well in the middle of a concrete patio. Use it alone or in groups in a natural setting such as along a woodland edge, or as a single tree along a rustic fence or against a wall. Complement in the winter with evergreen hollies, nandina, naturalizing daffodils, and soft-tip yucca.

Personal Favorites
'Council Fire' has orange-red berries that last until mid-March. 'Warren's Red' and 'Sundance' are also good selections. 'Byer's Golden' has orange berries. 'Red Escort' is a popular pollinator, as are any male American hollies (*I. opaca*). Another deciduous holly (*I. verticillata*), also called winterberry, is a smaller species.

Dogwood
Cornus florida

When, Where, and How to Plant

Container-grown dogwoods can be set out any time, but are more likely to survive if set out in the fall or early winter to get them better established before summer. While mature dogwoods have been grown in full sun, dogwoods grow naturally on wooded slopes—for the best chance of success, plant them in partial shade (morning sun is better than hot afternoon sun) in rich, slightly acid, well-drained soil. Place dogwoods at least 20 to 25 feet apart when using them in groups. When possible, add a little "dogwood dirt" to your native soil, dug from beneath a healthy mature dogwood; this adds beneficial soil organisms that are not present in potting soil. Mulch heavily to create a woodsy condition for roots.

Growing Tips

Water dogwoods deeply but not frequently—over-watering causes swampy soil conditions, exactly the opposite of what naturally drought-tolerant dogwoods require. Fertilize lightly at planting time and every spring.

Care

Prune dogwoods only to remove broken or dead limbs or branches, or to give them a more open, tree-like shape when they are young. Dogwoods suffer from different petal and leaf blights throughout the season, but most of these will not kill the trees. Trunk borers are a more serious problem. If they attack a prized dogwood, call your county Extension agent.

Companion Planting and Design

In addition to being "must have" understory trees for wooded lots—filling in vertically between taller trees and shade-loving shrubs and groundcovers—dogwoods, especially the pink ones, make good specimen trees in small gardens. Plant against a backdrop so the fine form of dogwoods can be seen all winter. Underplant with woodland wildflowers, mondo grass, liriope, ferns, or wintercreeper.

Personal Favorites

'Cherokee Princess' and 'Cloud 9' are popular white selections. The form *rubra*, 'Cherokee Chief', and 'Welch's Junior Miss' are good pink selections. 'Appalachian Spring' is a selection touted as resistant to anthracnose.

One of our showiest native trees, the dogwood brings four seasons of landscape pleasure—masses of white or pink blooms in spring, cooling shade in summer, fiery foliage color in fall, and bright red berries for the birds in winter. In its natural woodland setting, dogwood grows bent and gnarly, but when planted in a more open situation the tree's form is full and rounded. Dogwoods are difficult to get established (about half die, under the best of conditions), but are well worth the attempt. Unfortunately, dogwoods in cooler, higher elevations can suffer from a deadly fungus called anthracnose, but those in most parts of our states rarely get it. The Oriental or kousa dogwood (C. kousa), a later-blooming species, is disease resistant.

Other Common Name
Flowering Dogwood

Bloom Period and Seasonal Color
White, pink, rose blooms in March or April

Mature Height × Spread
15 to 30 feet × 15 to 25 feet

Eastern Red Cedar

Juniperus virginiana

The spicy scent of Eastern red cedar is unforgettable to anyone raised in the South—especially older folks who remember using its fragrant branches to clean and wax "smoothing irons" before electric irons were available. The native, cone-shaped evergreen was used as a charming Christmas tree long before folks began to buy fancy northern firs and spruces. Outdoors, birds enjoy the cedar's intriguing blue winter berries, and the trees provide ideal shelter and protection for nests. Though fairly slow growing, the tough, long-lived tree grows equally well from our highest elevations to coastal areas. It is tolerant of both city pollution and salt-water spray.

Other Common Names
Cedar, Juniper

Bloom Period and Seasonal Color
Evergreen foliage, blue winter berries

Mature Height × Spread
30 to 50 feet × 15 to 25 feet

When, Where, and How to Plant

Eastern red cedar is not widely available at smaller garden centers; however, young wild plants are very easy to transplant from along fencerows and meadows (with landowner permission), especially those under 3 feet tall (larger plants often don't survive being moved). The best time to dig and transplant is in the fall or early winter. Container-grown or balled-and-burlapped plants can be set out any time, but fall is best. Cedars grow best in full sun, in acidic to very alkaline soil, as long as the soil is well drained. The small plants fill out surprisingly fast; space them 10 or more feet apart.

Growing Tips

Water every two or three weeks during the first summer. Feed lightly every two or three years in the spring, and mulch with pine straw or pine bark until the trees get large enough to shade their own roots.

Care

The leading cause of cedar death is waterlogged soil. Do not plant where irrigation is installed, or where water stands for more than a few hours after a heavy rain. Cedar-apple rust, a fungus that depends on apples, crabapples, and related plants for transmission, causes strange reddish-orange globs to grow on young cedar twigs but poses little problem to mature trees. Prune only to remove wayward or cluttered branches and limbs.

Companion Planting and Design

Cedar makes an excellent windbreak or property boundary as a tall hedge, or can be used to create an old-fashioned allée along a driveway. When lower limbs are thinned, it makes an excellent, long-lived specimen tree. Underplant with azaleas, iris, spirea, hosta, ferns, and other shade- and drought-tolerant perennials, or ivy or euonymus groundcover. Plant in a small group at a woodland edge.

Personal Favorites

'Canaertii' is an old favorite with a compact, pyramidal form and bright green foliage; 'Emerald Sentinel' is columnar with dark green foliage; and 'Glauca' is very narrow and columnar with silvery-blue spring foliage that turns blue green in summer.

Flowering Cherry
Prunus hybrids

When, Where, and How to Plant
Plant young trees in the fall or winter, or be prepared to water during the summer. Flowering cherries require an acid soil that's moist but well drained. Although they are at flowering peak in full sun, cherry trees bloom well under high shade. Prepare a planting area three to five times the diameter of the rootball, adding organic matter to your native soil and a little fertilizer. Loosen a container-grown tree's roots; for a balled-and-burlapped tree, cut and remove all wires or rope holding the burlap in place. Set the tree on undisturbed solid ground so the rootball is level with the surrounding soil. Mulch the planting area. Allow 20 or 25 feet between trees.

Growing Tips
Flowering cherries need moisture in the hot summer, but do not want to be kept wet. Give trees a slow, deep soaking and wait until your soil dries to several inches below the surface before watering again. Fertilize very lightly in the late winter or early spring to promote healthy growth.

Care
Thin crowded limbs and branches as needed—this is better to do in the winter when you can see what you are doing. Cherry trees are susceptible to twig borers. If you see sudden signs of dieback in the spring or early summer, snip off a branch and see if a caterpillar is inside. Pruning off borer-infested twigs and getting rid of them is a good way to both control borers and help flowering cherries branch out for a fuller effect.

Companion Planting and Design
Use as an accent tree in the shady lawn or as a focal point in a small garden. Underplant with spring-flowering daffodils, or summer-flowering surprise lilies. Fast growing (up to 3 feet a year), several cherry trees planted together provide quick summer shade; groups of five or more provide even greater impact.

Personal Favorites
The hybrid 'Okame' (a cross between *P. incisa* and *P. campanulata*), Taiwan cherry (*P. campanulata*), and 'Kwanzan' (a cultivar of *P. serrulata*, with red new leaves) all flower well throughout our region, even on the Gulf Coast.

The Yoshino cherry trees (P. × yedoensis) in Washington, D.C., are stunning, but there is also a mid-March show in the Japanese garden at the Birmingham Botanical Gardens every spring. For two ethereal weeks, pink, rose, and white clouds settle in the garden, creating a picture-postcard oriental landscape. Several communities in both Alabama and Mississippi hold cherry tree festivals to welcome spring. Among the most beloved trees in the spring, flowering cherries are small, vase-shaped trees that do not yield edible fruit. Some landscaping professionals consider them "high maintenance," but this is only when they are improperly planted or over-cared-for. And though they are also relatively short lived (from twenty-five to thirty years), most gardeners who enjoy the cherry's spirited blooms still think they are worth the effort.

Other Common Name
Cherry

Bloom Period and Seasonal Color
White, rose, pink blooms in spring

Mature Height × Spread
15 to 30 feet × 20 to 25 feet

Fringe Tree
Chionanthus virginicus

An old-fashioned curiosity that draws much attention when in flower in early spring, the native fringe tree bursts into a cloud of delicate, fragrant, fringe-like blooms in loose clusters on stems up to 6 or more inches long. The small, usually multiple-stemmed tree has a spreading, almost shrub-like canopy. Male and female plants are separate, and though it is nearly impossible to tell them apart when young, the mature male trees have larger flowers; females bear beautiful, blue, olive-size fruits in late summer that are highly favored by birds. Fringe tree also has deep yellow fall color. It is readily available in the trade, but is often overlooked because its name is not familiar to new gardeners.

Other Common Name
Grancy Gray Beard

Bloom Period and Seasonal Color
White blooms in April, yellow fall foliage

Mature Height × Spread
15 to 30 feet × 15 to 25 feet

When, Where, and How to Plant
Plant container-grown trees in the fall or winter, or be prepared to water during the first summer. Fringe tree grows and flowers best in full sun but also has a fine display in high shade like that found under scattered pines. A long taproot makes moving wild plants difficult, even if you know what you are looking at (the tree is not very distinctive when not in bloom). Plant fringe tree in rich, moist soil or on a slope. Fringe tree is usually grown as a single specimen, but can get up to 20 feet wide, so space plants in a group at least 10 or 12 feet apart.

Growing Tips
Being a native, fringe tree is tolerant of wet winters and summer drought. Water only during prolonged dry spells; usually no more than once or twice a season is needed, if at all. Feed very lightly or expect rank, leggy growth.

Care
This small tree can sometimes look more like a large shrub for its first few years, so create a tree-like effect by thinning. In the winter when you can see what you are doing, cut off a few of the lower limbs (leave no stubs), then thin a few branches from the lowest limbs that are left. Fringe tree has no major insect or disease problems, other than being hit with the lawn mower or string trimmer.

Companion Planting and Design
The tree makes a handsome small specimen, especially when set off against an evergreen hedge or magnolias or camellias. It is also small enough to grow under power lines. It is at home in natural island beds and wooded settings with azaleas, rhododendrons, and oakleaf hydrangeas.

Personal Favorites
The native fringe tree (*C. virginicus*), with its large leaves and clusters of flowers, is often preferred over the large, multi-stemmed, earlier-blooming Chinese fringe tree (*C. retusus*). Both are often sold under the same common name.

Ginkgo
Ginkgo biloba

When, Where, and How to Plant

Ginkgo trees, both large and small, are widely available, and can be planted pretty much any time of the year, even in midsummer; many gardeners plant them in the fall after they have noticed their beauty in gardens around town. Plant in full sun in a well-drained site, by digging a wide hole and only slightly amending with organic matter, then carefully loosening the potting soil and roots. Mulch or underplant with a ground-cover, and water only as needed the first summer. If you choose to plant more than one ginkgo, space them at least 20 feet apart so they can each show off but still have a solid carpet of fall leaves.

Growing Tips

Be very careful to keep the lawn mower and string trimmer off the thin bark, or you can easily girdle and kill the tree. Water only as needed during extreme summer drought during the first summer or two. Water infrequently and deeply—regular, shallow irrigation can cause roots to grow close to the soil surface and be prone to disease. Feed lightly by broadcasting an all-purpose fertilizer over the entire area under the tree, or just feed the nearby lawn and let that be enough for the tree, too.

Care

Carefully thin competing limbs to reveal the interesting bark and lower trunk, and to help mowers get under the trees. No major insect or disease problems affect ginkgos.

Companion Planting and Design

A single ginkgo makes a fantastic specimen, especially set against the deep green background of pines or other evergreens, or a red brick or stone wall. Ginkgos are dramatic lining a long driveway, or in groups on a large, sloped landscape. Plant with spring-blooming bulbs such as daffodil, grape hyacinth, and others that come up in the late fall and winter, and do not interfere with the beauty of ginkgo leaves on the lawn or ground.

Personal Favorites

A few good male (non-fruiting) selections are: 'Autumn Gold', 'Princeton Sentry', and 'Shangri-la'.

If you want to make an artistic statement, plant a ginkgo. Its brilliant yellow fall foliage is stunning every single fall without fail, especially when the bark is wet and dark. The leaves hang on until the last minute, then shed to create a beautiful solid yellow carpet underneath the trees. This living fossil—there is petrified ginkgo wood all around us from dinosaur days—makes a handsome shade tree with unusual fan-like leaves on irregular branching. Ginkgos are long-lived, with female trees bearing fruit only after they are at least twenty years old. When there is fruit, it has a musky, ill-smelling odor—so it is better to plant male selections. Ginkgo gets its alternative common name from the resemblance of the foliage to maidenhair fern leaflets.

Other Common Name
Maidenhair Tree

Bloom Period and Seasonal Color
Golden yellow fall foliage

Mature Height × Spread
60 to 70 feet × 20 to 50 feet

Hawthorn

Crataegus species

With white flowers and red berries, native hawthorns are trees with several seasons of interest. Because they are small and tough, they are easy to use as street trees or even under power lines. Slender and multi-trunked, the Washington hawthorn (C. phaenopyrum) sports clusters of white, musky-smelling flowers in late spring, lustrous green leaves in summer, and striking red berries in fall and winter. It has gray-brown bark with spines and a bent, wizened form in the understory of the woods. Trees grown in full sun develop a more erect, vase-like form. Parsley hawthorn (C. laevigata) has parsley-like foliage and mottled bark, and is especially nice in light shade under taller trees; a good jelly is made from the late spring fruit of the native May haw (C. opaca).

Other Common Name
Tree Haw

Bloom Period and Seasonal Color
White blooms in late spring, red berries in fall and winter

Mature Height × Spread
25 to 30 feet × 20 to 25 feet

When, Where, and How to Plant
Plant hawthorns whenever you can dig a wide hole (not easy to do in midwinter or midsummer). It grows well in sun or moderate shade as an understory tree. Dig a wide hole and add organic matter to create a "woodsy" soil. Mulch with pine straw or shredded bark until it grows large enough to shade its own roots.

Growing Tips
Most hawthorns are "upland" species, meaning they will not tolerate heavy or wet soils. Heavy feeding or watering makes them more susceptible to fire blight; feed only lightly every spring or two, if at all.

Care
Twiggy hawthorns need thinning, especially when they are young and can be trained to have a more open form. Cut out cluttered, close, overlapping, or wayward limbs and branches, leaving no stubs to rot. Fire blight, a bacterial disease that spreads from wild pears, can cause twigs to die back; if you want to prevent it, spray the plants when in full bloom with a bactericide recommended for fire blight (it does not harm bees). Hawthorns are also susceptible to cedar-apple rust, which causes leaf spots and some fruit loss.

Companion Planting and Design
The berries and pretty bark of hawthorns make them great winter specimens or accents, and their showy spring flowers make up for the thorns. Hawthorns make ideal specimen trees at the edge of a natural area, or against a white or gray building, or a deep green background. Group together for impact or use under power lines as street trees. Interplant with evergreen groundcovers or low-growing evergreen shrubs such as nandina.

Personal Favorites
Washington hawthorn has several cultivars: 'Clark' (heavy fruiting), 'Fastigiata' (columnar type), and the hybrid 'Vaughn' (heavy fruiting, susceptible to rust). Green hawthorn (C. viridis) has a popular cultivar named 'Winter King'. May haw (C. opaca) tolerates low, wet soils and has delightful crabapple-like fruit prized for making jelly.

Hemlock
Tsuga species

When, Where, and How to Plant
Plant hemlock in the fall or in winter, or be prepared to water during the first summer. Give the plants plenty of room to spread out, planting them 15 or 20 feet apart. Hemlock is fairly shallow rooted, and grows best in moist, well-drained, acid soil. In the mountain or high hills areas of our states, plant hemlock in full sun; in central areas hemlock suffers from heat stress unless grown in afternoon shade, which also means it grows more slowly. It suffers from night heat and lack of winter chill along the Gulf Coast. Dig a wide hole and lightly amend with acid-forming organic matter such as peat moss. Add a controlled-release, nitrogen-rich, tree-and-shrub fertilizer at planting time, and loosen container-grown plant roots. Mulch the entire area with pine straw.

Growing Tips
Water the shallow-rooted plants every three or four weeks during prolonged droughts, and feed very lightly in the spring with an acid-forming azalea-camellia type fertilizer.

Care
There are few major pests, though the fairly new wooly aphid can cause a drought-stressed plant to die. Shear new growth, but do not cut back beyond where there are needles, or the entire branch may die.

Companion Planting and Design
Hemlocks make nearly perfect accents or specimens, but can be planted in rows as screens or windbreaks, and can be sheared to thicken them up like other evergreen shrubs. Underplant with hosta, ivy, pachysandra, or other drought-tolerant groundcover, and use as a backdrop to showy spring flowering shrubs such as azaleas or forsythia. Small trees also make handsome potted specimens on outdoor decks, especially with holiday lights; they can be planted into the larger landscape later.

Personal Favorites
Canadian hemlock has many small, shrubby cultivars, including 'Pendula', the Sargent weeping hemlock. Carolina hemlock is slower growing and stiffer than the Canadian hemlock, with darker green needles arranged all around the twigs instead of in opposite rows.

Some plant experts say the hemlock was pushed south with the last Ice Age, and found refuge in the Appalachian Mountains and its deep canyons. Today, you can see virgin Canadian hemlock stands (T. canadensis) in the Smoky Mountains as tall as church spires. Closer to home, this popular northern plant only grows well in the upper third or higher elevations of our states where it gets plenty of winter chill. However, Carolina hemlock (T. caroliniana), which is native to the Southeast, is a better choice for us, except along the Gulf Coast. Hemlocks have a rugged appearance, and tolerate ice loads well in the winter—they really stand out when covered with a light snow.

Other Common Names
Canadian Hemlock, Carolina Hemlock

Bloom Period and Seasonal Color
Evergreen foliage

Mature Height × Spread
25 to 70 feet × 15 to 30 feet

Japanese Maple
Acer palmatum

The Japanese maple may well be the perfect small tree— or trees, depending on how many different types you want to grow. It comes in many sizes, forms (even weeping), and leaf types that range from the classically beautiful maple shape to hand-shaped or finely textured, and can be green, red, or almost purple. Large types of Japanese maples provide convenient shade in summer, but smaller ones have incredibly varied sculptural forms that add interest to the winter garden. Dwarf and cut-leaf selections are best for containers. While fancy grafted forms are the most popular, seedling trees can be faster growing, more rugged, and drought tolerant. With the huge diversity of choices, there is a Japanese maple for every garden.

Bloom Period and Seasonal Color
Gold, red, burnt orange fall foliage

Mature Height × Spread
6 to 25 feet × 4 to 20 feet

When, Where, and How to Plant
Japanese maples frustrate many Deep South gardeners by developing burned leaf tips and dead branches—both of which can be easily avoided by planting in light shade or at least with protection from hot afternoon sun, and not near concrete or brick paved areas. However, heavy shade can cause the leaves to have a faded color. Well-drained soil is a must, or roots will rot; but prolonged drought also causes root damage. Plant specimen trees according to their mature spread, which can vary widely depending on the selection. Mulches are crucial for keeping roots cool and moist, and can cut down dramatically on how often you will need to water.

Growing Tips
Japanese maples need to be kept slightly moist, not wet. Water regularly, especially in hot, dry weather, and maintain a thick mulch. Too much fertilizer can result in leggy growth and poor leaf coloration, so give them a light application of all-purpose fertilizer in the spring, and a second application in midsummer to compensate for what washes away during regular watering.

Care
Prune only to shape, by removing cluttered branches. Japanese maples can be easily trained into "bonsai" shapes. Aphids and whiteflies may be temporary problems, but no control is usually needed.

Companion Planting and Design
Japanese maple selections can be used as understory trees in light shade with pines or other tall trees, or to offset the coarse-textured, evergreen foliage of camellias. Many are ideal as specimens or accent trees in small gardens, flower borders, or rock gardens, and in large containers if kept out of hot sun and drying wind. Companions include hellebore, liriope, mondo grass, and dwarf bulbs, including daffodils and grape hyacinth.

Personal Favorites
'Atropurpureum' is the classic Japanese red maple. 'Bloodgood' is a large, 15- to 20-foot red-purple selection resistant to leaf scorch in the sun; 'Crimson Queen' is an 8- to 10-foot bronze to crimson tree; 'Butterfly' has blue-green leaves edged with white.

Lacebark Elm

Ulmus parvifolia

When, Where, and How to Plant

Plant this deciduous tree in the fall, so roots can continue to grow during the winter and be well established by the next summer and require little or no care. Plant in full sun or at the edge of woodlands where the tree can develop its sturdiest growth, in well-drained soil that does not stay soggy in the winter. Dig a wide hole and only lightly amend the native soil with organic matter. Loosen roots at planting time to encourage them into a wide-ranging growth pattern. Mulch lightly, but do not mound up mulch on the trunk.

Growing Tips

Noted for its landscape toughness, the lacebark elm rarely needs any watering once it is established; if irrigation systems are run too often it can cause root problems. Feed only very lightly, or not at all if the tree is grown in or near a fertilized lawn where nutrients are readily available for foraging roots.

Care

Prune only to thin cluttered or wayward branches, or to "limb up" young trees into more mature forms for street planting and to make mowing underneath easier where grass is grown underneath. This elm is even somewhat resistant to Japanese beetles and the elm leaf beetle that eats patterns in leaves.

Companion Planting and Design

Growing as much as 3 feet per year, lacebark elms make good street trees. Use as specimens in patio centers, in small grouping in lawns, or for lining a driveway (the roots do not pose serious problems to pavement). Underplant with groundcovers, small shrubs, or shade-tolerant perennials such as hosta, ferns, and cast-iron plant, or spring flowering bulbs that need winter sunshine.

Personal Favorites

'Allée' and 'Athena' have particularly showy bark. 'Burgundy' has reddish fall color. 'True Green' and 'Drake' are evergreen in the southern counties, but are less cold hardy and may suffer dieback in northern or upland counties.

Ever since Dutch elm disease wiped out the American elm, homeowners have been searching for a substitute. Many turned to lacebark or Chinese elm. Fast growing, lacebark creates a quick canopy of shade. Rounded with high, arching branches, the tree is as handsome as it is useful. And its mottled, peeling bark, which gives the tree its name, is striking in winter as well as summer. The trees turn a deep gold in the fall, and along the Gulf Coast they hold their leaves well into winter. Some selections may be evergreen. Do not confuse lacebark elm (U. parvifolia) with the inferior Siberian elm (U. pumila), which is sometimes also labeled Chinese elm by nurseries.

Other Common Name
Chinese Elm

Bloom Period and Seasonal Color
Deep gold fall foliage

Mature Height × Spread
40 to 60 feet × 25 to 40 feet

Leyland Cypress
×*Cupressocyparis leylandii*

Few plants are called upon to solve as many problems as the Leyland cypress. Need an instant hedge? A Christmas tree? A screen or evergreen backdrop for other plantings? Call on the exotic Leyland cypress, a feathery blue-green hybrid that, in spite of a couple of serious pests, is currently one of the most popular trees in the landscaping trade. A fast-growing, dark green spire, Leyland cypress takes on a fuller pyramid shape when it is mature. It adds drama, vertical interest, and evergreen mass to any landscape. Some gardeners enjoy using it for a year in a container, until it grows so tall it must be planted in the ground. Economize and buy small, container-grown trees; they will be over your head in no time.

Bloom Period and Seasonal Color
Evergreen foliage

Mature Height × Spread
60 to 70 feet × 15 to 20 feet

When, Where, and How to Plant
Plant small, fast-growing trees any time you can dig a decent hole, but larger plants are best set out in the fall. Plant in full sun. When grown as a hedge near other trees, they tend to be smaller where competition for sun, water, and nutrients is greater. Though they are tolerant of a wide range of soil types, wet soils lead to root rot. Plant no closer than 10 feet apart for best growth, even for hedges. Dig a hole several feet wider than the root-ball, loosen potting soil, and spread roots out when planting. Mulch well.

Growing Tips
Water newly planted trees deeply as needed, but do not keep them wet. Feed very lightly every year or so, but not too much or you will get lots of loose, weak growth.

Care
Prune by shearing new growth. Two serious drawbacks to Leyland cypress are stem diseases that kill twigs, for which there is no good control—this is the single best reason to not over-plant this popular plant—and split trunks during ice storms (plant single-trunk specimens in the northern half of our states). It is also susceptible to bagworms, which can be removed or sprayed with a biological worm spray as they appear.

Companion Planting and Design
Excellent as an evergreen hedge or screen, as a buffer against strong winter winds, or as a background for azaleas and other flowering plants. Good as a short-term investment around new properties, but plant other trees as well in case leaf or root diseases start to kill your Leyland cypress just as it reaches its peak of beauty and usefulness.

Personal Favorites
'Castlewellan Gold' has golden new foliage and an upright, narrow growth habit; 'Emerald Isle' is popular as a Christmas tree for its bright green foliage; 'Naylor's Blue' has grayish blue foliage.

Live Oak
Quercus virginiana

When, Where, and How to Plant

Live oak can be planted any time of the year, but fall planting is best so plants can get established by summer. Young trees can be grown in light shade but will be denser at maturity in full sun. The trees tolerate all but the heaviest clay, but grow best in well-drained soil. Mature trees spread very wide, so give them 25 or more feet to grow in all directions—not too close to buildings. Their roots can displace sidewalks and break up thin driveways. Loosen roots and potting soil at planting time, and mulch after planting.

Growing Tips

Do not over-water young live oaks or place irrigation under mature trees, which can rot their roots. Feed only lightly in the late winter or spring, or not at all if nearby lawn areas are fed at least every two or three years (wide-ranging roots will find fertilizer many yards away from tree trunks).

Care

Live oaks are very durable even during hurricanes, but can break up in ice storms. Thin out cluttered growth and excess small limbs every few years to maintain an open growth habit that is less likely to break. Do not allow tree workers to climb trees with "boot spurs," which puncture trees and lead to decay. There are few serious pests, though "oak blister" and certain gall-forming insects may cause leaf shed. No controls are needed or recommended.

Companion Planting and Design

Live oaks are best as either specimen trees or in long allées beside drives. Their deep shade and shallow roots make it nearly impossible to grow grass underneath for very long, so use natural bark mulch or underplant with ivy, vinca, liriope, cast-iron plant, or other shade-loving groundcovers.

Personal Favorites

There are no cultivars, just the native species. However, in northern parts of our states, it is best to plant trees grown from locally collected seeds, to help ensure hardiness.

No other tree says "Deep South" like our native evergreen "live" oaks, grand old ladies who often wear veils of Spanish moss on their massive, Medusa-like branches. The wood from live oak has been prized by ship builders for centuries. In a generous gesture several years ago, the city of Mobile donated one of its older, dying trees for use in the renovation of the ship nicknamed Old Ironsides, the historic USS Constitution. Live oak is tough and resistant to salt spray, but often freezes in the northern third of our states, especially in higher elevations where its bark can literally break loose from the trunk.

Bloom Period and Seasonal Color
Evergreen foliage

Mature Height × Spread
50 to 70 feet × 50 to 125 feet

Oak

Quercus species

Oaks are the workhorses of the Southern landscape. The native trees, though considered somewhat slow growing, can easily shade a house in practically no time—and shade out the lawn as well! A few oaks can frame and cool even the largest landscape, while providing excellent screens for large views. They help control erosion with their matted roots and copious leaf fall. Offering strong trunks, beautiful limb and twig patterns, cooling leaves, acorns for wildlife, and plenty of material for hungry compost piles, they sometimes even have decent fall color. Because oaks are long lived, study your options carefully so you can choose the right one for your landscape needs—both now and down the road.

Bloom Period and Seasonal Color
Red or yellow fall foliage colors

Mature Height × Spread
60 to 90 feet × 40 to 70 feet

When, Where, and How to Plant
Plant or transplant small bare-root trees in the fall or winter. Container plants can be set out any time. Oaks grow best in full or part sun, and though they grow close together in the woods, landscape trees do better with room to spread out—20 feet or more in any direction, per tree. Dig wide holes, barely amend with organic matter to get roots started, and mulch a wide area for roots to grow into.

Growing Tips
Oaks are heavy feeders, and oak roots forage a long way for water and nutrients. Lawn irrigation can damage oak roots! Fertilize by broadcasting under the outer spread of the branches and beyond; if you rake leaves, it is helpful to aerate the soil every few years, a process normally done by earthworms as they eat decomposing leaves.

Care
Prune oaks only to limb them up for mowing, to let light penetrate a lawn underneath, or to remove dead branches. Unraked leaves feed the soil as they compost over the winter. Oak pests include leaf-eating caterpillars, aphids, twig galls, and leaf spots, but none are usually serious enough to warrant sprays.

Companion Planting and Design
Use oaks as specimens, for shade, or in naturalistic groups. They drop leaves, flowers, and acorns, so place them in a natural or low-maintenance area. Underplant with drought-tolerant groundcovers such as ivy, Asiatic jasmine, liriope, vinca, or cast-iron plant, all of which absorb excess leaf litter in the fall. Since oaks are tall, they provide high shade for such smaller trees as fringe tree, dogwood, and red buckeye, or acid-loving shrubs (fallen oak leaves are acidic) as azaleas and rhododendrons.

Personal Favorites
Post oak (*Q. stellata*) has beautiful cross-shaped leaves and thick, spooky-looking gnarly limbs. Pin oak (*Q. palustris*) has a pyramidal shape and good fall color, and works beautifully in suburban neighborhoods. Willow oak (*Q. phellos*) and water oak (*Q. nigra*) offer filtered shade and make excellent street trees. The highly adaptable Shumard oak (*Q. shumardii*) grows in moist or dry soil, with its leaves turning a flaming red in the fall.

Ornamental Pear

Pyrus calleryana

When, Where, and How to Plant

Set nursery-grown, grafted trees out any time of the year, but be prepared to water during the first summer. Plant in full sun in well-drained soil, loosening roots at planting time. Place no closer than 25 to 30 feet apart. Stake large new specimens a year or two to reduce excess movement in high winds. Fertilize lightly and add mulch to protect trunks from mower or trimmer damage.

Growing Tips

Water deeply every few weeks in the summer, and fertilize lightly in the spring (no need to fertilize if grown in a well-fed lawn). Excess water or fertilizer creates more leaf and twig mass that can be damaged by wind and ice, and lush growth that is more susceptible to fire blight.

Care

Do not shear ornamental pears, which destroys their natural shape. Remove only a few lower limbs at a time to make mowing underneath easier (do not leave stubs). If a tree splits, simply remove it rather than try to patch it back together. Fire blight, spread by bees in the spring, kills twigs by early summer; plant resistant varieties, or spray with a recommended "fire blight spray" when in full flower. No need to prune—dead twigs usually just shed.

Companion Planting and Design

Ornamental pears are handsome as single accents, as lawn specimens (watch that mower and string trimmer!), in rows or allées, or as "parking lot island" trees. Their shallow roots preclude much being grown underneath, but groundcovers such as liriope or Asiatic jasmine will grow well, interplanted with daffodils, and can protect trunks from equipment damage.

Personal Favorites

Avoid the overplanted 'Bradford' that breaks apart easily and 'Redspire' which is very prone to fire blight. Instead, choose blight-resistant 'Aristocrat', 'Chanticleer' (sometimes sold as 'Cleveland Select' or 'Select'), or 'Trinity' for their sturdier branching. 'Capital' and 'White House' are narrow, columnar selections that grow only a third as wide as they are tall.

Unlike the pears grown for their large, sweet fruits, ornamental pears (which do make small fruit) are grown primarily for their teardrop shape, dazzling white spring flowers that show up just before leaf break in the spring, their glossy foliage, and intense fall colors of yellow, orange, scarlet, or burgundy. Normally considered fast growing but "short lived" trees (usually beginning to decline before 20 or 25 years), they are boldly dramatic in any landscape style—formal, suburban, or cottage. Some popular selections (most notoriously the one named 'Bradford') hold up poorly in heavy wind and rain, and often break apart under ice loads in the winter, but there are outstanding cultivars that hold up much better.

Other Common Name
Bradford Pear

Bloom Period and Seasonal Color
White flowers in late winter and spring, fall color

Mature Height × Spread
30 to 50 feet × 25 to 40 feet

Pine

Pinus species

Several species of pines are used for landscaping. The tall, handsome evergreens are popular for windbreaks and in naturalistic groups, and in mixed woodland gardens. Their shedding needles are collected and sold as pine straw, one of the South's best natural mulches. There are many different pine species, each with its own size, bark color, seed cone size, and leaf arrangement (the slender needles can be in bundles of two, three, or five). Pines are quite specific about where they will—or will not—grow. Young trees tend to be pyramidal, with older ones spreading out. Pines in general are not resistant to urban air pollution, but grow well in small towns and suburbs. The longleaf pine, with its long, lush needles and stately presence, is Alabama's state tree.

Bloom Period and Seasonal Color
Evergreen foliage, brown seed cones

Mature Height × Spread
50 to 100 feet × 20 to 30 feet

When, Where, and How to Plant
Plant small container-grown pines any time, but bare-root plants must be set out in the winter, without ever letting roots dry out. Plant in full sun, well-drained deep or sloped soil, and give them plenty of room: 20 to 30 feet between trees. Mulch the entire area with a 2- to 4-inch layer of (what else?) pine straw.

Growing Tips
Once trees are established, water only during extreme droughts, but soak them deeply. Feed by broadcasting an all-purpose fertilizer over a large area around trunks, or just fertilize nearby lawn areas; do not overfertilize, or expect leggy, weak growth.

Care
Thin out small limbs from young pines to shape them. Even without thinning, pines are "self pruning;" they naturally drop lower limbs, which can be a problem in close quarters or over houses and cars. Use a pole saw to remove those that are showing fading foliage. Pine needles can accumulate very quickly, leading to disposal problems. Pests include sap-sucking insects that drip sticky sap; "fusiform rust" disease that disfigures trunks; and pine bark beetles, which are mostly a problem on trees stressed from drought, root damage, or lightning strikes.

Companion Planting and Design
Plant pines in large or small groups, or as specimens far from the house where you can see their overall shape better. Underplant with azaleas, spirea, oakleaf hydrangea, wax myrtle, ferns, cast-iron plant, or English ivy. When not too close to a structure, a dead pine can be left as a long-lasting wildlife habitat.

Personal Favorites
Longleaf pine (*P. palustris*) is the classic Southern pine with huge cones, but it needs deep soils. Loblolly pine (*P. taeda*) is great for poor soils. White pine (*P. strobus*) has silky, blue-green needles and grows best in northern areas. Virginia pine (*P. virginiana*) is a scrubby tree grown for Christmas trees. Slash pine (*P. elliottii*) and spruce pine (*P. glabra*) grow well near the coast.

Red Buckeye

Aesculus pavia

When, Where, and How to Plant

Plant container-grown buckeyes any time of the year, but expect to water every two or three weeks during the first summer. Transplant small seedlings in the fall or winter. Harvest and plant seeds an inch deep in the late summer when the husks first split—they will get nearly a foot tall by winter. Plant buckeyes in the shade, on a slope or in well drained soil, with at least 10 feet between trees.

Growing Tips

Water deeply during hot, dry summers, or expect leaves to burn and then shed early. Feed lightly if at all with an all-purpose fertilizer, or just rake leaves into a thick mulch under the trees in the fall, which will feed the trees as the leaves decompose.

Care

Prune irregular branches or remove lower limbs that interfere with mowing or walking along a path. There are no major pests other than an occasional and non-threatening woodland caterpillar, but count on an early leaf shed, especially when buckeyes are grown where they get a little sun, or after an unusually hot, dry summer (though this is not a problem to the tree).

Companion Planting and Design

Buckeyes are outstanding understory trees for shaded lots, especially when naturalized on a wooded slope or along a creek bank. Plant close to a window so you can enjoy the hummingbird show when it flowers. Native woodland perennials, ferns, and naturalized bulbs are perfectly at home under the light shade of buckeyes.

Personal Favorites

Other than the straight species, Texas buckeye (*A. glabra* var. *arguta*) has pale yellow flowers and a heavy fruit load. There are much larger buckeyes, including red horse chestnut (*A.* × *carnea* 'O'Neil Red'), sweet or yellow buckeye (*A. flava*, with yellow flowers), and hybrid *A.* × *arnoldiana* 'Autumn Splendor' with showy yellow and red flowers and brilliant fall colors.

One of the earliest late-winter sources of nectar for hungry migratory hummingbirds, the native buckeye is a cheerful harbinger of spring, especially in shady gardens. As newly unfurled, hand-shaped leaves of five to seven leaflets begin to expand from each branch, they serve as a backdrop to a bouquet of nearly foot-long, upright spikes of red, salvia-like flowers. In the late summer, the showy, leathery, light-brown seed capsules, each up to 3 inches around, split to reveal two or three or more large, glossy, seeds (from which the tree gets its common name), each of which can be planted immediately for new trees by fall. Keep a seed in your pocket for good luck.

Other Common Name
Buckeye

Bloom Period and Seasonal Color
Late winter, early spring red flowers

Mature Height × Spread
15 to 20 feet × 10 to 15 feet

Redbud

Cercis canadensis

Redbud, one of the first natives to bloom in the late winter, starts showing its magenta-pink flowers on hillsides and woodland edges just as everything else begins to green up. Wads of pinkish-red flower clusters pop out like beads on the dark branches even where no leaves will grow. Redbud (whose flowers are edible!) looks like a lanky shrub with crooked stems when it's small, but grows to be an upright, spreading tree. Heart-shaped leaves provide light summer shade before turning a mellow yellow in the fall. It's one of the most brilliant small, native trees—not as showy as dogwood, but a lot tougher. If magenta is not your color, try the white-flowered form.

Other Common Names
Judas Tree, Eastern Redbud

Bloom Period and Seasonal Color
Magenta blooms in March, yellow fall color

Mature Height × Spread
25 to 30 feet × 15 to 20 feet

When, Where, and How to Plant
Redbud seedlings can be "rescued" from old house sites and the woods, but dig only small seedlings, as large ones do not transplant well. Replant immediately. Set out container plants in the fall or winter. Redbud grows best in light shade or morning sun, but has better flowers in full sun. It requires well-drained soils (it grows even in rocky rubble on mountainsides), but will tolerate moist soil that stays wet for hours on end. Dig a wide hole for fast root growth until plants can get established. Plant no closer than 15 feet to allow ample room for crown development.

Growing Tips
Water only to get established, and fertilize very lightly—again, the tree can grow in almost nothing but gravel, and being in the legume (pea) family, it makes its own nitrogen fertilizer; too much fertilizer will cause weak, succulent stems that can break in ice storms.

Care
Prune dead wood from branches after the tree has finished flowering, and remove crossing or cluttered branches. Root rot is a major disease made worse in heavy clay or overly wet soils, aggravated by too much fertilizer.

Companion Planting and Design
It makes a good specimen in a natural island bed of pines, a prominent corner of the yard, or a small garden. For a natural look, plant several trees in a drift along a woodland edge, or beside a rustic or picket fence. Underplant with native woodland edge perennials such as spiderwort and wild blue phlox, or accent with a birdbath or rock wall.

Personal Favorites
'Forest Pansy' is a striking purple-leaf type. 'Alba' is a white selection. 'Pinkbud' is a bright pink. 'Wither's Pink Charm' is pastel without a purplish tint. Texas redbud (*C. canadensis* var. *texensis*) has thick, dark green leaves. 'Avondale', a cultivar of Chinese redbud (*C. chinensis*), has thick clusters of flowers.

Red Maple
Acer rubrum

When, Where, and How to Plant

Plant or transplant in the fall or winter, in full sun for best fall color. Red maple tolerates heavy wet soils, so situate it toward the bottoms of slopes. Lawns with irrigation systems are ideal, though sooner or later the tree shades out grass underneath. Give the trees plenty of room to spread their shallow roots and broad crown—at least 40 or 50 feet apart—and mulch to keep roots moist through the summer.

Growing Tips

Water as needed, to keep moist in the hottest summers, especially if other plants are grown underneath these thirsty trees. Fertilize to keep new growth coming on strong, but don't overdo it, or lose some of the fall color and make plants brittle during ice storms.

Care

Prune lower limbs as the trees grow, leaving no stubs, and thin out those that are left for a more open tree form. Also thin out some of the branches to allow more sunlight to penetrate the dense foliage to the grass and other plants below. There are no major pests to worry about on red maple.

Companion Planting and Design

This is a large, fast-growing tree (as wide as it is tall), so give it plenty of room, such as an open lawn or on the edge of woods. Use it more formally to line a driveway or street. If planted on the south or west side of the house (at least 25 feet away), red maple provides shade in summer, so it's a favorite of new homeowners. It's pretty against a backdrop of pines. Because it is very shallow rooted, it can be difficult to grow a garden beneath its spreading limbs, but liriope, mondo grass, and Asiatic jasmine will do just fine.

Personal Favorites

Many good cultivars are available now, including 'October Glory', 'Red Sunset', 'Autumn Flame', and the tall, narrow selection 'Columnare'.

Many folks admire this large, native tree for its typical "shade tree" shape and summer shade, and its rich coloring in the fall. But its spring show is equally impressive when red maple blooms with clusters of scarlet red flowers. They appear before the tree leafs out and are among the first spots of color in the woods. Indeed, this and its red twigs are where the "red" in the tree's name comes from. Still, the maple reigns supreme in fall, when its stunning scarlet, yellow, and bright orange colors force us to acknowledge the changing seasons. Red maple is not the best urban street tree, but unlike its upland sugar and silver maple cousins, it tolerates even heavy or wet soils.

Other Common Name
Swamp Red Maple

Bloom Period and Seasonal Color
Early spring red flowers and fruit, scarlet, yellow, and orange fall foliage

Mature Height × Spread
54 to 60 feet × 40 to 50 feet

River Birch

Betula nigra

River birch is a very popular and versatile native river-bank tree for use in landscapes. The broadly pyramidal tree grows in moist or irrigated soils, and provides dappled summer shade under which many plants can be grown. It has a modest yellow fall color on leaves that are easy to rake or blow away. Its most stunning feature is the shaggy bark—cinnamon-colored papery shards that peel and curl away from young trunks and limbs to reveal orange-pink beneath. Popular with landscapers for its fast growth and multiple trunks, river birch tends to drop leaf and twig litter throughout the summer, making it a nuisance around patios, but is well worth the effort to see such an all-season plant up close.

Bloom Period and Seasonal Color
Yellow fall foliage, attractive winter bark

Mature Height × Spread
50 to 80 feet × 40 to 60 feet

When, Where, and How to Plant
Set out river birches any time you can provide water, especially through the first summer. Plant in full or nearly full sun. River birch is native to river-banks, not swamps; while it may tolerate long periods of wet soil, it still grows best in deep, moist, well-drained soils. Dig a wide hole, lightly amended with organic matter plus a little sand in very heavy clay soils to help increase drainage. Spread roots out to get them established more quickly, and mulch to keep roots moist. River birches can be planted as close as 10 feet apart for a near-hedge effect, but mature trees need 40 feet or more for good growth.

Growing Tips
River birch drops leaves in the middle of the hot summer, especially in heavy soils where roots may be shallow and more subject to drought; deep soakings every two or three weeks help prevent this. Fertilize lightly or expect tender leaves to shed more quickly.

Care
Prune lower branches and limbs, especially those growing inward or crossing others, to better display multiple trunks, or remove all but one strong trunk for a single-trunk effect. Leave no stubs when pruning branches. Minor leaf spot diseases and aphids can cause leaf shed and some sap dripping, but there is no good control for either—just proper watering and fertilization without overdoing it.

Companion Planting and Design
Use as a specimen tree or in a naturalistic grove in the lawn or along a pond or creek bank. It can provide shade in the late afternoon, but do not plant where limbs will grow directly over a patio, or leaf and twig drop and sticky insect-drippings may be a problem. Plant with ferns, hosta, impatiens, and other shade- and moisture-loving plants, even antique orange daylilies that echo bark colors.

Personal Favorite
'Heritage' is an improved cultivar with darker leaves and brighter inner bark.

Saucer Magnolia

Magnolia × soulangiana

When, Where, and How to Plant

Set out container-grown or balled-and-burlapped plants in the fall or winter, or be prepared to water deeply every two or three weeks through the first summer. Saucer magnolias are poor choices near the beach because of salt spray. Locating them on the north side of the house decreases their tendency to bloom too early, and light shade helps trees stay cool and retain foliage longer in the summer. Saucer magnolias tolerate dry spells but hold their leaves longer into the fall when kept slightly moist in well-drained soils. Prepare a wide planting hole and mulch deeply to keep roots cool and moist. Fertilize at planting time. Space 20 to 30 feet apart.

Growing Tips

Do not let saucer magnolias stay dry for long, or expect leaves to fade, burn on the edges, and shed early. It is especially important to water deeply once or twice in late summer (if hurricanes don't take care of it for you) to help flower buds form properly. Fertilize according to directions in the spring with a slow-acting all-purpose fertilizer.

Care

Prune only to remove dead branches or those that crowd or cross over others. If a tree suffers serious damage, cut it nearly to the ground to let it resprout like a large shrub; do this in spring or early summer so flower buds have time to form on new growth. No major insects or diseases to worry about, if plants are kept watered and lightly fed.

Companion Planting and Design

Saucer magnolia is best grown as a specimen tree against a protective wall. Give it a prominent location and lots of space to spread out. Underplant with small azaleas, oakleaf hydrangeas, or evergreen hollies.

Personal Favorites

'Rustica Rubra' is a large specimen with deep reddish purple flowers and showy, 6-inch red seedpods. Later bloomers that usually do not get freeze damage include 'Lennei', 'Brozzonii', and 'Verbanica'.

Saucer magnolia is one of several exotic deciduous magnolias that stop traffic in late February or March. The fat buds, 6 or 7 inches long, open into exotic-looking tulip-shaped flowers in white and hues of purplish pink to apricot. The flowers seem to come right in time for the last freeze of the season, but when they survive (especially late-blooming cultivars), they announce spring with a bang. The trees, multiple-trunked with slender, upright branches and long, wide leaves, are not very showy most of the year (in fact, they can look ratty and thin toward fall), but grow fast to provide summer shade against small buildings—ideal for east-facing walls (south walls can cause them to warm up and bloom too early).

Other Common Names

Tulip Magnolia, Japanese Magnolia

Bloom Period and Seasonal Color

White, pink, apricot blooms in February and March

Mature Height × Spread

20 to 30 feet × 20 to 30 feet

Serviceberry

Amelanchier species

Serviceberries are a group of small, quietly beautiful, native trees more deserving of landscape use. They bloom as early as February with drooping clusters of delicate white flowers that float like clouds in the still-gray woods. It's "service berry" name comes from pioneers on the frozen western plains, who could finally bury their winter-deceased at the same time Amelanchier blooms. In summer, serviceberry produces large, sweet, edible purple berries for jams and pies. Its foliage, which starts out purplish then turns to summer green, makes serviceberry one of the best small trees for red, orange, or yellow autumn foliage color. An all-season tree, serviceberry is one of a number of native species gardeners are bringing into their landscapes.

Other Common Names
Appleberry, Juneberry, Shadbush, Sarvisberry

Bloom Period and Seasonal Color
White blooms in February, summer fruit, orange fall foliage

Mature Height × Spread
15 to 25 feet × 10 to 20 feet

When, Where, and How to Plant

Plant trees in the fall or winter, or whenever you can find them for sale! Serviceberry grows best in light shade as an understory plant, or its leaves will scorch by August, especially if planted near a heat-retaining wall or patio. Plant in a moist, well-drained soil that does not have standing water for days on end, and loosen roots when planting so they can spread out. Do not fertilize heavily at planting, so young trees can get root-established before being forced into lots of top growth. Mulch heavily.

Growing Tips

Make sure serviceberry is watered during dry spells and kept well mulched. Fertilize lightly, as this native woodland tree has trouble coping with lots of excess tender growth and foliage.

Care

Prune only to create a tree-form effect and to remove wayward or cluttered branches. There are no major pests to control, but birds like the edible berries, as do people, so prune to create a more compact plant that a bird net can fit over easily if you are planning to eat the fruit.

Companion Planting and Design

Serviceberry grows in a multi-trunk "clump form" that works best in naturalistic "drifts" at wood's edge, or toward the back of shrub borders. It is an excellent addition to a natural island bed as long as it is not in a lot of sun or heat. Underplant with purple coneflowers, blazing star, ferns, trillium, and other native woodland perennials, and add visual interest with a rustic fence or birdbath.

Personal Favorites

A. × grandiflora 'Autumn Brilliance' is a popular selection for fall color; 'Autumn Sunset' has excellent heat and drought tolerance. Others worth growing include shadblow (*A. canadensis*); Juneberry (*A. arborea*), with large dark purple berries; and Allegheny serviceberry (*A. laevis*), which can reach 40 feet tall with very sweet small fruits. When possible, ask for plants propagated in the South, which can be more heat tolerant than those from northern sources.

Silverbell

Halesia species

When, Where, and How to Plant

Silverbell, which does not transplant well, is best set out as a container-grown specimen, which can be done any time. Plant in a rich, well-drained "woodsy" soil with a fair amount of organic matter worked into the native soil, in light shade or part sun. Spread roots out to help them get quickly established into your garden, and mulch deeply.

Growing Tips

Silverbell is easy to ignore during the summer, needing very little water or fertilizer other than what it gets from rainfall and composting leaves. During a severe, prolonged drought, give plants growing in more sun an occasional deep soaking. In the fall, spread fallen leaves that will feed the tree as they decompose.

Care

Train to a single trunk when young or you may end up with a large silverbell shrub. Thin low or wayward branches and limbs as needed, leaving no stubs. No major pests affect silverbell, though some leaf-eating caterpillars may occasionally defoliate entire limbs (they turn into attractive native butterflies, and the leaves grow back).

Companion Planting and Design

Silverbell is not much to look at in the summer or winter, so interplant with other woodland trees and shrubs. Its flowers show off best when set against a darker background, and are dazzling when viewed from underneath—plant silverbell along woodland walks, on a slope, or near a shady patio. Its shade is very light, so most naturalizing bulbs, wildflowers, and ferns can be grown underneath with no problems.

Personal Favorites

There are several species of silverbell, but two favorites are Carolina silverbell (*H. carolina* or *H. tetraptera*), because it flowers before leaves come out in the late winter; and two-winged silverbell (*H. diptera* var. *magniflora*) whose flowers are larger and showier, but come out during and just after leaf break. *H. monticola* 'Rosea' has light pink flowers.

This is the best, and most underused, solution to the dogwood dilemma. Where dogwoods are tricky to grow, this tough native will thrive. Silverbell can be used nearly anywhere and is not fussy about soils or treatment. The small tree, very elegant in woodland gardens, has clusters of snow white, bell-shaped flowers that droop along the entire length of graceful branches in the late winter and spring. Some species bloom earlier than others, before or during spring leaf break. The fruit, which is either two- or four-winged (depending on the species), persists through most of the following winter. Oval, pointed leaves usually turn a medium yellow before shedding in the fall.

Other Common Name
Carolina Silverbell

Bloom Period and Seasonal Color
Early spring white flowers, yellow fall color

Mature Height × Spread
30 to 40 feet × 25 to 30 feet

Sourwood
Oxydendrum arboreum

The tall, lanky sourwoods in the woods hanging off hillsides in our states welcomes us to spring when they first leaf out in glowing green with bright red stems. Then in summer, tiny, white, bell-like flowers bloom in fragrant drooping sprays that are up to 10 inches long, hanging over the foliage like lace caps. In the fall the foliage turns a stunning red, almost neon. In the winter the tree is loaded with birds coming to feast on its pretty yellow seeds—leaving its stark branches to outline the sky. Sourwood, a slender tree with irregular, upright branches, is one of the best small- to medium-sized native trees for the home landscape—if you have a slope to plant it on.

Other Common Name
Sorrel Tree

Bloom Period and Seasonal Color
White blooms in summer, red fall foliage

Mature Height × Spread
25 to 40 feet × 15 to 20 feet

When, Where, and How to Plant
Plant in the fall or winter, giving plants plenty of time to get established, especially on slopes and far-out landscape spots where water may not be readily available. Sourwood has the best flowers and foliage in full, all day sun, but works well at a woodland edge if it gets at least six to eight hours of hot, direct sun. The plants grow best with excellent drainage, so plant on a slope or raised mound rather than at level ground. Loosen the soil all around the planting hole to help roots grow farther, faster. For a naturalistic planting, stagger plants at least 20 or 25 feet apart.

Growing Tips
Sourwood, though native, can suffer in the heat of summer, especially if grown in a flat garden and roots are shallow. On slopes, give a plant a slow soaking once or twice over a dry summer to increase its ability to hold its foliage. Fertilize very lightly or risk losing the show of fall color.

Care
Prune only to shape the tree, or to remove broken lower branches. Bagworms may be a bit of a nuisance, but rarely cause serious damage; handpick those you can, or spray with a biological worm spray that won't harm other creatures. By all means keep mowers and string trimmers away from the thin bark, or risk losing trees to trunk decay.

Companion Planting and Design
In the home landscape, use sourwood in a grouping at the edge of a green, piney woods or near a Southern magnolia, where its shape and colors really stand out. It naturalizes well on wildflower slopes too steep to mow, and provides just the right amount of summer shade for oakleaf hydrangeas. Underplant with naturalizing spring bulbs and black-eyed Susan.

Personal Favorites
'Chameleon' is a bit more upright and has brilliant fall colors, including lime green and blackish purple, while 'Mt. Charm' has earlier fall color—plant one of each to prolong the show.

Southern Magnolia

Magnolia grandiflora

When, Where, and How to Plant

Plant magnolias any time, but fall and winter are best. Magnolias grow in nearly any type of soil except rocky and swampy, but will tolerate water standing for a day or so after a rain. Their foliage is thick and full in the sun; they are more open and have fewer flowers in the shade. Space trees 25 to 35 feet apart, in wide holes amended with organic matter (add more organic matter to sandy soils). Mulch to keep roots cool until trees can shade their own roots.

Growing Tips

Freshly planted large magnolias will need slow, deep soakings every two or three weeks their first summer—but no more than every week or two, or risk root rot. Smaller trees may need staking in high-wind areas until their roots can hold them upright in strong gusts. Feed very lightly by broadcasting all-purpose fertilizer under the outer spread of branches.

Care

Avoid pruning if at all possible—once pruned, a magnolia never develops new lower branches, and the view of very shallow roots and the large amount of slow-to-decompose leaves can be unsightly. Magnolias get occasional leaf spot diseases, which are sometimes severe enough to partially defoliate the trees, but they usually recover on their own. Sapsucker-type woodpeckers often girdle trunks, but again, it's not worth doing anything about.

Companion Planting and Design

Magnolias are superb specimen plants where there is room, especially when lower limbs drape the ground. They are solid barriers even to noise, and can be used as large hedges. They can be espaliered against a wall. Underplant with cast-iron plant or liriope, which not only grows and flowers under magnolias, but also completely absorbs and hides leaf litter.

Personal Favorites

The dwarf hybrid 'Little Gem' is smaller (about 20 feet) and narrower, with smaller flowers and the longest flowering period of all. Other favorites for their shape, luxurious foliage, and flowers include 'Bracken's Brown Beauty', 'Majestic Beauty', and 'D.D. Blanchard'.

The South's most spectacular flowering tree is revered in songs and gardens all over the world (there is even a Hardy Magnolia Society in Ohio). This stunning, large evergreen has big, glossy leaves that are often fuzzy, reddish brown underneath. Its pure white flowers—which can be over a foot across—fill the spring and early summer air with strong, citrus-like fragrance before shedding petals to reveal prehistoric-looking cones that produce bright red seeds. Grafted trees usually flower within a year or two of being planted; seedlings take several years to mature. Native magnolias are often seen in the understory of rich woods. Its splendid foliage is used in flower arrangements year-round. It serves as both Mississippi's state tree and state flower.

Other Common Name

Bull Bay Magnolia

Bloom Period and Seasonal Color

White blooms in spring and summer, evergreen foliage

Mature Height × Spread

20 to 80 feet × 25 to 50 feet

Vines *for Alabama & Mississippi*

"A vine is to a bit of architecture what a dress is to a woman. It may serve to enhance beauty or to cover defects," observed Loring Underwood in *The Garden and Its Accessories*. Most vines do a little of both: enhance and conceal. Technically, vines are flexible stems that are too flimsy to stand on their own and carry the weight of leaves, flowers, and fruit. The stems help the plants get up and over obstacles to reach sunlight. Some, including gourds, tomatoes, and cypress vine, are annuals to be replanted every year. Everyone knows about perennial monsters such as kudzu and woody perennials that live for many years, including grapes and climbing roses. And of course there is the famous native vine with gorgeous autumn color, *Toxicodendron radicans* or poison ivy, identified by its three leaflets ("leaves of three, let it be").

Careful selection of vines can give your garden vertical appeal throughout the year, plus color from spring to fall. Some have very showy flowers, or useful or delicious fruits. However, it also helps in choosing appropriate vines to know the four basic ways different vines grow:

- Trailing vines, such as Lady Banks' rose, do not attach themselves. They need to be tied or laid over the support of a fence or arbor to keep them from sprawling over other plants or the ground.
- Twining vines, such as Carolina yellow jessamine, Confederate jasmine, coral honeysuckle, moonvine, and morning glory, have stems that twist and wrap themselves around supports.
- Climbing vines, either produce tendrils (as muscadine grape) or use their leaf petioles (as clematis) to coil around supports.
- Clinging vines, such as creeping fig and trumpet creeper, attach themselves to supports with aerial rootlets growing off stems and actually grow into structures; they can damage wood on walls, doors, and windows, and other surfaces such as stucco.

Clematis

Words to the Wise

Some vines can quickly turn into fast-growing thugs that get out of bounds, causing you to spend precious time or resources pruning to control them in your own landscape. And some can also escape into nearby natural areas, outgrow native plants, and destroy wildlife habitat. Take special care with vines that can easily "get away from you," including wisteria, Japanese honeysuckle, kudzu, and bittersweet. Not that you can't grow them, just monitor them and be sure you have them well under control, and take responsibility if you find them getting

Coral Honeysuckle

out of bounds. Some other popular weedy vines are cypress vine, trumpet creeper, and English ivy.

Helping Vines Grow

Some vines, such as gourds and moonflower, are very fast-growing annuals. Others, especially climbing roses and other woody vines, seem to just sit there until they catch their second wind, then they really jump. (There's an old saying about woody vines: "First year they sleep, second year they creep, third year they leap.") To help vines grow stronger and more quickly, consider the following advice:

- If you are in a race with yourself or a peeking neighbor, choose a fast-growing vine.
- Place vines in sunny locations (the roots of some vines, such as clematis, should be shaded) so they will get the energy needed for sturdy growth.
- Dig a wide hole, not necessarily a deep one, so roots can easily grow outward. Amend heavy clay soils or sandy soils with organic matter, up to one part organic matter to two parts native soil—never more than that.
- Fertilize lightly to stimulate growth, but not heavily, which causes new growth to be tender and weak.
- Water only as needed, but deeply, then let the soil surface dry before soaking the roots again. Too much water is often worse than none at all.
- Help the vine get started climbing by using twine or a stake to get it growing upwards.

Many popular vines get much larger than most gardeners realize and quickly outgrow their supports—especially cute but flimsy store-bought metal or lattice arbors. The rule of thumb is to provide a support that looks way too big at first, but by the time the vine matures it will look right and not threaten people who try to walk underneath. After being sunk into the ground, arbor posts should still be at least 8 feet above the ground to give vines room to grow and cascade a little, yet still allow headroom for the gardener and visitors.

Vines are the free spirits of the garden, climbing skyways, sideways, all ways. They lift the gardener's view off the ground, and levitate it along fences, up walls, into trees, over arbors, and across rooftops, providing that "extra dimension" that many modern gardens lack. They tone down sharp angles and long fences—perfect elements of *feng shui* that help make gardens calmer, at least visually. *Viva la vine!*

Carolina Jessamine

Gelsemium sempervirens

Every spring our woodland roadsides are awash in masses of golden yellow trumpets of what many gardeners call "yellow jasmine"—really named Carolina jessamine. This native vine with its delicate, glossy green leaves climbs by twining around nearby shrubs and trees, easily reaching 20 feet high or more. It can spread into a mass thick enough to also serve as a groundcover on a bank, where it sprawls at will. It is evergreen (semi-evergreen in northern areas), and is one of the earliest vines to start flowering in a massive show. It continues to spritz out a few flowers the rest of the spring and summer.

Other Common Name
Yellow Jasmine

Bloom Period and Seasonal Color
Yellow blooms in spring

Mature Length
20 feet

When, Where, and How to Plant
Plant container-grown Carolina jessamine any time of the year, loosening roots and potting soil to encourage fast new root growth. When planting flowering vines in the spring, some flowers will shed from the stress but it's no big deal. Fall planting allows plants to get established before they put on their spring show and then endure summer heat. An ideal location for this woodland native would be where it gets morning sun but protection from hot afternoon sun or reflected heat from a wall or walk. Plant in morning sun or partial shade in rich, moist, well-drained soil, then mulch the roots to simulate natural woodland conditions. Space vines 8 feet apart.

Growing Tips
The first summer, water vines every week or two but do not keep them wet. Carolina jessamine is drought tolerant, but benefits from a good soaking every few weeks when there is no rain. Fertilize lightly in the late winter or early spring, and spread a little compost over the root area to "feed" the soil naturally.

Care
Prune after flowering by simply cutting out excess growth but leaving some to continue the vine effect. Carolina yellow jessamine is pest free. Note: Beekeepers report that when honeybees bring a lot of jessamine pollen to hives, very young bees can be poisoned—but they are quickly replaced with a new brood. Do not let young children "suck" the flowers as they might a honeysuckle blossom.

Companion Planting and Design
The relatively small vine makes an ideal cover for small arbors and even porch railings and tones down chain link fences, where its evergreen effect is very desirable. It is often planted around mailboxes but requires annual pruning. There are not a lot of good companions other than airy cypress vine, because jessamine is such a tight grower.

Personal Favorites
'Plena', sometimes sold as 'Pride of Augusta', is a double-flowering form sometimes offered by garden centers.

When, Where, and How to Plant

Plant any time you can find a container-grown plant. If in full bloom, be very careful when loosening roots, and don't over-water to compensate for the resulting wilt and flower drop. Plant clematis in morning or full sun in rich, well-drained soil. Allow 8 feet between plants if planting a row of them along a fence. Dig a wide hole and backfill with a mixture of native soil and a generous amount of compost or soil conditioner, plus a little slow-release fertilizer. If planting a bare-root vine, spread the roots out over a cone of soil, then water to settle the soil mix around them.

Growing Tips

Clematis usually takes a season or two to get completely established. Help the vine get a good start by tying it to a string attached to the top of its support. Think "rose" when it comes to watering and feeding—keep soil evenly moist but not wet, and fertilize in early spring, using a slow-release fertilizer and a shovelful of compost.

Care

Just like climbing roses, some clematis bloom on old previous-season's growth and may need thinning right after flowering; others bloom on new growth and can be pruned fairly heavily in the late winter to stimulate strong new flowering growth in the spring. If plants suffer from clematis wilt, don't despair—they usually grow back from the roots.

Whether it's encircling a mailbox, flirting with a stair rail, or hugging a shrub rose, clematis reigns supreme as the "Queen of Climbers." The long-lived deciduous climbing vine grows slowly, eventually reaching 5 to 12 feet. Some selections bloom almost three months in the spring and summer; others bloom only in spring or fall. The most spectacular have large daisy-like flowers up to 10 inches across! Hundreds of hybrids exist today, many with giant blooms in pink, ruby, lavender, blue, and white. Armand clematis (C. armandii) is evergreen, with showy white flowers in spring. Sweet autumn clematis (C. terniflora) is an almost weedy vine that becomes a cloud of tiny, fragrant, white flowers in the fall.

Companion Planting and Design

A small climbing vine, clematis is perfect for mailboxes and small arbors, but also complements small trees such as crape myrtle, and will grow perfectly well among the canes of climbing roses for a "double duty" effect. It also looks great clambering through and blooming over the foliage of evergreen shrubs such as privet.

Bloom Period and Seasonal Color
Pink, ruby, lavender, blue, white blooms in spring or fall

Mature Length
5 to 12 feet

Personal Favorites

The most popular clematis are *C. × jackmanii* cultivars, *C. henryi*, and *C. armandii*. The native *C. crispa* has bell-shaped lavender or purple flowers, and the vigorous sweet autumn clematis (*C. terniflora*) is evergreen with white flowers.

Climbing Rose
Rosa species and hybrids

The allure and romance of climbing roses goes back many centuries, and should not be resisted. However, most climbing roses, which have to be tied to their supports at first, are just as susceptible to pests as their shrub counterparts. Some notable exceptions, if planted well, can provide many years of nearly carefree enjoyment. Clusters of often-fragrant flowers appear in mid-spring, with ever-blooming types repeating heavily in the fall and a few lighter flushes between; some also have attractive fall fruits. Tricks to growing great climbing roses include selecting good cultivars, preferably ones that are not grafted, and giving them a large, sturdy support—even with occasional pruning, their vigor surprises novice gardeners.

Bloom Period and Seasonal Color
Yellow, red, pink or white blooms in April through fall

Mature Length
15 to 30 feet or longer

When, Where, and How to Plant
Plant in winter or early spring when plants are most readily available. Set out rooted cuttings when they get large enough, in a location with at least seven or eight hours of direct sunshine and rich, well-drained soil. Loosen roots of container-grown plants during planting; spread roots of bare-root plants over a cone of soil, then cover with soil, and water deeply to settle soil around roots. Cover the planting area with mulch.

Growing Tips
Water deeply every two or three weeks if your garden goes without rain. Feed lightly in March or April and again in late August to help the fall flower display be lush. Apply compost annually.

Care
Tie new canes of climbing roses loosely, and remove unruly or wayward canes when they start to get too long for the space, cutting branches off where they start growing (leave no stubs to rot). Thin crowded climbers in the late winter when you can better see what you are doing. If you need to completely rejuvenate old plants, do it right after enjoying the first main flower flush. Aphids and thrips often damage flowers, but several selections are rarely seriously bothered by insects or even blackspot disease.

Companion Planting and Design
Climbing roses are ideal for tall arbors, walls, fences, and growing over outbuildings. Underplant with daffodils and perennials that tolerate occasional watering, and let a clematis climb the rose trunk for dramatic contrasting flowers.

Personal Favorites
Lady Banks' (both yellow and white forms) is a vigorous, pest-free, thornless once-bloomer; 'New Dawn' is a huge vine with large, stunning, fragrant, pink-white flowers in spring and fall; 'Zephirine Drouhin' is nearly thornless and more mannerly on small arbors; 'Red Cascades' creates a prolific, nonstop production of clusters of bright red flowers from spring to frost; 'Climbing Old Blush' has nonstop medium-pink flowers all summer and fall.

Coral Honeysuckle
Lonicera sempervirens

When, Where, and How to Plant
Plant container-grown honeysuckle any time. Fall-planted vines will be better established before spring blooming begins. The vine grows well in sun or part shade. Be careful when loosening roots or first-season flowers may shed. Do not over-water at planting time. Coral honeysuckle likes its roots in the shade and its flowering sections in the sun. Dig a wide hole and mix plenty of organic matter into your native soil, which fluffs it up and increases drainage in the winter and moisture-holding capacity in the summer. Individual vines are usually planted, but vines planted 6 or 8 feet apart will grow together in two years.

Growing Tips
Help the somewhat vigorous but slow-to-start vines get started climbing by tying a string to the top of the support structure and lightly tying the new vine to the string. Coral honeysuckle is drought tolerant, but benefits from occasional deep soakings during periods of drought. Fertilize sparingly in early spring, using a slow-release, all-purpose fertilizer or compost.

Care
Prune in late spring after the main flush of flowering has passed; usually only light thinning of tangled or old stems is needed. Coral honeysuckle sometimes has aphids—which hummingbirds and ladybugs love to pick off—and bouts of powdery mildew; if the situation becomes overwhelming, cut the vine back hard and it will resprout.

Companion Planting and Design
This honeysuckle is vigorous on lightly shaded fences and small arbors, but not too overwhelming on a mailbox—with occasional pruning. Unlike other vines, it will not tear up lattice with age. Companion plants include daisy, salvia, black-eyed Susan, daylilies, and other low perennials that hide the lower stems and shade roots in the summer.

Personal Favorites
'Sulphurea' is a common and pretty yellow selection. 'Magnifica' has larger, bright red trumpets that are yellow on the inside. Great hybrids include the popular *L. × brownii* 'Dropmore Scarlet' and goldflame honeysuckle (*Lonicera × heckrottii*), which has pink buds that open into bright coral flowers with rich golden throats.

One of the earliest natural sources of nectar for hungry late winter and early spring hummingbirds, this non-invasive native honeysuckle vine is winter hardy all the way into Canada. Its clusters of bright red trumpets, which form on a short stalk that grows out of the center of a pair of fused blue-green leaves, are followed by luminescent orange-red berries that birds love. It begins flowering in late February or March and is in full bloom by April, with a few clusters of flowers through summer. Like the invasive Japanese honeysuckle, it climbs by twining, but never takes over or gets out of control. Coral honeysuckle is evergreen along the coast, but loses most of its winter leaves in higher elevations.

Other Common Names
Scarlet Woodbine, Trumpet Honeysuckle

Bloom Period and Seasonal Color
Red, yellow blooms in spring and summer

Mature Length
10 to 20 feet or longer

Creeping Fig
Ficus pumila

It's hard to believe that this little vine is in the same milky-sap family as fruiting fig trees and rubber trees. Creeping fig is a slow but steady creeper for sun or shade, where its small dark green leaves grow flat and dense on tenacious vines that inch up everything their clinging rootlets touch. Toward the coast it can get up to thirty feet or more high in just three or four years. In northern areas the vines usually die back to the ground, leaving lacy skeleton vine tracings on walls; it usually rebounds quickly in the spring, but makes a superb potted plant in areas too cold for its roots to survive.

Other Common Name
Fig Vine

Bloom Period and Seasonal Color
Evergreen foliage

Mature Length
30 feet or more

When, Where, and How to Plant
Plant creeping fig in late spring, when danger of frost has passed, in a moist but well-drained soil and full sun or light shade. Avoid planting on west- or south-facing walls that warm up too much in the winter, especially in northern areas. Gently loosen tangled roots at planting time. Fig vine roots very quickly from summer stem cuttings. For mass planting, you do not need to plant closer than 2 feet apart.

Growing Tips
The first spring, summer, and fall, water the fig every week or so to encourage fast rooting; do not keep it wet or roots may rot. This tropical vine is accustomed to humidity and it benefits from regular watering during periods of drought. No need to train this vine: Like barnacles, it clasps everything it touches.

Care
Prune in late winter or early spring, cutting out old stems and winterkill. Newly planted vines grow slowly, but be patient. Fertilize in early spring, using a slow-release, all-purpose plant fertilizer and an annual application of compost around roots to enrich the soil. If creeping fig dies back in the winter in northern areas, prune old stems back to the ground, and wait to see if new growth shoots up from roots in the spring. Keep vines thinned to prevent insect infestations.

Companion Planting and Design
In addition to climbing brick, stucco, or stone surfaces, it works well as a groundcover, planted between paving stones, and across the vertical risers below steps. It can completely cover statuary. It grows too thickly to have good companions, but some bulbs such as lycoris will push up through its dense foliage.

Personal Favorites
The variegated form is a very durable potted plant, and 'Quercifolia' has small lobed leaves that look like miniature oak leaves. 'Minima' is a cute miniature that grows almost perfectly over topiary frames.

Cross Vine

Bignonia capreolata

When, Where, and How to Plant

Plant container-grown cross vine any time you find the plants for sale, although fall or winter is better for plants to get established before spring and summer stress. Plant cross vines no closer than 6 or 8 feet apart, and even then they will quickly grow together. Cross vine tolerates a wide range of soils, but grows best in loose, well-drained woodsy soils high in organic matter. It grows well in the shade, creating interesting semi-evergreen patterns on tree trunks, but only the portions in full sun—at woodland edges or in the tops of trees—will bloom. Keep new plants moist until well established.

Growing Tips

The first summer, water vines every week or two but do not keep wet. Help get plants started by loosely tying new shoots to supports, and the many-branched vines will quickly take it from there. Fertilize lightly in the late winter or early spring, and spread a little compost over the root area to "feed" the soil naturally.

Care

Prune after flowering by thinning out cluttered stems and wayward vines. Cross vine is pest free.

Companion Planting and Design

Given good growing conditions, cross vine will overtake nearly any nearby plant, so it is best to use this vigorous vine as a specimen on an arbor or tree trunk, or to tone down chain link or other fences. Their flowers make an attractive red and gold carpet as they fall, so try to grow it over a patio, walkway, or mulch where the fallen flowers can be showy. An interplanting of cypress vine will add to the texture and prolong the flowering vine effect without shading cross vine.

Personal Favorites

Free-blooming 'Tangerine Beauty' has exceptionally bright, apricot-orange flowers, which continue to bloom throughout the entire summer and fall, and 'Dragon Lady' has red flowers with orange throats. Hard-to-find 'Atrosanguinea' has reddish-purple blooms and longer, narrower leaves than the wild species.

You have to look up to notice cross vine, one of our showiest late winter and early spring native wildflowers. At every leaf joint are two pairs of paired leaves looking like overlapping butterfly wings. Against these are massed clusters of dusty red trumpets with golden yellow inside, creating a smoky blaze throughout trees at the edge of woodlands. Hummingbirds and bees crawl into the thumb-size flowers. It gets its common name from the "X" seen when looking down the cut ends of vines (like looking down a drinking straw). Using tendrils to grab supports, this vine climbs so high that the only way you will often notice cross vine is from the spent flowers carpeting the ground underneath.

Bloom Period and Seasonal Color
Orange and yellow blooms in spring

Mature Length
20 to 50 feet

Gourds
Lagenaria, Luffa, and *Cucurbita* species

These ancient vines, native to the Americas but found growing thousands of years ago in Africa and Asia, are no longer a novelty plant. Their kudzu-like fast growth and dense foliage caused a friend to call his gourds "vegetal whiteout" for their ability to completely smother his specially-built "gourd house" arbor. Gourds grow over the ground or climb nearby structures using coiled tendrils to wrap around supports. Features include big bold foliage; pretty pollinator-attracting yellow or white flowers; and incredible diversity in fruit shape, size, and uses—from interesting ornaments to dippers and eating utensils, birdhouses, and even musical instruments including folk art banjos (there is even an American Gourd Society!). Gourds are among the toughest and most productive annual vines around.

Bloom Period and Seasonal Color
Vines and flowers all summer, fruit in fall

Mature Length
15 to 25 feet

When, Where, and How to Plant
Gourds require warm soil or their roots will quickly rot. Plant seeds or set out transplants in the spring after temperatures are in the 60s and all danger of frost is past, in full sun or near a support where they can grow toward the sunlight. Gourds grow best in well-drained soil that is moderately fertile and does not stay wet after long rains. Plant seeds in small "hills" spaced according to the size of the gourds (2 to 3 feet for small gourds, 5 or 6 feet for larger types). Keep soil moist until seeds sprout, then gradually water more deeply and less frequently until plants are established.

Growing Tips
Gourds require good air circulation, so thin seedlings to two or three per hill. They also require pollination by bees or by hand for fruit set; make sure flowers are visible to pollinating bees, or call your county Extension Service office for information on "hand pollination" of gourds and squash. For straight "necks" on dipper and birdhouse gourds, provide a trellis from which fruit can hang. For giant gourds, thin fruit to one or two per vine early in the growing season.

Care
Water regularly, especially in hot weather, but do not keep wet or foliage diseases can seriously threaten foliage and fruit. Insects are the same as for squash and cucumbers in vegetable gardens.

Companion Planting and Design
Small ornamental gourds can be very attractive on lattice and fences, but larger types need a lot of space to grow. They can overwhelm nearby small trees! The vines are too vigorous to grow with anything else, but winter bulbs can be grown in the same area in different seasons.

Personal Favorites
Small ornamental gourds have pretty yellow flowers; large birdhouse, dipper, and basket gourds have large white flowers. Loofah or "dishrag" gourds are interesting and very easy for children to grow over the summer.

Hyacinth Bean
Lablab purpureus

When, Where, and How to Plant
Sow seed directly into warm, moist garden soil after the danger of frost is past, or start indoors three weeks before planting outside (they are fast growing). Plant in full sun or at least six to eight hours of direct sun, near a trellis, arbor, or fence where they can quickly begin to climb. Keep soil moist until seedlings appear, then slowly start watering more deeply but less frequently as plants become established. Space vines 3 to 4 feet apart if you're trying to thickly cover a long fence.

Growing Tips
Allow the vines to wrap themselves around small support stakes or poles. Fertilize lightly after the vines get established, keeping in mind that—as with all beans and other legumes that collect nitrogen from the air through nodules on their roots—too much fertilizer will lead to mostly vine growth with few flowers and beans. Water only during extreme drought, or risk rotting the vines.

Care
Tip-prune new shoots early in the season to get them to branch out for more flowers and seedpods later. Allow some seedpods to dry on the vine to collect seeds for planting the next spring or to share; store seed in a cool, dry location indoors. Hyacinth bean is susceptible to aphids, leaf miners, spider mites, and leaf spots during wet seasons, but no control is usually needed. At most, spray with insecticidal soap or neem oil to control pests without harming beneficial insects.

Companion Planting and Design
Grow hyacinth bean where visitors will be able to marvel at it. Cover and shade a tall arbor, or create a flowery allée by planting them on pairs of rustic cedar posts connected at the top with more cedar poles. This is an ideal vine for children to plant around a pole teepee, grown with moonflower, morning glory, and cypress vine. Plant marigolds, melampodium, or other annuals at the base.

Personal Favorites
There is a white-flowering form of hyacinth bean ('Giganteus'), but the species is stunning without any improvements.

Grown by Thomas Jefferson at Monticello, his Virginia mountaintop home, this vine still never fails to stop traffic. Its green, small heart-shaped leaves are held on burgundy stems, on burgundy vines that twine and wrap around supports to climb 10 feet or more. Upright stems of lavender-purple or white flowers look like those of hyacinth bulbs, and are showy enough by themselves. But the real kicker with this heirloom vine is the clusters of wine-red bean pods, short and fat with two or three beans per pod held above the foliage. The pods are edible, but turn green upon being cooked. The seeds are black with attractive white edges, easy and interesting for kids to collect and save for spring planting.

Other Common Name
Lablab Bean

Bloom Period and Seasonal Color
Purplish blooms and burgundy seedpods in summer and fall

Mature Length
10 to 15 feet

Mandevilla
Mandevilla × amabilis

Caramba, *as we say in Spanish, this festive, easy-to-grow tropical vine is exciting and very showy as it clambers up deck supports, arbors, porch rails, poles, and mailboxes. The large leaves and broadly lobed rich pink trumpet flowers provide the perfect finishing touch to tropical gardens. Mandevilla, which can easily grow to 15 or 20 feet in a season, can flower nonstop from spring to frost. Like its bougainvillea and allamanda cousins, the tender tropical will not survive a dip below freezing, making it an annual in all but perhaps coastal areas. It is grown in the ground or in pots from April through October, then potted up and overwintered indoors, or simply replaced each spring.*

Other Common Names
Brazilian Jasmine, Scarlet Pimpernel

Bloom Period and Seasonal Color
Warm weather pink flowers

Mature Length
15 to 20 feet

When, Where, and How to Plant
Plant tropical mandevilla in late spring after all threat of frost has passed. Mandevilla prefers light shade, and moist, well-drained soil high in organic matter, whether grown in the ground or in pots. Stem cuttings root fairly readily and can be transplanted quickly after forming roots.

Growing Tips
Water planted vines regularly, keeping them moist but not wet. Container-grown vines require more frequent watering, sometimes every couple of days in hot weather, depending on container size, amount of sunshine, and drying winds. Feed lightly and regularly with a balanced all-purpose fertilizer without overfeeding, or you will get only lush foliage.

Care
Be attentive to container-grown plants. In October, cut the vine back, pot it up, and let it go into winter dormancy. Water sparingly while the vine is dormant. In early spring, cut back old foliage and fertilize the vine with a slow-release, balanced fertilizer. Set it out again after the threat of frost has passed, and it will quickly sprout new flowering growth. If growing vines permanently in containers, renew part or all of the soil once a year and add slow-release fertilizer.

Companion Planting and Design
Grow mandevilla as a single specimen vine on a support, or cascading from large pots on high porches or decks. For a lush tropical effect, interplant with larger plants such as canna and elephant's ear, or with pots of pentas. Feathery red cypress vine will climb throughout mandevilla for richly contrasting foliage and flowers.

Personal Favorites
'Red Riding Hood' has deep red flowers; 'Summer Snow' has sparkling white 3- to 4-inch flowers against dark foliage; 'Yellow' has wide, bright yellow flowers and is lower growing and shrubbier than the species, and is superb in hanging baskets. *M. splendens* has smaller, white flowers that are fragrant. *M. × amoena* is another hybrid; 'Alice du Pont' is a popular cultivar. A similar-looking, yellow tropical vine, *Allamanda cathartica*, or golden trumpet vine, is frequently sold along with mandevilla and requires similar growing conditions.

Moonflower
Ipomoea alba

When, Where, and How to Plant

Sow seeds outdoors after the threat of last frost is past, between April 15 and May 15. Plant moonflower seed in poor-to-average, well-drained soil. To speed germination, scratch the hard shell of the seed with a knife or nail clippers and soak seeds in water overnight. Plant the seeds where the vine is to grow since the plant doesn't like to be moved. Keep soil evenly moist until seeds sprout.

Growing Tips

Water these drought-tolerant vines only during extreme dry spells, and feed lightly or risk having all vine and few flowers.

Care

Train the vine by pinching the new growth early in the spring to cause more branching and provide a somewhat rough support, or wrap new growth loosely around a string tied to the top of the support. Pick off faded blossoms, and save a few seeds to share with others (especially with children, but warn them that the seeds are poisonous). Moonflower is relatively pest free except for midsummer whiteflies, which are difficult to control.

Companion Planting and Design

Excellent for arbors and trellises where visitors can enjoy the flowers, fragrance, and nectar-seeking wildlife. It grows too thickly to combine with roses, but is excellent in mixed plantings with morning glory and cypress vine for a morning, noon, and night effect. This is a perfect plant for kids to plant on homemade vine houses or teepees.

Personal Favorites

There are no moonflower hybrids, but two very close relatives are worth mentioning: Cypress vine (*I. quamoclit*) is a vigorous summer climber with delicate, feathery, cypress-like foliage and brilliant red or white trumpets that are butterfly magnets, but can reseed itself into the weed hall of fame; Spanish flag (*I. lobata* or *Mina lobata*) has very showy one-sided spikes of flowers that fade from red to orange, yellow, and white.

Moonflower is a showy antique annual vine with large, triangular leaves that twines around any support it can find. It produces big luminous white flowers up to 8 inches across that open with a snap at dusk, releasing a puff of fragrance. Its shiny white seeds are pretty and easy to save for sharing with others. Closely related to old-fashioned morning glory (I. purpurea and I. tricolor), as well as the weedy "tie vine." Moonflower is a perfect excuse to linger on the patio at dusk to watch late-afternoon hummingbirds and evening moths as they sup.

Other Common Name

Moon Vine

Bloom Period and Seasonal Color

White flowers from late spring to fall

Mature Length

20 to 30 feet

Muscadine
Vitis rotundifolia

Muscadines are the South's most famous native grape, so they were brought into gardens and landscapes for the shiny, slick leaves, golden yellow fall color, and loose clusters of large, luscious berries used for pies, juices, jellies, wine, and of course fresh eating. The deciduous vines are thick in the woods and many a childhood includes memories of swinging Tarzan-like on the tough, flexible stems. In gardens they can be vigorous and long-lived. Dozens of modern named selections, when grown on simple wire trellises, are far superior to unpredictable wild vines because they produce many more pounds per vine of larger, sweeter, less pulpy berries.

Other Common Name
Scuppernong

Bloom Period and Seasonal Color
Berries in late summer

Mature Length
20 to 40 feet

When, Where, and How to Plant
Plant bare-root or container-grown muscadines in ordinary but well-drained soil of moderate fertility, in full sun for the heaviest berry production. Unlike "bunch" grapes, muscadines are very difficult to root from cuttings, but container-grown types are readily available from garden centers or new vines can be "layered" (bury portions of long branches still attached to the "mother" plant in the ground in the summer, and cut off the rooted "offspring" in the winter). Give them plenty of room to stretch out, allowing at least 20 feet of trellis per plant. Add a slow-release, all-purpose fertilizer to the soil, cover the planting area with mulch, and water thoroughly.

Growing Tips
Muscadines are vigorous growers in need of a very sturdy support. Place a stake beside a new vine and train it to the stake until it gets close to a cross wire or beam. Pinch off side shoots so the end growth will go as far as possible the first season, then pinch the growing tip to promote branching. Keep vines well watered the first summer.

Care
Once vines are established, prune regularly in the winter to remove most of each year's growth, leaving only short 3- to 4-inch stubs for new growth to sprout from the next spring. If you miss a year pruning, the work triples. Muscadines have no major pests.

Companion Planting and Design
Once a staple of country gardens, a single vine looks charming when grown on an arbor or along a fence. However, avoid using muscadine over patios, or learn to live with the messy fruit drop every September. Also avoid growing other plants on muscadine vines, or pruning becomes a real headache.

Personal Favorites
Wild muscadines are either male or female plants, and both are required for fruit production. 'Scuppernong' is an old, female-only variety that won't fruit by itself. Flavorful, self-pollinating muscadine selections include light-skinned 'Carlos' and purplish-skinned 'Noble'. They will pollinate themselves and other nearby vines (including 'Scuppernong').

Trumpet Creeper
Campsis radicans

When, Where, and How to Plant
Plant bare-root vines dug from around wild plants in the winter or container-grown hybrid vines any time of the year. Plant in very well-drained, dry soils and full sun. Loosen tight roots of new plants when setting out. Allow plenty of room for trumpet creeper to grow, and plant far enough away from desirable flower beds or structures where its ivy-like rootlets can damage wood; the vines themselves can edge their way inside windows or underneath shingles. There is no need to enrich soil or add fertilizer, but water new plants to help get them established.

Growing Tips
There is simply nothing you need to do to help this rugged, drought-loving native vine, other than provide a sturdy support and fasten new growth of young vines to supports until aerial rootlets can take over. Or plant on a tall pole that you can walk around to keep runners from spreading into nearby flower beds. Trumpet creeper needs no fertilizer.

Care
Thin out side shoots that are produced close to the ground or they may invade nearby plantings. Prune plants in early spring to encourage flowering on new wood and keep vines from growing so heavy at the top. In short, never let pest-resistant trumpet creeper get the upper hand.

Companion Planting and Design
Grow trumpet vine on fences, walls, the tin roofs of sheds or barns, and even up trees. Grow over old stumps or even tall (10 feet high) solitary posts. It can be very attractive when paired with morning glory, moonflower, or evergreen yellow jessamine. Hide a birdhouse in its foliage for feathered visitors in summer and for winter interest.

Personal Favorites
'Flava' has golden yellow flowers, and 'Crimson Trumpet' is a glowing deep red with no trace of orange. Chinese trumpet creeper (*C. grandiflora*) is not as invasive as the native and has larger red flowers. A hybrid between it and our native, *C. × tagliabuana* 'Mme Galen' is bright orange to red.

Wildlife-conscious gardeners appreciate this vigorous native vine commonly seen covering roadside trees, fencerows, telephone poles, and other supports. The vine twines and attaches with aerial roots to achieve astounding heights—often covering abandoned homes. It is common to see nectar- and pollen-hungry bumblebees and even hummingbirds crawling inside the orange trumpets from midsummer to fall. Attractive, large, canoe-shaped seedpods up to 6 inches long crack open to release gossamer-winged seeds that float like dandelion seed. In the fall the leaves, each of which has up to nine pointed leaflets, turn yellow, then shed to reveal attractive pale tan shoots and dried seedpods. The pods have long been used for homemade Christmas ornaments and other crafts.

Other Common Name
Trumpet Vine

Bloom Period and Seasonal Color
Orange, yellow, red blooms in summer

Mature Length
25 to 40 feet

Water and Bog Plants
for Alabama & Mississippi

Anyone who has ever rooted a sweet potato, avocado seed, or philodendron cutting in a glass jar in the kitchen window, pretty much has all the basics of watering gardening down pat. Everything else—adding a goldfish to the pool, or situating a small splashy fountain or waterfall—is finesse. You can make an easy water garden from a preformed plastic water garden tub, set on top of the ground with soil or mulch piled up to the edge (there are even plastic liners that fit half whiskey barrels). Or you can make a water garden from a cheap kiddie wading pool, aluminum foot tub, old bathtub, five-gallon paint bucket, or trash can cut in half.

If you want sound and movement from a waterfall or fountain, you will need a pump, flexible hose to run water from the pump to your fountain or waterfall, and a nearby electric outlet. (**Caution:** Always use a "ground fault interrupter" electric outlet like those found in bathrooms, which will pop out a button-like fuse if you run into trouble with electricity; it is cheap, and can save your life.) Choose a pump according to two things besides price: how much water it pumps and the height to which you will need the water pumped (refer to the chart on the side of the pump's box).

Some basic guidelines for a simple water garden:
- Any container that holds water will do.
- Maintain the water level by replacing whatever evaporates during hot spells.

- Drain and clean the pond at least once a year to remove sunken debris that can build up and cause water quality problems.
- Mosquitoes breed in still water, and can be a problem unless you have fish or moving or splashing water (a waterfall or fountain).
- You do not need to have fish in a water garden; if you do have them, don't overfeed!
- If your water stays murky or green, plant a shade tree over the pond, or have two-thirds or more of the water surface covered with plants. A filter can help, as can "quick fix" algaecides.

Water and Bog Plants
Aquatic plants come in three basic categories: floating, submerged, and "marginal" or bog. Each has a wide range of foliage and flower

Water Garden

Louisiana Iris

types, and are used like any other plants in design. Some are tall and narrow, some are frilly or round, and some are very low growing and used like groundcovers are in regular garden settings. One important note on invasive species: Some popular water garden plants, including water hyacinth, purple loosestrife, and elephant's ear, have escaped into natural waterways and caused ecological and economic problems. Either avoid planting them, or be very careful to keep them on your own property—dispose of excess plants in the compost, not in a lake or river. Below are a few general guidelines for planting and maintaining aquatic plants:

- Most water garden plants need at least half a day of sunshine to grow well and bloom.
- Plant them in wide containers with gravel in the bottom, especially shallow bog plants, which need to be bottom heavy so they won't tip over in sudden gusts of wind.

A Container Bog Garden with Pitcher Plants, Rush, and Lady's Tresses Orchid

- Plant just like ordinary potted garden perennials, only in good (even heavy clay) garden soil, not potting soil.
- Cover the top of the soil with at least 2 inches of gravel or sand to keep the soil in, especially in a water garden with fish.
- Fertilize plants annually with plant pellets made just for them, or with a slow-release fertilizer such as Osmocote.
- In the winter, cut back frost-damaged foliage. In northern counties, tropical water lilies will need to be pulled out of the water, pots and all, sealed in plastic bags, and kept in a cool, frost-free place over the winter.
- Divide water garden plants in the spring or as needed.

239

Floating Plants

Free-floating kinds of plants have very small or furry roots that hang beneath masses of foliage that spread over the surface of the water. Their leaves are usually very attractive, waxy, and naturally water repellent. Most provide important food for fish, and can cover the water surface to help keep algae down. Many are so fast-spreading they have to be thinned regularly to keep from covering the water completely. A handful of common ones include the following plants:

Fairy Moss (*Azolla caroliniana*) is a small, fern-like floater that forms a solid mass of finely curly green foliage with red tints. It can completely cover a small water garden in just weeks, but is easy to dip out and compost. Koi fish in your water garden will eat a lot of it.

Parrot Feather

Parrot Feather (*Myriophyllum aquaticum*) is perhaps the most useful foliage plant for the water garden. It grows as a tangled mass of stems that are completely covered with very small narrow leaves, making each stem a feathery plume of green. It grows both as a floater and as a bog plant (and can survive outdoors in wet ditches in southern counties). Its foliage is partly submerged, partly out of the water. It is an excellent filter plant for algae.

Water Lettuce

Water Lettuce (*Pistia stratiotes*) is a rapidly spreading floating plant that grows into a 4- or 5-inch wide rounded "rosette" of pale green leaves. It creates a peaceful look, but can completely cover a small water garden in just a few weeks. It can be easily dipped out and composted.

Submerged Plants

Submerged plants are planted in pots of garden dirt (just like garden plants) that are sunk beneath the water, needing 6 inches to 2 feet of water above their soil surface to give long stems and wide leaves room to grow up and float. Plant in real dirt because organic matter in potting soil will float away or rot and cause root problems. Every spring, poke water garden plant food into the soil.

Arrowhead (*Sagittaria latifolia*) is a native perennial submerged plant that reaches 3 feet tall with glossy, dark green leaves in narrow triangular arrowhead shapes. It is very hardy, often evergreen along the Gulf Coast.

Arrowhead

Four-Leaf Water Clover (*Marsilea mutica*) is a favorite submerged plant that grows best in shallow water, with spreading, floating four-lobed leaves with a distinctive pattern of green, yellow, and red. *M. quadrifolia* holds its solid green leaves above the water.

Golden Club (*Orontium aquaticum*) is a hardy native submerged plant for southern counties, which needs to be at least 6 or 8 inches below the water's surface. Its large glossy leaves cup up out of the water and surround very slender flower spikes, which are pure white with 2 or more inches of the tip a golden yellow.

Lotus

Lotus (*Nelumbo* species) is one of the surprises of the water garden. This submerged plant, which needs at least 6 or 8 inches of water above its soil, sends up huge, waxy, green, dinner-plate-shaped leaves over a foot across, held above the water on slender stalks. The flowers are as beautiful as any water lily, in reds, pinks, and yellows. The very interesting seedpods are popular for dried arrangements. The plant is winter hardy into Canada. If planted in the ground in a large pond it can become quite aggressive.

Water Lily (*Nymphaea* species) are almost always the focal point of the water garden with their beautiful round, glossy green leaves, 6 or 8 inches or more across. They need at least 6—but no more than 18—inches of water above the plants to give leaves room to spread out on the surface. The dense foliage provides much-needed shade for the water and cover for fish. Water lilies—of which there are many dozens of wonderful varieties available—flower mostly in the day, though there are some tropical night-flowering types. Their blossoms are fist-sized, single or double and daisy-like, and sometimes fragrant.

Tropical types have to be brought indoors in the northern counties (kept in plastic bags, pots and all), but can be left outside along the Gulf Coast. *Nymphoides* species are similar to water lilies, with small, heart-shaped leaves and lots of 1- or 2-inch-wide, fringed, snowflake-like flowers.

Bog Plants

Bog plants—often called "marginal" plants because they grow naturally between land and water—are usually tall and flowering, and grow in shallow water. They will need to be set atop bricks or plastic "milk crates" so the top of their soil is at or just below the water surface. Planting bog plants in a mixture of soil and potting soil is fine. Instead of growing bog plants directly in the water garden, consider planting them just outside the edge, so they look like they are in the water, complementing the scene without taking up precious water garden space. Place taller plants toward the back of your view, and smaller, softer-edged ones closer around the water garden to help conceal its edges. Many water-tolerant bog beauties are common garden plants already described in this book. These include canna, miscanthus grass, ruellia, cardinal flower, Louisiana iris, butterfly ginger, hibiscus, and elephant's ear. A select few very commonly grown bog plants include the following:

Bullrush (*Scirpus lacustris* or *Schoenoplectus lacustris*) is a bog plant for the edge of big ponds. The large clump-forming plant reaches up to 5 feet tall and is an explosion of dark green, very narrow needle-like leaves with small eruptions of brown flower clusters appearing near the tops of the leaves. Variegated forms are available.

Calla Lily

Calla Lily (*Zantedeschia aethiopica*) grows outdoors perfectly well in all but our northernmost counties, with spring and summer canna-like leaves and very exotic flowers of white, yellow, or pink. It grows very well in low areas, but needs protection in cold winters.

Common Rush (*Juncus effusus*) is a much smaller bog plant than bullrush, and forms less of a clump. A favorite form is the dwarf 'Spiralis' with its very interesting, unusual, tight corkscrew foliage.

Dwarf Cattail (*Typha minima*) is much more manageable than "regular" cattails, which are native plants that can reach 6 or more feet tall and will completely take over wet areas. Dwarf cattail is a bog plant that only gets 3 or 4 feet tall, with very narrow, blue-green foliage and 1-inch, oblong cattails that look like miniature hot dogs on skewers.

Horsetail (*Equisetum hyemale*) can be a real thug in moist soil, but can be contained easily in pots in a water garden. Its colonies have many upright, 3- or 4-foot-tall stems that are dark green, hollow, jointed, and leafless, with a small club-like cone at the tip (horsetail does not have flowers in the traditional sense). It is an excellent native evergreen for even the coldest parts of our states, and can be left out all winter.

Papyrus (*Cyperus papyrus*) is a bog plant with many tall, stiff, triangular stems topped with attractive "mop heads" of needle-like foliage. The heavy clusters cause stems to weep gracefully. Use as a strong accent plant or specimen. Dwarf papyrus (*C. haspan*) is smaller with golden-green flowers that turn rusty bronze in the late summer.

Pickerel Weed (*Pontederia cordata*) is an upright native bog plant with 3- or 4-foot stems topped with narrow, canna-like leaves, each one cradling an erect stem of very showy blue or pink flowers from spring to fall. It grows well with horsetail and parrot feather.

Pitcher Plant (*Sarracenia* species) is one of the oddest plants on earth—yet it is native to our southern counties, where it colonizes low-fertility, wet bogs. It has a narrow, hooded, hollow, pitcher-like leaf, which traps and drowns insects as a food source. The many varieties range from 6 inches to nearly2 feet tall; they can be white, green, yellow, or red, and usually have distinct vein markings. The flowers hang upside down on narrow stalks beside the pitcher leaves

Pitcher Plant

Umbrella Sedge (*Cyperus alternifolius*) is a very popular marginal plant, often grown as a potted plant indoors. It is similar to papyrus, but with umbrella-like foliage atop stiff stems. It provides an upright accent, and its roots can be a great natural filter for pond water. 'Gracilis' is a smaller, more erect, narrow-leaved variety. It can be brought indoors in the winter in northern counties.

Umbrella Sedge

The Low-Maintenance Lawn

The lawn ideal—a perfectly flat, low-growing mat of turfgrass—holds most gardeners in a powerful grip, yet you don't have to be a slave to it to enjoy its benefits. Advantages as well as disadvantages to lawns aside, there are ways you can reduce the amount of time, labor, equipment, water, and pesticides your lawn demands.

A Quick History

Early in our country's settlement by Europeans, open swaths of turf were adopted by a relatively small group of landscape gardeners as a sign of "Old World" culture and prestige. They were based on elements taken from old European manor "garden park" landscape designs. Most were mowed every month or two with long-handled scythes, or grazed by sheep and cattle; the development in the 1800s of clumsy mechanical cutting machines (often pulled by people), then gas mowers, made the lawn more appealing to average gardeners and homeowners, who saw the wall-to-wall green as representing a democratic ideal by which everyone who worked hard enough could be seen as equals.

In the early 1900s, newly-organized chapters of The Garden Club of America pushed the U.S. Department of Agriculture to develop more uniform lawn grasses, which helped standardize lawn care; soon equipment, seed, and fertilizer companies began promoting the benefits of their products in ways which today would border on brainwashing, with ads which suggested that "if you don't have a nice lawn, you aren't as good or smart or patriotic as your neighbors." Until recently, advice on lawn care—from the size of your mower and edger and leaf blower, to the amount of fertilizer and weed killer, and even your lawn's color—has been driven by the marketplace philosophy of "more is better." The trend now is towards smaller, more easily managed turf areas that highlight the landscape, rather than dominate it.

Lawn Benefits

There is no question that having a neat lawn is beneficial in several ways. Beyond the physical exercise provided by caring for the lawn (assuming you don't ride your mower), and the obvious leisure activities made possible by a uniform surface of turfgrass, a thick turf has environmental benefits:
- A thick turf holds the soil against erosion.
- Lawns keep dust and pollen down in the summer.
- A thick turf reduces mud tracked indoors in the winter.
- Grass shades soil from direct sunshine, which has a dramatic cooling effect for the entire landscape.
- The lawn generates an incredible amount of fresh oxygen while "scrubbing" pollutants from the air.

Plus, a neat lawn provides an important design element to the landscape or garden. Its strong shape contrasts with other plants, it can serve as a walkway between flower borders, it creates a vista which leads the eye to a focal point, and it can become a crucial "unifying" element overall.

Kinds of Turfgrass

The most commonly grown summer lawn grasses in our states are St. Augustine, centipede, bermuda, and zoysia. Each has advantages and disadvantages, and its own unique needs. Bermudagrass has fine-textured, thin leaves, is fast-growing, and spreads by underground runners. "Common" bermudagrass is available from seed, but hybrid types are transplanted as sod or plugs. Good bermudagrass lawns are high maintenance, requiring close mowing, regular feeding (two or three times a year), and watering or they will go dormant in the summer. Bermudagrass requires full sun, and will tolerate and recover quickly from foot traffic.

St. Augustinegrass is a coarse-textured (wider-bladed) grass that spreads by aboveground runners. It is only available as sod or sprigs, and though it won't grow for long in dense shade, it will tolerate a fair amount—more than any other grass type. It is a moderate-maintenance turf, requiring mowing on the highest lawn mower setting and light fertilizing every year or two for best growth. It is generally drought tolerant.

Centipedegrass is a coarse-textured, pale green grass that has the lowest maintenance all turf types. Its aboveground runners are fast growing, and it needs to be mowed at a moderate setting. It will tolerate less shade than St. Augustine, and grows and recovers from wear quickly. Fertilize centipedegrass less than any other lawn—its yellow-green color makes people want to feed it, which simply kills it.

Zoysia is a deep green, fine-textured turf that tolerates nearly as much shade as St. Augustine. It grows from sod or plugs, spreading slowly but steadily from short, sturdy underground and aboveground runners. It needs to be mowed at a moderate setting, fed once a year, and watered during extreme drought.

Ryegrass and other "cool season" lawn grasses grow well in cold weather and are often used to "overseed" summer lawns for winter green. They are available from seed, are sowed in the late summer or fall, fertilized lightly, and mowed until they start to burn out in spring heat.

Grass in the Shade

If you have over fifty percent shade, you are out of the lawn business. Period. Hundreds of thousands of frustrated gardeners who have tried *everything* to get grass re-established where it has died out in the shade, even solid sodding, careful watering, and fertilizing. Yet no one can point out a single success story except along the Gulf Coast where winters are mild. Not one.

The solution—even in front yards, where grass has too long been the accepted norm—is to forget the grass and use either a natural layer of leaf mulch, store-bought mulch, or planting low-growing groundcovers such as English ivy, mondo grass, liriope, periwinkle, ajuga, pachysandra (northern counties only), or even moss. There are other plants that will work, of course, but these are the most commonly used and lowest maintenance. You can create a landscaped effect keeping a neat edge between where grass is, and where it is not. Edging materials and low-growing border plants—especially liriope—can highlight combinations of taller shade plants such as ferns, hostas, and iris, making a nice scene. Complete the effect with stepping stones, a bench, urn, sculpture, birdbath, or other "hard" feature—which creates a focal point that takes attention away from your lack of grass.

Labor Saving Ideas

Some gardeners love their lawns as a hobby, others have them maintained by professionals as a means of proving their social intentions or standing; most of us, however, simply "mow what grows"—and then only grudgingly. The most important things you must understand are *there is no such thing as a low-maintenance lawn*—even the most slovenly lawn is the single most labor-intensive feature of any landscape—and *no two grasses are alike when it comes to maintenance needs*—each has distinct requirements for mowing, watering, feeding, and weed control.

Here are a few tips on how a reasonably neat lawn can be maintained without becoming a taskmaster; they are listed in order of importance for the lawn and your neighbors:

- Find out what kind of grass you have, or what kind you should plant based on your desires and its needs.
- Mow at the right height for your type of lawn.
  —High for St. Augustine (3 inches or the highest mower setting)
  —Medium for centipede, zoysia, and "cool season" fescue and ryegrasses
  —Low for hybrid bermudagrass
- Create a distinct edge by digging a small ditch around the lawn, or line the lawn with material such as bricks, rocks, broken pottery, or store-bought edging material and keep the edge crisp and neat with regular cutting. This creates a dramatic appearance for even a ragged turf.
- Water *only* when the lawn is about to die from drought.
- Fertilize lightly at least every three or four years, but no more than once a year. Really!
- Weed control is nearly impossible without the use of strong chemicals; if you follow the earlier tips, your lawn will compete much better with weeds and bad weather.
- Don't look at the lawn too closely, or you will find imperfections that are not as glaring as you think. Look at the big picture—even a poor-quality lawn that is mowed regularly and edged occasionally can still look good overall.

Dandelion is one of many common lawn weeds.

Mower Care

A lawn mower engine can last for many years if it is not worn out from improper care or lack of basic maintenance. Get the most out of your power equipment by keeping blades sharp, oil and air filters clean, and changing the spark plug as needed. Every winter, drain the gas tank and run the engine dry to keep fuel from turning into a gummy mess—the leading cause of starting problems in the spring. (And believe it or not, string trimmers are designed to be run "flat out"—the engines are more efficient at high speeds.) By the way, keeping mower blades sharp is the easiest trick to a neat, crisp lawn. A dull blade batters the grass rather than cutting it, leaving ragged tips that quickly turn brown and give a dingy cast to the entire lawn. Mowing with a sharp blade makes a clean cut that really makes a difference in the appearance for days afterwards. Buy a second mower blade, so you can keep one on the mower while the other is being sharpened.

Reduce Your Lawn Size

Consider the arrangement of golf courses, with a tightly mowed "putting green," a lesser quality but still-neat "fairway," and the wilder "rough." This is the same way a garden can be set up, with a lawn area, groundcover and flower beds, and shrub borders and trees. By having all three elements your landscape will be fuller and more lush, but still look neat. The trick is to reduce the lawn from a "wall-to-wall carpet" to a "throw rug."

Start by deciding how much lawn you really want to have—or want to maintain. Use a garden hose or long string to lay out a potential shape, moving it around until you find just the right shape and size. Take several days if you want to get a feel for how it looks. Then simply mow the area you want to remain turfgrass, and let the other area grow taller for a week or so to see if you really like the design. If you can create this effect by just mowing one area more often than another, it can look purposeful, even if you never plant a wildflower. Just the mowing pattern can look interesting, while cutting your mowing chores dramatically!

Once you get the shape of the lawn right, you can either spray the non-lawn area with a safe herbicide, or simply cover it up with flattened cardboard boxes covered with grass clippings and natural leaf or bark mulch. Within just a few weeks the grass underneath will be completely smothered and dead, and you can either continue to cover it with mulch, or begin planting flowers or groundcovers.

Create a Wildflower Meadow

Wildflowers are a natural alternative to a large lawn, but they need to be planted and maintained neatly or the area will look messy—and your neighbors will complain. Think of a meadow as an irregular, informal flower bed. There are some easy tricks to get started. First of all, simply stop mowing part of the lawn for a couple of weeks, to get the shape of the meadow you want. Secondly, add a "hard feature" in the area, to accessorize the scene. Easy ones include a short section of split rail fence, a scarecrow, large interesting log, add a group of birdhouses or bird feeders—anything that looks "naturalistic" and lets neighbors know you are doing something on purpose, not just letting your lawn go to

Meadow of Wildflowers

Lawns provide many benefits—dust control, playing surfaces, and garden bed framing.

weeds. Spray the grass with a safe herbicide such as Roundup or similar product, or mulch heavily to smother the lawn. Then plant a few wildflowers (native or not).

Avoid the "meadow in a can" approach, in which lots of wildflower seed are mixed for a general effect; it rarely works well. Instead, arrange a few hardy perennial wildflowers in groups and drifts—don't just dot plants here and there. Good ones to start with (all described in other parts of this book) include purple coneflower, obedient plant, narrowleaf sunflower, coreopsis, phlox, blazing star, oxeye daisy, asters, goldenrod, and naturalizing orange daylilies and daffodils. Then sow seed of easy, dependable wildflowers, including coreopsis, black-eyed Susan, Queen Anne's lace, crimson clover, zinnias, cosmos, and cleome. Before you know it, you will have a beautiful area filled with flowers, artistic features, butterflies, and songbirds. Mow on the high side once a year, after frost, to keep taller plants under control while letting reseeding winter annuals and low-growing spring wildflowers and bulbs get the sun they need to flower best.

Hold Your Head Up

The common wisdom of the past half-century was that a perfect lawn was attainable and desirable. The truth is, neither is completely correct, with a lot of "wiggle room" for gardeners who just want a neat lawn to offset the rest of their landscape. If you think some of these recommendations are radical, consider how little maintenance—especially irrigation, fertilizer, and weed killers—is needed around cemeteries, school yards, country churches, and old home sites—none. In the long run, the route to having a low-maintenance lawn is easier than most folks realize, at least physically. But mentally it is hard to let go of that desire for perfection. Plus there are social pitfalls to either avoid, or learn to live with. It's your landscape, your spare time.

If you understand and follow the few tips listed in this short section, your lawn will be better than most lawns around you—without the fuss and attention given by the hard-core "lawn fanatics." However, if you want to slightly improve your lawn's appearance, and reduce the mowing frequency (weeds need mowing more often than turf), you will need more detailed tips on lawn care. For this, contact your county or parish Agriculture Extension Service Office, or get a copy of *The Perfect Alabama Lawn* or *The Perfect Mississippi Lawn* published by Cool Springs Press.

General Pest Control

Sooner, rather than later, all gardeners have to deal with bugs and blights, and things that bump around the garden in the night. In the past, we just "went with the flow" and replanted, or planted enough for everyone—including the pests. Then we got into a race to find ever-more-potent chemical solutions, a "shotgun" approach that often caused more problems than it solved. But in recent years the term "pest control" has changed and now means "abatement" rather than total eradication—eliminating the worst of the problem, and living with a certain amount of pest damage. It does not mean lowering your standards, but getting in line with reality. As the saying goes, "If you can't fix it, flee it, fight it, or flow with it."

Integrated Pest Management

These days, rather than a total warfare against all pests (which is a losing proposition in the long run), a moderate approach is being used, called "Integrated Pest Management" or IPM. It simply involves using several different practices chosen from a wide array of options, including the following (more or less in order of importance):

- Choose pest-resistant plants to begin with, or replace problem plants.
- Plant well—good soil preparation goes a long way towards healthy plants.
- Fertilize lightly, not heavily (overfed plants are weak and tender).
- Water deeply and infrequently—only when plants really need it. Hint: Water in the morning, or early enough in the evening, for plants to dry before dark.
- Spend time in the garden, so you can see problems when they first appear.
- Learn to live with a moderate amount of damage.
- Remove diseased plants or plant parts, or damage that can lead to diseases.
- Encourage beneficial insects, birds, even spiders and lizards, which eat pests.
- Hand pick or wash insects off plants with soapy water.
- Use traps, baits, repellents, or other non-toxic measures.

Planting correctly is one of the best defenses against pests and diseases.

- As a last resort, choose a safe pesticide that is recommended for the specific pest, on the specific plants, and only as directed. Read and follow all label directions, including those on "natural" materials. Use only as needed.

There are other measures, but these are all just "good gardening practices" used by gardeners for many centuries. The use of chemical or even natural pesticides can be easily overdone, and affect "non-target" creatures. It should be a last resort only.

Prevention or Cure?

Two very common misconceptions are that pesticides can be used to prevent insect attack or to cure plant diseases. The truth is, insecticides and fungicides work in the completely opposite way. Most insecticides do not last very long, and depend on contact with or ingestion by the insect to work; this means they are best used to kill existing insect pests, must be applied after the insects appear, and reapplied as needed. Fungicides, do not cure diseases—they are mostly used as a preventive coating on the plant, so they need to be applied before a disease shows up or starts to spread.

Modern insecticides and fungicides do not last very long—usually only a couple of weeks or through a couple of rains, whichever comes first—so they must be reapplied regularly when the pest or disease is present. Below are a few tips on getting the most out of pesticides:

Spraying with soapy water is a safe way to fight pests.

- Choose the right material for the pest.
- In general, liquid sprays work better than dusts or granules because they have better coverage.
- Mix and apply exactly according to directions, never stronger.
- Get good coverage, on both tops and bottoms of leaves. (Hint: Add a teaspoon of liquid dish detergent to every gallon of spray, to help the pesticide spread out and stick to the plant.)
- Reapply as needed for control.
- Most insecticides lose strength quickly after being mixed with water, so always mix a fresh batch before every use.

Slug Damage on Hosta

Common Pests

There are many, many kinds of pests, most of which cause temporary or relatively minor damage (meaning they don't actually kill the plants) and, believe it or not, can often be ignored; they will typically go away or be eaten by beneficial creatures. Below are just a few of the most troublesome pests, and some very general comments on how to avoid them, prevent them, control them, or ignore them. None of the accompanying recommendations is written in stone; there are usually several different approaches—including chemicals and home remedies—that work well for some gardeners, but not for others. The following recommendations are from the authors' personal experiences from many years of working with gardeners, their pests, and a wide variety of resources. For more detailed pest descriptions, identifications, and control recommendations, contact your county Extension Service staff, Master Gardeners, or trained garden center employees.

Insects:

Aphids are small, soft-bodied insects that suck sap from tender plant tips and the undersides of leaves. Spray to coat the pests with soapy water or insecticidal soap, and allow beneficial insects to take care of the rest.

Fire Ants create mounds filled with thousands of stinging ants, and are difficult to eradicate on a large scale. Treat individual mounds with insecticides rather than using poisons wall-to-wall across the landscape. Re-treat as necessary.

Japanese Beetles and **May Beetles** are shiny green or dull brown beetles that crowd onto and eat leaves and flowers of many plants, especially in northern counties. Hand pick or spray with a recommended material. Do not crush Japanese beetles since that releases a pheromone which will attract more beetles; experts disagree as to the effectiveness of traps (some say traps actually draw more beetles to the garden).

Scale insects attach themselves to stems and the undersides of leaves, especially on camellias, hollies, and euonymus, and suck sap. Prune badly infested plant parts, or spray in the late winter with a dormant oil.

Whiteflies are very tiny flying insects that suck sap from undersides of leaves and their drippings cause "sooty mold." Spray the undersides of leaves with insecticidal soap.

Other Animal Pests:

Moles leave mounded trails as they burrow under the lawn and flower beds, but they just eat worms and insects, not plants. Use a plunger-type mole trap.

Slugs and Snails crawl around at night and chew leaves and stems. Get rid of their hiding places (moist rocks, old boards, unused flower pots). Hand pick what you can, and use a snail bait. Toads eat them.

Squirrels and Chipmunks may be prevented from digging up bulbs and tender roots somewhat by covering beds with chicken wire and covering with mulch.

Voles are very small, mouse-like rodents that burrow and eat plant roots. There is no completely effective control other than lining flower beds with buried "hardware cloth." But try baiting mouse-traps with peanut butter, and placing them by burrow entrances.

Deer are perhaps the most frustrating of all pests because they are so large, and they will eat nearly anything—sooner or later. Deer resistant plants are not always deer proof! Repellents must be reapplied constantly, and often lose their effectiveness as deer get used to them. The only sure

Deer Fencing

control is a fence 6 to 8 feet tall. A few usually deer "resistant" plants include boxwood, bald cypress, crape myrtle, fig, magnolia, pine, abelia, butterfly bush, lantana, artemisia, crinum, narcissus, English ivy, flowering quince, most grasses, hellebore, juniper, oleander, petunia, ginger lily, dusty miller, oregano, rosemary, prickly pear cactus, tulip, yarrow, yaupon holly, yucca, and zinnia. Good luck!

Major Plant Diseases:

Black Spot affects primarily roses, and is best controlled by regular fungicide sprays—at least every couple of weeks—or by planting resistant varieties.

Blackspot on Rose Leaf

Fire Blight is caused by a bacterium that is spread by bees from flower to flower, and causes twigs and fruit to look like they have been scorched. Plant resistant varieties, or spray (only during flowering) with a commonly available fire blight spray. Pruning off infected branches may actually cause bacteria to spread via the pruning shears.

Powdery Mildew shows up as a grayish-white powdery material that covers leaves and flower buds, and distorts new growth. Choose resistant plant varieties, or spray regularly with a recommended fungicide or neem oil.

Root Rot affects all kinds of plants that are either planted in heavy soils with poor drainage, or are being watered too much or too often. Replant in prepared beds, and do not water except when plants absolutely need it.

Sooty Mold is a very common black, sticky covering on leaves. It is a simple mold that grows on the sticky drippings of insects eating leaves or plants; treat by washing with soapy water, and by controlling aphids, scale, and other sucking-type insects.

Virus infections, spread by sucking insects or pruning equipment, cause leaves and flowers to be distorted, twisted, or variegated. There are no controls other than plant replacement.

Pesticides seem to constantly change in availability, content, and strengths. Some very common ones have been taken off the market because of environmental or health concerns, leaving the field wide open for new products to come forward. Some of the most exciting include those made from natural ingredients, including pyrethrins (made from a chrysanthemum flower), neem oil (made from the oil of the tropical neem tree), insecticidal soaps made from natural fats, and caterpillar-controlling bacteria.

Rather than list them all here, it would be best for you to find a local expert who has the health and wellbeing of both you and your garden in mind. Contact your county Extension Service office, Master Gardeners, or trained garden center employees, and always read labels before purchasing and using any pesticide.

Landscaping with Native Plants

Nothing says "South" more than using native plants in the landscape, which by their very nature attract native creatures—including butterflies, hummingbirds, and songbirds. By choosing and carefully placing a variety of plants, you can create a strong "sense of place" that not only looks right, but also works well. Here are a few great garden-quality native plants that you can easily see growing naturally in our states, and which can be perfectly beautiful—and at home—in your landscape, without a lot of maintenance. They are available from a variety of sources, such as local garden centers and mail-order nurseries. Digging from the wild is not generally a good idea, since some species are rare or endangered, or don't transplant well; get permission from the landowner before attempting any digging.

Big Trees

American Holly	Hemlock	Southern Magnolia
Bald Cypress	Longleaf Pine	Sweet Gum
Eastern Red Cedar	Red Maple	Tulip Poplar
Ginkgo	River Birch	Willow, Water, and Live Oaks

Small Trees and Large Shrubs

Bottlebrush Buckeye	Magnolia 'Little Gem'	Sourwood
Cherry Laurel	Parsley Hawthorn	Sumac
Deciduous Holly	Red Buckeye	Wax Myrtle
Dogwood	Redbud	Wild Plum
Fringe Tree	Serviceberry	Yaupon Holly
Leucothoe	Silverbell	

Shrubs

American Beautyberry	Fothergilla	Strawberry Bush
Deciduous Azaleas	Oakleaf Hydrangea	Sweetshrub
Dwarf Yaupon Holly	Rabbit-Eye Blueberry	Virginia Sweetspire
Florida Anise	St. John's Wort	Yucca

Vines

Carolina Jessamine	Cross Vine	Smilax
Coral Honeysuckle	Muscadine Grape	Trumpet Creeper

Perennials and Grasses

Asters (many species)	Columbine	Obedient Plant
Bee Balm	Coreopsis	Phlox (many species)
Black-eyed Susan	Ferns (many species)	Prickly Pear Cactus
Blazing Star	Goldenrod	Purple Coneflower
Bluestar	Hibiscus	River Oats
Broomsedge	Joe Pye Weed	Spiderwort
Cardinal Flower	Narrowleaf Sunflower	Stokes' Aster

Plants to Attract Butterflies and Hummingbirds

Flowers are not pretty and fragrant just for the benefit of gardeners—those attributes are mostly designed to attract pollinating birds, bees, butterflies, and other insects. Even the white color and sweet fragrance of most night-blooming flowers are to help night-flying moths find their nectar-rich targets. To gardeners, the romance of beautiful flowers and delicious fragrance is only enhanced by the presence of the very creatures they benefit most. And don't forget, to have beautiful butterflies and moths you also need to provide host plants for their caterpillars; learn to recognize the caterpillars of prominent species and resist the urge to kill them when they are eating your plants—the plants will recover once the caterpillars have eaten their fill. Here are a few selected plants—including trees, shrubs, vines, perennials, annuals, and bulbs—noted for their attractiveness to butterflies, moths, and hummingbirds. Note, however, that many of them are also visited by bees, so don't plant them too close to walks or doorways! Single asterisks indicate exceptional attractors; double asterisks indicate the plant is food for butterfly caterpillars.

Abelia*
Bee Balm*
Black-eyed Susan*
Blazing Star*
Blueberry
Buddleja*
Butterfly Weed**
Canna
Cardinal Flower*
Chaste Tree*
Cleome*
Columbine
Coreopsis
Cosmos*
Cypress Vine*
Dutchman's Pipe**
Elderberry
Fennel**
Four-o'-Clock*
Foxglove
Gaillardia*
Gladiolus
Goldenrod*
Gomphrena*
Hibiscus
Hollyhock
Honeysuckle*
Impatiens*
Joe Pye Weed*

Lantana*
Lily
Marigold (single flowering)
Mimosa*
Moonflower
Morning Glory
Palmetto
Parsley**
Passion Vine**
Pentas*
Phlox*
Privet
Purple Coneflower*
Queen Anne's Lace*
Rue**
Salvia*
Scarlet Runner Bean
Sedum
Snapdragon
Sumac*
Sunflower*
Trumpet Creeper*
Verbena*
Viburnum
Weigela
Wisteria
Yarrow
Yucca
Zinnia*

Landscape Tips for Winter Interest

In spite of our relatively mild climate and wide range of plant choices, during our "two months of winter" we often find our landscapes and gardens bare of color and texture. Here are a few ways to spice up this otherwise dreary season:

Pansy

- Place a "hard feature" in the land-scape, such as a large rock, birdbath, sculpture, urn, trellis, gate, or small section of fence (wrought iron, picket, or whatever suits your style).
- Enlarge small plantings by working up the soil in a wide curve or other shape, and cover with mulch (pine straw or shredded bark), which gives instant good looks until you get around to planting more. Add a few sections of liriope or mondo grass to give extra definition to the bed.
- Add shrubs and small trees with interesting foliage, bark, or berries, including nandina, soft-tip yucca, pyracantha, crape myrtle (especially 'Natchez' for its mottled bark), dwarf palmetto, aucuba, mahonia, arborvitae, holly, and many more. Break up lines of shrubs with plants having contrasting leaf shapes and foliage color.
- Include winter-flowering shrubs such as *Camellia sasanqua* (which blooms in fall and early winter), *Camellia japonica* (winter and early spring flowers), winter honeysuckle, flowering quince, clove currant, mahonia, or flowering almond.
- Plant bulbs, hollyhocks, parsley, and other perennials (store-bought or divided from your own garden) in the fall so they can get settled in before winter and perform much better next year.
- Replace summer annuals with winter annuals such as pansies and violas, sweet William, ornamental cabbage and kale, snapdragons, even colorful winter salad greens.
- Position perennials with winter foliage for best effect, including yarrow, iris, dianthus, cast-iron plant, liriope (both green and variegated), and holly fern. Hellebore is a handsome evergreen perennial, and a winter-bloomer. Ornamental grasses are attractive additions to winter gardens, with their tan foliage and silvery flower heads.
- Overstuff a large pot on a sunny porch with several kinds of cold-hardy plants, including winter annuals, bulbs, cascading groundcovers, small "textury" shrubs, etc. Group several kinds of indoor potted plants together near a window for a tropical touch (grouping also helps them cope with low humidity indoors).
- Make sure weeds and frost-damaged perennials (ferns, lantana, cannas, etc.) are cut and composted, the lawn edged, and the garden raked free of leaf clutter. Clean up the garden, remove stakes, apply fresh mulch, and just generally neaten the landscape.
- Set up a simple platform-type bird feeding station. Stock with black-oil sunflower seed. Thistle feeders will attract goldfinches.
- Install and position low-voltage night lighting to illuminate steps for visitors as they come to and leave your home at night.

Resources

Extension Service Offices

Master Gardener classes, publications, soil tests, and often highly dependable plant or pest identification services are available through university outreach offices located in every county. The Extension Service can be found in the phone book under county government listings. For more information, contact your state Extension Service office.

Alabama

Auburn University
Department of Horticulture
101 Funchess Hall
Auburn, AL 36849
(334) 844-4862 (telephone)
(334) 844-3131 (fax)
www.ag.auburn.edu

Mississippi

Mississippi State University
Department of Plant and Soil Sciences
Box 9555, 117 Dorman Hall
Mississippi State, MS 39762
(662) 325-2311 (telephone)
(662) 325-8742 (fax)
www.msucares.com

Public Gardens

We are lucky to have outstanding public gardens where you can see how native and exotic plant species perform, learn about historic gardens, and discover new things happening in garden design and gardening techniques. Include them in your travel plans, or if you live close to a garden, become a member. Most of these gardens offer special events, classes, activities, and plant sales. Many also have websites with information on the garden's history, plant collections, and calendar of events.

Alabama

Bellingrath Gardens and Home

12401 Bellingrath Gardens Road
Theodore, AL 36582
(334) 973-2217

These internationally famous gardens include 65 landscaped acres with flower-lined paths, giant oaks, sculptures, lakes, and native waterfowl; numerous specialty gardens, including a spring show featuring over 250,000 azaleas.

Birmingham Botanical Gardens

2612 Lane Park Road
Birmingham, AL 35223
(205) 879-1227

With 67 acres in the heart of metropolitan Birmingham, this regionally acclaimed facility showcases many fine specialty gardens including Japanese, wildflower, Alabama woodlands, rhododendron, rose, fern, herb, bog, the Southern Living garden, and great garden sculptures.

Cullman Native Plant Society Wildflower Garden

Sportsman Lake Park
Cullman, AL 35055
(205) 734-4281

This small but charming 4-acre garden is dedicated to the preservation of native plants, shrubs, and trees. It's a refreshing stopover when traveling north or south on Interstate 65.

Donald E. Davis Arboretum

(corner of Garden Drive and South College)
101 Rouse LSB, Auburn University
Auburn, AL 36849
(334) 844-5770

This beautiful arboretum has 13 acres of Alabama trees and shrubs, many of which are labeled; a guide map is available in the pavilion.

EcoScape

Birmingham-Southern College
Birmingham, AL 35254
(205) 226-4770

This exciting demonstration garden and outdoor environmental classroom reflects the "New American Garden." It is good for design ideas, environmentally friendly gardening techniques, choices of native and drought-tolerant plants, and enjoying fun, oversized animal sculptures. Call ahead for tours.

Huntsville-Madison County Botanical Garden

4747 Bob Wallace Avenue
Huntsville, AL 35805
(205) 830-4447

Huntsville is not just for space buffs. With 112 acres, this garden includes impressive displays, such as a beautiful aquatic garden, herbs, roses, bulbs, native plants, ferns, daylilies, and a Lunar Greenhouse that kids love.

Mobile Botanical Gardens

P.O. Box 8382
Pat Ryan Drive, Langan Park
Mobile, AL 36608
(334) 342-0555

This 100-acre botanical oasis in the hills of West Mobile showcases Alabama and Gulf Coast plants and includes an herb garden and gazebo, outstanding nature trails, native and exotic azaleas, camellias, hollies, magnolias, and ferns. This is a fun garden to visit in the winter.

Noccalula Falls Park

1500 Noccalula Road
Gadsden, AL 35999
(205) 549-4663

The botanical gardens surround the recreational park and feature a fabulous spring show, including more than 25,000 azaleas.

University of Alabama Arboretum

4400 Arboretum Way (off Pelham-Loop Road)
Tuscaloosa, AL 35487
(205) 553-3278

Just inside Tuscaloosa's eastern city limits, the arboretum has a 60-acre plant collection for botanical education and appreciation. It includes a native woodland, an ornamental area, the wildflower garden, an experimental garden (with herbs, medicinal plants, and organic gardening displays), plus a nearby bluebird trail.

Mississippi

The Crosby Arboretum

370 Ridge Road (Hwy 43 and I-59)
P.O. Box 1639
Picayune, Mississippi 39466
(601) 799-2311
crosbyar@datastar.net

The Crosby Arboretum is a unique native plant conservatory for over 300 species of carefully selected native trees and shrubs, plus many more annual and perennial wildflowers and grasses found in south-central Mississippi and southeast Louisiana. Its 64-acre Interpretive Center (adjacent to Interstate 59 south of Picayune, Mississippi) serves as the focus of arboretum activities and development. Additionally, the arboretum manages over 700 acres in seven associated natural areas. Its pavilion and wooden bridges, which span an extensive display of native water plants in their natural setting, won a national architectural design award.

Mynelle Gardens

4736 Clinton Boulevard
Jackson MS 39209
(601) 960-1894

This cozily-designed estate garden, now owned and operated by the city of Jackson, is 6 acres of relatively small garden "rooms" each with its own distinct character and plant palette, all connected with a meandering, slightly raised concrete walk making it accessible in all seasons. It is an astounding collection of hardy, low-maintenance trees, shrubs, perennials, groundcovers, wildflowers, and garden accessories, with displays of annuals and garden sculptures.

Bibliography

Every gardener has his or her favorite resources (usually kept on a groaning bookshelf). It would not have been possible to write a book of this scope without references. The following books were of great help to the authors:

Armitage, Allan. *Herbaceous Perennial Plants: A Treatise on Their Culture and Garden Attributes*. Athens, GA: Varsity Press, Inc., 1989.

Bender, Steve. *The Southern Living Garden Book: Second Edition*. Birmingham, AL: Oxmoor House, 2004.

Bender, Steve and Felder Rushing. *Passalong Plants*. Chapel Hill, NC: University of North Carolina Press, 1993.

Chaplin, Lois Trigg. *The Southern Gardener's Book of Lists*. Dallas, TX: Taylor Publishing Co., 1994.

Dean, Blanche E. *Trees and Shrubs of the Southeast*. Birmingham, AL: Birmingham Audubon Society Press, 1988.

Dean, Blanche E., Amy Mason, and Joab L. Thomas. *The Wildflowers of Alabama and Adjoining States*. Tuscaloosa, AL: The University of Alabama Press, 1973.

Dirr, Michael. *Manual of Woody Landscape Plants*. Champaign, IL: Stipes Publishing, 1990.

Givhan, Ed. *Flowers for South Alabama Gardens*. Montgomery, AL: Ed Givhan, 1980.

Halfacre, R. Gordon and Anne R. Shawcroft. *Landscape Plants of the Southeast*. Raleigh, NC: Sparks Press, 1979.

Hériteau, Jacqueline and Charles B. Thomas. *Water Gardens*. New York, NY: Houghton Mifflin Co., 1994.

Hill, Madalene and Gwen Barclay with Jean Hardy. *Southern Herb Growing*. Fredericksburg, TX: Shearer Publishing, 1987.

Lawrence, Elizabeth. *A Southern Garden*. Chapel Hill, NC: University of North Carolina Press, 1991.

McClinton, Victoria Headley. *The Shade Design Workbook*. Montevallo, AL: The Good Earth Press, 1997.

Miller, Carol Bishop. *In a Southern Garden: Twelve Months of Plants and Observations*. New York, NY: Macmillan Publishing Co., Inc., 1994.

Odenwald, Neil. *Identification, Selection, and Use of Southern Plants for Landscape Design: Third Edition*. Baton Rouge, LA: Claitor's Publishing Division, 1996.

Odgen, Scott. *Garden Bulbs for the South*. Dallas, TX: Taylor Publishing Co., 1994.

Ottesen, Carole. *Ornamental Grasses: The Amber Wave*. New York, NY: McGraw-Hill Publishing Co., 1995.

Pleasant, Barbara. *Warm-Climate Gardening*. Pownal, VT: Storey Communications, Inc., 1993.

Rushing, Felder. *Tough Plants for Southern Gardens*. Nashville, TN: Cool Springs Press, 2003.

Tenenbaum, Francis, series editor. *Taylor's Guide to Gardening in the South*. New York, NY: Houghton Mifflin Co, 1992.

Wasowski, Sally and Andy Wasowski. *Gardening with Native Plants of the Southeast*. Dallas, TX: Taylor Publishing Co., 1994.

Welch, William C. *Perennial Garden Color*. Dallas, TX: Taylor Publishing Co., 1989.

Welch, William C. *The Southern Heirloom Garden*. Dallas, TX: Taylor Publishing Co., 1995.

Wilson, Jim. *Bulletproof Plants for the South*. Dallas, TX: Taylor Publishing Co., 1999.

Glossary

Acid soil: soil whose pH is less than 7.0. A pH of 6.0 to 7.0 is mildly acid. The pH in which the widest range of flowers thrive is slightly acid, in the pH 5.5 to 6.5 range. Except for areas where limestone is prevalent, most garden soil in America is in this range. This pH is also suited to most plants described as acid loving.

Alkaline soil: soil whose pH is greater than 7.0. It lacks acidity, often because it has limestone in it.

All-purpose fertilizer: is available in three forms: powdered, liquid, or granular. It contains balanced proportions of the three important nutrients—nitrogen (N), phosphorus (P), and potassium (K). It is suitable for most plants.

Annual: a plant that lives its entire life in one season. It germinates, produces flowers, sets seed, and dies the same year.

Balled and burlapped: a tree or shrub grown in the field and dug, whose soil- and rootball are wrapped with protective burlap and held together with twine or wire "basket."

Bare root: describes plants without any soil around their roots, often packaged by mail order suppliers. The rule of thumb is to soak the roots ten to twelve hours before planting.

Bedding plant: usually annuals that are massed (planted in large groups) in a bed for maximum show.

Beneficial insect: insects and their larvae that prey on pest organisms and their eggs. Some that are well known include the ladybug and praying mantis.

Botanical name: plant names given in Latin accurately identifying the genus, species, subspecies, variety, and form. Here's an example: *Picea abies* forma *pendula* is the 1) genus, 2) species, and 3) form (*pendula*, meaning "pendulous" or "weeping") that is the botanical name for weeping Norway spruce. *Picea abies* 'Nidiformis' is the 1) genus, 2) species, and 3) variety. When the varietal name is between single quotation marks, it's what is called a "cultivar"—a cultivated variety, or a variety that has been cultivated and given a name of its own.

Bract: a modified leaf structure resembling a petal that appears close behind the flower or head of flowers. In some flowers, that of flowering dogwoods for example, the bract may be more showy than the flowers themselves.

Bud union: a thickened area above the crown on the main stem of a woody plant. This is the point at which a desirable plant has been grafted, or budded, onto the rootstock of a plant that is strong but less ornamental.

Canopy: the overhead branching area of a tree, including its foliage.

Cold hardiness: the ability of a plant to survive the winter cold in a particular area or zone.

Common name: there is no such thing as an accurate "common name" for a plant. Names commonly used for plants are rarely common the world over, or even in a single country or state. Because they can vary from region to region, they are not as much help in locating plants as the scientific botanical names. Many are British "antiques" which continue to be used for their charm—for example, love-in-a-mist, fleabane, and lady's mantle. Botanical names also find their way into common gardener language. Examples are: impatiens, begonia, petunia, salvia, zinnia, aster, astilbe, phlox, iris. In time, you will find yourself remembering many of the botanical names of the plants that interest you most.

Compost: organic matter, such as leaves, weeds, grass clippings, and seaweed, that has undergone progressive decomposition until it is reduced to a soft, fluffy texture. Soil that has been amended with compost holds air and water better and also has improved drainage.

Corm: an energy-storing structure, similar to a bulb, but actually a specialized stem, found at the base of a plant, such as crocosmia and crocus.

Crown: the base of a plant where the roots meet the stems.

Cultivar: the word stands for "cultivated variety." Cultivars are varieties named by gardeners and gardening professionals. They are developed, or selected, variations of species and hybrids.

Deadhead: the process of removing faded flower heads from plants in order to improve their appearance, stop unwanted seed production, and most often to encourage more flowering.

Deciduous: refers to trees and shrubs that loose their leaves in fall, a sign that the plant is going into dormancy for the period of weather ahead.

Division: the splitting apart of (usually perennial) plants in order to create several smaller plants. Division is a way to control the size of a plant, multiply your holdings, and also to renovate crowded plants that are losing their vitality.

Dormancy: the period, usually the winter, when plants temporarily cease active growth and rest. However, heat and drought can throw plants into summer dormancy. Certain plants, for example oriental poppies, spring-blooming wildflowers, and certain bulbs, have their natural dormancy period in summer.

Established: the point at which a new planting begins to show new growth and is well rooted in the soil, indicating the plants have recovered from transplant shock.

Evergreen: plants that do not lose all their foliage annually with the onset of winter.

Exfoliating: to peel away in thin layers, as with bark.

Fertility/fertile: refers to the soil's content of the nutrients needed for sturdy plant growth. Nutrient availability is affected by pH levels.

Floret: a tiny flower, usually one of many forming a cluster, comprising a single flower head.

Foliar: refers to the practice of making applications to just the plant's foliage of dissolved fertilizer and some insecticides. Leaf tissue absorbs liquid quickly.

Germinate/germination: refers to the sprouting of a seed, the plant's first stage of development.

Graft/union: the point on the stem of a strong, woody plant where a stem (scion) from another plant (usually one that is more ornamental) has been inserted into understock so that they will join together into one plant.

Hardscape: the permanent, structural, non-plant part of a landscape, such as walls, sheds, pools, patios, arbors, and walkways.

Herbaceous: plants with soft stems, as opposed to the woody stem tissue of trees and shrubs.

Humus: almost completely decomposed organic materials such as leaves, plant matter, and manures.

Hybrid: a plant that is the product of deliberate or natural cross-pollination between two or more plants of the same species or genus.

Leader: the main stem of a tree.

Loam: a mix of sand and clay. When humus is added, loam is the best soil for gardening.

Low water demand: describes plants that tolerate dry soil for varying periods of time. They are often succulent and or have taproots.

Microclimate: pockets on a property that are warmer or cooler than the listed climatic zone. Hilly spots, valleys, nearness to reflective surfaces or windbreaks, proximity to large bodies of water can all contribute to altering the surrounding temperature.

Mulch: a layer of material (natural or man-made) used to cover soil to protect it from water or wind erosion, and to help maintain the soil temperature and moisture. Mulches also discourage weeds.

Naturalized: a plant that adapts and spreads in a landscape habitat. Some plants we think of as "native" are imports that have "naturalized", for example Queen Anne's lace.

Nectar: the sweet fluid produced by glands on flowers that attract pollinators such as bees, butterflies, and hummingbirds.

Organic fertilizer: a fertilizer that is derived from anything that was living, such as bone meal, fish emulsion, manure, plants.

Organic material/organic matter: any substance that is derived from plants.

Peat moss: acid organic matter from peat sedges (United States) or sphagnum mosses (Canada) often mixed into soil to raise its organic content and sometimes as a mild acidifier.

Perennial: a flowering plant that lives for more than one season; the foliage often dies back with frost, but their roots survive the winter and generate new growth in the spring.

Perennialize: sometimes confused with "naturalize." The two words are not synonymous. Tulips many perennialize, that is come back for a few years, but they don't become wild plants. "Naturalize" applies to a garden plant that becomes a wildflower of a region that is not its native habitat. It could be a native plant or an exotic plant.

pH: pH stands for potential of hydrogen. A measurement of the relative acidity (low pH) or alkalinity (high pH) of soil or water. Based on a scale of 1 to 14, pH 7.0 being neutral.

Pinch: to remove tender stem tips by pressing them between thumb and forefinger and clipping them off. The purpose is usually to deadhead, or to encourage branching and compactness. Hand shearing achieves the same purpose on plants whose stem tips are too small and/or numerous to pinch out one at a time, mums for example.

Planting season: refers to the best time to set out certain plants. The most vigorous growth occurs in spring. Early spring is the preferred planting time in cold zones, particularly for woody plants and for species that react poorly to transplanting. Early fall, after summer's heat has gone by and before cold comes, is an excellent time for planting, provided the climate allows the roots two months or so to tie into the soil before cold shuts the plants down. Traditional planting seasons are spring and fall; availability of plants in containers/pots has added a new and valuable season to plant—the summer, as long as ample water is provided.

Pollen: the yellow, powdery grains in the center of a flower which are the plant's male sex cells. Pollen is transferred by wind and insects, and to a lesser extent by animals, to the female plant parts, whence fertilization occurs.

Raceme: describes a flower stalk where the blossoms are an arrangement of single-stalked florets along a tall stem; similar to a spike.

Rhizome: an energy-storing structure, actually a specialized stem, similar to a bulb, sometimes planted horizontally near the soil surface (iris), or beneath the soil surface (trillium). The roots emerge from the bottom and leaves and flowers grow from the upper portion of the rhizome.

Rootbound/potbound: the condition of a plant that has been confined in a container too long. Without space for expansion, the roots wrap around the rootball or mat at the bottom of the container.

Root division/rooted divisions: sections of the crown of a plant, usually of a perennial, that has been divided. This is most often the source of containerized perennial plants. A root division will perform exactly like the parent plant.

Rooted cuttings: cuttings taken from the stems of perennials, usually, or from woody plants, that have been handled so as to grow roots. Rooted cuttings will perform exactly like the parent plant.

Seedling: plantlets started from seed. Flats and containers of annuals are often seedlings. Seedlings of perennials, and especially of hybrids, may perform exactly as the parent did, but can't be counted on to do so. Which is why perennial growers of quality plants sell root divisions or rooted cuttings rather than seedlings.

Self-sow: some plants mature seeds, sow them freely, and the offspring appear as volunteers in the garden the following season.

Semi-evergreen: tending to be evergreen in a mild climate but deciduous in a colder climate.

Shearing: the pruning technique where plant stems and branches are cut uniformly with long-bladed pruning shears or hedge trimmers. Shearing is also a fast and easy way to deadhead plants with many tiny blooms, pinks for example.

Slow-release fertilizer: fertilizer that does not dissolve in water and therefore releases its nutrients gradually. It is often granular and can be either organic or synthetic.

Soil amendment: anything added to change the composition of the soil. Most often the element called for is humus or compost.

Succulent growth: the production of (often unwanted) soft, fleshy leaves or stems. Can be a result of over-fertilization.

Suckers: shoots that form underground stems which can be useful, or not, depending on the plant. Removing lilac suckers keeps the parent plant strong and attractive.

Summer dormancy: in excessive heat some plants, including roses, slow or stop productivity. Fertilizing or pruning a partially dormant plant will stimulate it into growth.

Tuber: similar to a bulb, a tuber is a specialized stem, branch, or root structure used for food storage. It generates roots on the lower surface while the upper portion puts up stems, leaves, and flowers. Dahlia and caladium are examples.

Variegated: foliage that is streaked, edged, or blotched with various colors—often green leaves with yellow, cream, or white markings.

Variety: the only accurate names for plants are the scientific botanical names and these are given in Latin—genus, species, subspecies, variety, and form. In botany, "variety" is reserved for a variant of a species that occurs in the wild or natural habitat. It should not be used instead of, or confused with "cultivated variety," which has been shortened to "cultivar."

Wings: the tissue that forms edges along the twigs of some woody plants such as winged euonymus; or the flat, dried extension on some seeds, such as maple, that catch the wind and enable the seeds to fly away to land and grow in another place.

Index

Featured plant selections are indicated in **boldface**.

Meet the Authors

Felder Rushing

Felder Rushing is a 10th-generation Southern gardener whose ancestors moved from Virginia to South Carolina in the 1600s, then to Alabama and Mississippi in the late 1700s. His quirky, overstuffed cottage garden, which he shares with his wife and long-time best friend Terryl and their teenage son and daughter in Jackson, Mississippi, has been featured in many magazines, including *Southern Living, Garden Design, Landscape Architecture, House and Garden, The New York Times,* and *Better Homes and Gardens.*

For many years he served as Mississippi State University's statewide home garden expert. He continues to write twice-weekly garden columns and hosts a call-in radio program. Felder gives over a hundred lectures every year from coast to coast and has appeared on many television programs. Hundreds of his articles and photographs have been in various issues of over two dozen national magazines.

Once one of only six members of the garden advisory board for *Southern Living,* he has been a contributing editor for *Garden Design* and *Country Living Gardener,* and currently serves in that capacity for *Horticulture* magazine. Felder is on the board of directors of the American Horticultural Society, and is an honorary member of the Garden Clubs of Mississippi, of which his horticulturist great-grandmother was a 1936 charter member. He has spent a lifetime trying to make gardening as easy as it is fun.

Jennifer L. Greer

Jennifer L. Greer is a veteran journalist and author whose career spans more than twenty years. A former newspaper and magazine writer, Jennifer is the author of the *Alabama Gardener's Guide,* and has co-authored five *Southern Living Garden Guides* and *Alabama Gardens Great and Small: A Guided Tour.* She and her husband, Robert Gandy, a professional forester, live and work on 25 acres of woods near Harpersville, Alabama. In her free time, Jennifer enjoys growing herbs, vegetables, cottage flowers, and native plants.

When asked why she has written so much about Alabama gardens, Jennifer says: "Because there are no other places like them in the world. Alabama gardeners are philosophers, scientists, activists, artists and romantics. They reveal all of this—and more—in their gardens. In fact, I have often thought that what we make of our gardens is not nearly so important as what they make of us."